Pathologies of Climate Governance

International Relations, National Politics
and Human Nature

Earth's climate is in crisis. Climate governance has failed. This book diagnoses climate governance as if it were a sick patient, uncovering the fundamental factors causing the worsening climate crisis. It distills decades of global climate negotiations to reveal the features of international relations that are impeding climate action, and it identifies political obstacles to climate governance across a variety of countries in the Americas, Asia and Europe. The psychosocial aspects of climate change are explored to show how human nature, overconsumption and global capitalism conspire to stymy climate action. Remedies are suggested for how to overcome hurdles to effective climate governance internationally and nationally, with ideas provided for individuals to help them align their own interests with those of the global environment. Covering all of the major recent events in climate politics and governance, this is an accessible book for concerned readers who want to understand the climate crisis.

PAUL G. HARRIS has written or edited 25 books on global environmental and climate change politics, policy and ethics, including: *What's Wrong with Climate Politics and How to Fix It* (Polity Press, 2013), the *Routledge Handbook of Global Environmental Politics* (Routledge, 2014), *Global Ethics and Climate Change* (Edinburgh University Press, 2016) and *Climate Change and Ocean Governance* (Cambridge University Press, 2019). He is the Chair Professor of Global and Environmental Studies at the Education University of Hong Kong and a Senior Research Fellow in the Earth System Governance global research alliance.

Pathologies of Climate Governance

International Relations, National Politics and Human Nature

PAUL G. HARRIS

CAMBRIDGE UNIVERSITY PRESS

CAMBRIDGE
UNIVERSITY PRESS

University Printing House, Cambridge CB2 8BS, United Kingdom

One Liberty Plaza, 20th Floor, New York, NY 10006, USA

477 Williamstown Road, Port Melbourne, VIC 3207, Australia

314–321, 3rd Floor, Plot 3, Splendor Forum, Jasola District Centre, New Delhi – 110025, India

79 Anson Road, #06–04/06, Singapore 079906

Cambridge University Press is part of the University of Cambridge.

It furthers the University's mission by disseminating knowledge in the pursuit of education, learning, and research at the highest international levels of excellence.

www.cambridge.org
Information on this title: www.cambridge.org/9781108423410

DOI: 10.1017/9781108526029

First published 2021

A catalogue record for this publication is available from the British Library.

ISBN 978-1-108-42341-0 Hardback
ISBN 978-1-108-43753-0 Paperback

Additional resources for this publication at www.cambridge.org/harris2021

Contents

Acknowledgements

Climate change and climate governance are moving targets for scholars. New research, new events and new interpretations of them are being reported every day. As such, it has to be acknowledged that any book about climate change can give readers only a snapshot of what has been happening and what is known about it. To keep up with changing events, and to give readers – especially students and their instructors – additional information, a companion website has been created to supplement this book. The website includes updates to topics covered in each chapter, a bibliography listing almost 1,000 sources, discussion questions, PowerPoint slides and links to websites and other resources. Readers can access the website here: https://paulgharris .net/pathologies-of-climate-governance/.

I have benefited from information and ideas found in a wide range of literary sources, including books, scholarly journal articles, official reports from governments and international organizations, expert research assessments, analyses from nongovernmental organizations, and newspaper articles, among others. I have tried to provide a rich list of references to these sources. Readers who wish to dig more deeply into the topics that are discussed here will find Internet (i.e., World Wide Web) hyperlinks in the list of references that provide direct access to the sources, when available, or additional bibliographic information. Readers who are studying or doing research on climate governance may also find the more detailed bibliography on the companion website to be particularly useful. As hyperlinks to sources change, the online bibliography will be updated accordingly. Readers are encouraged to notify me via the website if they find that hyperlinks are not functioning.

The roots of this book can be found in many of my previous books (Harris, 2001a, 2001b, 2002, 2003, 2005, 2007a, 2009b, 2009c, 2009d, 2010b, 2011a, 2011b, 2012, 2013, 2014, 2016a, 2016b, 2016c, 2019a, 2019b), book chapters and journal articles (see www.paulgharris.net/articles), as well as the literature cited therein. In particular, this book builds on a number of ideas that I shared in some detail in *What's Wrong with Climate Politics and How to Fix It* (2013, Polity). Much as in that book, in this one I identify major structural, political and psychosocial causes of the climate crisis and propose some solutions to them. Chapter 8 of this book distills several chapters of that one, and some of the prescriptions for climate governance in Chapter 9 here resemble proposals that were made there. I have tried to integrate much of the feedback that I received on *What's Wrong with Climate Politics and How to Fix It* from scholars, reviewers, students, activists and other readers. I am indebted to all of them for sharing their comments with me.

I gratefully acknowledge permission to reproduce several figures. Figure 2.1, "Fossil CO_2 emissions," is a black-and-white reproduction of figures from Friedlingstein *et al.* (2019: 1806) under the Creative Commons Attribution 4.0 License. Figure 2.2, "Atmospheric CO_2 at Mauna Loa Observatory," is reproduced with permission of the NOAA Global Monitoring Division. Figure 7.1, "World total population," is reproduced with permission of Creative Commons license CC BY 3.0 IGO. Figure 7.2, "Percentage of CO_2 emissions by world population," and Figure 7.3, "Lifestyle consumption emissions of CO_2 per capita," are black-and-white reproductions of illustrations in Gore (2015: 4), used with the permission of Oxfam, Oxfam House, John Smith Drive, Cowley, Oxford OX4 2JY, UK, www.oxfam.org.uk. (Oxfam does not necessarily endorse any text that accompanies the figures.)

I am indebted to the individuals at Cambridge University Press who have helped to make this book possible, especially Matt Lloyd, publishing director for Earth and environmental sciences, and Sarah Lambert, senior editorial assistant, as well as members of the Cambridge University Press Syndicate (the press's editorial board) and everyone involved in the publication process, not least Beth Morel, Esther Migueliz Obanos and Charlotte Porter. I also wish to acknowledge appreciatively the anonymous reviewers, commissioned by Matt, who provided very helpful comments for strengthening the analysis and presentation.

My thanks go to my students, especially those in my long-running course on the politics of climate change, who have shared their observations during classroom discussions and debates. What those students have to say is especially pertinent because they will be affected by climate change throughout their lives and they have the ability, if they choose to use it, to avoid and ameliorate the mistakes of their forebears who caused the climate crisis.

As always, I want to acknowledge with much gratitude the support and companionship at home – where all of this book was written – of Keith K.K. Chan and Mobie.

Finally, my gratitude goes to people around the world who have selflessly devoted themselves to finding and implementing more effective and just methods for governing climate change. It is to them that this book is dedicated.

Figures and Tables

Figures

Tables

Abbreviations and Acronyms

AOSIS	Alliance of Small Island States
BRICS	Brazil, Russia, India, China and South Africa group
C&C	contraction and convergence
CBDR	common but differentiated responsibility
CCP	Chinese Communist Party
CCS	carbon capture and storage
CDM	Clean Development Mechanism
CDR	carbon dioxide removal
CO_2	carbon dioxide
COP	Conference of the Parties (of the UNFCCC)
EGD	European Green Deal
EPA	Environmental Protection Agency (United States)
ETS	Emissions Trading Scheme
EU	European Union
G7	Group of Seven economically advanced economies
G20	Group of 20 governments, central banks and the European Union
G-77	Group of 77 developing states
GDP	gross domestic product
GDR	greenhouse development rights
GHG	greenhouse gas
GND	Green New Deal (United States)
GNH	Gross National Happiness
GPI	Genuine Progress Indicator
GtC	gigaton of carbon
HDI	Human Development Index
HFC	hydrofluorocarbon
HPI	Happy Planet Index
ICAO	International Civil Aviation Organization
IEA	International Energy Agency
IIED	International Institute for Environment and Development

IISD	International Institute for Sustainable Development
IPCC	Intergovernmental Panel on Climate Change
LDC	Least Developed Country group (in UNFCCC negotiations); least-developed country
METI	Ministry of Economics, Trade and Industry (Japan)
MOFA	Ministry of Foreign Affairs (Japan)
NASA	National Aeronautics and Space Administration (United States)
NDC	Nationally Determined Contributions (to the Paris Agreement)
NDRC	National Development and Reform Commission (China)
NET	negative-emissions technology
NGO	nongovernmental organization
NOAA	National Oceanic and Atmospheric Administration (United States)
NRDC	Natural Resources Defense Council
OHCHR	Office of the High Commissioner for Human Rights (United Nations)
OPEC	Organization of the Petroleum Exporting Countries
ppm	parts per million
R&D	research and development
SDGs	Sustainable Development Goals
SEI	Stockholm Environment Institute
SIDS	Small Island Developing States group (in UNFCCC negotiations); small-island developing states
SUV	sport utility vehicle
UK	United Kingdom
UN	United Nations
UNDESA	United Nations Department of Economic and Social Affairs
UNDP	United Nations Development Program
UNEP	United Nations Environment Program
UNFCCC	United Nations Framework Convention on Climate Change
UNHCR	United Nations High Commissioner for Refugees
US	United States
USGCRP	United States Global Change Research Program
WHO	World Health Organization
WMO	World Meteorological Organization
WTO	World Trade Organization
WWF	World Wide Fund for Nature

PART I

Problems

1

Dysfunction in Climate Governance

The term "climate change" has become shorthand for the large-scale, unnatural, human-caused (anthropogenic) environmental changes brought about primarily by the emissions of greenhouse gases (GHGs) from human activities. Efforts to combat climate change have been on the world agenda for decades, but these efforts have barely slowed the increasing pollution of Earth's atmosphere. Despite international agreements brokered by the United Nations (UN), national policies to encourage the use of renewable energy and climate-friendly pledges by governments, countless nongovernmental organizations (NGOs) advocating action and increasing awareness of environmental sustainability among industries and publics, global emissions of carbon dioxide (CO_2) and other greenhouse gases continue to rise (Hausfather, 2019). This rise in climate-changing pollution is occurring even as scientists warn that emissions must be all but eliminated very soon if international objectives are to be realized (IPCC, 2018). That is, globally the causes of climate change are not yet being diminished; they are growing. Adding insult to injury, the financial and other resources being made available for adaptation to the inevitable impacts of climate change are a tiny fraction of what is required, especially in the poorest communities least responsible for causing the problem. At every level of governance – from the global to the local – policies and practices to mitigate climate-changing pollution and to deal with its impacts are increasing in number, yet simultaneously they are grossly inadequate to the task. In a word, they have been too little, too late.

If governing climate change is about reducing its causes and impacts, then climate governance has failed. This failure must be addressed because many millions of human lives, not to mention the vitality of societies and ecosystems, depend on finding ways to govern climate change far more effectively. If climate governance is to be effective in the future, it will require an honest

3

accounting of climate governance in the past and present. A prerequisite for doing this is to identify the most important reasons for failure up to now.

Considering the Governance of Climate Change

Governance can be conceived of as "a social function centered on efforts to steer societies or human groups away from collectively undesirable outcomes (e.g., the tragedy of the commons) and toward socially desirable outcomes (e.g., the maintenance of a benign climate system)" (Young, 2009: 12). Fundamentally, climate governance involves changing many prevailing policies, practices and human behaviors so that humanity collectively addresses climate change effectively. These changes may come in the form of actions or inactions: doing things that we do now differently – for example, using carbon-neutral public transport instead of private cars to get about – or doing what we do now much less often, or not at all – for example, reducing or eliminating environmentally unsustainable travel, not least holiday travel via airlines. Many changes will have to be structural – for example, through potentially dramatic changes in economic systems. Others will require transformation in energy systems – for example, through the replacement of centralized fossil-fuel energy infrastructure with localized carbon-free energy sources (e.g., from coal- or gas-fired power stations to regional wind-energy farms and rooftop solar arrays), thereby enabling people to more or less continue doing much of what they are doing now without in the process exacerbating climate change. Our actions may be inherently collective, as when government regulations induce changes across societies, or they can be individual steps that contribute to collective outcomes that are environmentally sustainable. They will be performed by all kinds of actors – international organizations, national and local governments, corporations, individuals and so forth. Particular acts of climate governance will involve mitigation or adaptation or some combination of both. If climate governance is to be effective, it will involve an end to the status quo.

It is important to note that much is already being done to govern climate change more effectively. There is no shortage of activity around the world to limit the causes of climate change and to address its impacts. In some places, GHG pollution is declining, and in others the rate of increase is being reduced. But to focus on this progress, great as it is, would be to ignore that even substantial global cuts in climate-changing pollution, which one might optimistically assume (despite historical precedent) will materialize in coming decades, will not stop the problem from growing worse. Past and present failures of climate governance, and specifically the painfully slow manner in which the world is responding to climate change, mean that further global warming and other manifestations of climate change are inevitable (IPCC, 2014b). What is more, multiplying even tenfold all funding and resources currently being generated from all sources, public and private, for adaptation to climate change will not prevent monumental human suffering around the world. Regardless of how one looks at the problem, climate change has out-paced – and is continuing to outpace – all of the policies and practical solutions meant to address it.

Climate change is a problem generated by humans that has, so far, defied human-generated solutions. Almost everything about the way that the world is governed today has contributed, in one way or another, to creating this problem. The climate regime – the collection of formal and informal agree-ments, rules, precedents and norms that foster and guide governance and action on climate change – suffers from a pathological inability to catch up with accelerating trends of climate change and to reverse the associated environmental and human impacts (cf. Dryzek and Pickering, 2019). There has been a chronic and *pathological* failure to govern climate change effect-ively – an inability that is akin to an incessant disease that permeates governance institutions and individual actors, compelling them toward long-term self-harm.

Why have governments, communities, industries, individuals and other actors failed to govern climate change effectively? In other words, what are the fundamental pathologies that have undermined climate governance? Answering these types of questions is the primary objective of this book. Bearing in mind the explanations for the pathological failure of climate governance, what might be done to realize more effective responses to the problem? Put another way, what are some of the most important therapies and prescriptions for improving climate governance, and how might those be applied among nation-states, within them and indeed among and by their citizens? Answering these types of questions is the secondary objective of this book. In the process of answering these questions, other important issues will be addressed, such as whether global politics as currently practiced might eventually govern climate change effectively – the answer is, in general, a negative one – and whether human well-being needs to be sacrificed to govern climate change effectively (as critics of robust action might argue) – the answer is that it does not.

The book is divided into three parts. Part I (which includes this chapter) introduces the dysfunction in climate governance and describes the worsening climate crisis – the problem that has arisen largely due to the governance pathologies. Chapter 2 shows how the momentum of climate change is going from bad to worse: the pollution that causes climate change continues to increase even as governments and other actors are beginning to take major steps to address the problem. Some of the science of climate change is described, showing that expert knowledge about the problem has grown and become more precise, thereby doing more over time to expertly inform international and national governance. As the science has improved, however, it has also been politicized by actors that view action on climate change as a threat to their economic or other interests. This process of politicization has undermined the ability of science to inform national and international climate governance to the extent that is required. Cultivated uncertainty has itself cultivated inadequate policy responses to climate change.

Part II of the book illustrates how climate change has been such a difficult governance problem by dissecting the pathologies of climate governance. It identifies *fundamental* pathologies underlying the failure of governments and other major actors to respond more effectively to climate change. It looks at the international and national politics of climate change to reveal the processes that have delayed more effective policy responses, and it examines the role of human nature in accelerating the pace of climate change.

Part III of the book describes proposals for overcoming the pathologies of climate governance and moving toward more effective policies and responses. Potential prescriptions for improving climate governance internationally and nationally are outlined. Some methods for individuals to beneficially align their own interests with those of the global environment are suggested.

In doing all of this, it is important to be honest about something: it is easier to see where climate governance has failed (and is failing) than to identify practical pathways for ending that failure, especially if one wants to do so relatively quickly (which is what is required). If readers are disappointed with the prescriptions for climate governance here, one defense is to humbly admit that the climate crisis has become so complex, so widespread, so all-encompassing and so controversial – in no small measure because those actors that want to maintain the status quo have tried to make it so – that it may be impossible to propose solutions that will satisfy many people. But that is all the more reason to take the approach of this book – to identify what is *most fundamentally pathological* about climate governance and to identify therapies that are appropriate for that pathology. Doing so will not quickly end the worsening crisis of climate change, but it may be the best way to mitigate it, and perhaps one day even to end it, sooner rather than later.

Pathologies of Climate Governance: A Preview

The chapters in Part II explore three major groups of pathologies of climate governance that have largely caused the climate crisis and greatly determine the world's responses to it. The first group of pathologies, examined in Chapter 3, are found in the prevailing international system of sovereign nation-states, each of which is individually focused on protecting and promoting its perceived national interests. (For literary license, throughout the book nation-states are variously referred to as *states*, particularly when referring specifically to the legally sovereign entities; *countries*, especially when referring to whole nation-states and their governments; and *nations*, specifically when using the adjective "national.") The international system in which we live today originated before the Industrial Revolution and the enormous growth in global pollution from human activities that has culminated in the climate crisis. The international system has certainly changed and adapted over the centuries, and there is no doubt that recent developments in international cooperation have contributed to action on climate change. Without that cooperation, climate change might be even worse. However, because the archaic international system is premised on promoting the relatively short-term perceived interests of its members, in its current form – at least under the current norms by which it operates – it is not up to the task of fostering effective governance of climate change. The system itself is a major source of the problem and an impediment to effective action.

The second group of pathologies of climate governance are found in countries' national politics. These pathologies are described in Chapters 4–6, which can be read together, with introductory remarks in Chapter 4 and concluding observations in Chapter 6. China and the United States, which together are the focus of Chapter 4, have been vitally important to global climate governance. The pathologies of national politics in these two countries are described in greater detail than are pathologies in other countries because China and the United States are the world's first- and second-largest sources of GHG emissions and together they produce two-fifths of the global pollution causing climate change (Environment and Climate Change Canada, 2019: 5). Neither of them is proposing, let alone implementing, national policies that are likely to trim their GHG emissions anywhere near as much as is necessary to prevent dangerous climate change. The United States is a case study in how the institutions of democracy can be exploited to the benefit of actors and forces interested in preventing effective climate governance. China is a case study in how authoritarian governments can similarly be "captured" to foster policies that severely exacerbate climate change.

Elsewhere, whether in Europe, Russia or other industrialized countries of the Global North, which are the focus of Chapter 5, or in the developing countries of the Global South, which are the focus of Chapter 6, different forms of governance have been ineffective in addressing climate change. While several member countries of the European Union (EU) are starting to address their large contributions to climate change, and as such the EU is the closest thing to a global leader on climate action, they are doing so too slowly. Russia's government is betting on further development and export of fossil fuels. Many developing countries face a choice of whether to bet their economic development on fossil fuels, with some of them, such as India, being large importers of energy, while others, such as Saudi Arabia, are large exporters. Meanwhile, numerous other developing countries, not least many small-island developing states, are on the frontlines of climatic impacts, with little responsibility for causing them and insufficient means to cope.

The third group of pathologies of climate governance, described in Chapter 7, are found in human nature. The material consumption of the world's expanding global middle class (not to mention the growing class of very wealthy people around the world) now largely characterizes modern life and increasingly serves as a substitute for traditional sources of well-being. As the population of global consumers grows, so too does GHG pollution. To be sure, human population is a driver of climate change: more people result in more consumption of natural resources, which directly and indirectly contributes to climate change. But what is more important than the numbers of people are the ways that increasing numbers of people live. More people are adopting modern lifestyles that are measured in terms of material growth. Consumerism is colonizing the world. People who can afford to consume do so; those who cannot yet afford to consume aspire to do so. The consequence is that GHG pollution is still increasing globally even as it stabilizes, or even falls, in some communities and countries.

Broadly speaking, these pathologies are respectively structural, arising from the structure and nature of the international system; political, arising from national politics, particularly its domestic aspects but also its external influences; and psychosocial, arising from human traits that are shaped and stimulated by social, economic and other forces. All of the groups of pathologies, and the individual pathologies within them, undergo myriad interactions, reinforcing one another across time and space (see Figure 1.1). The pathologies spread and mutate at an accelerating pace, resulting in new strains of pathologies that challenge climate governance in new and sometimes unexpected ways.

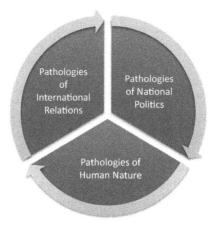

Figure 1.1 Interactions among the pathologies of climate governance

Prescriptions for Climate Governance: A Preview

Governing climate change more effectively requires, among other things, recognizing and confronting the international, national and human pathologies that have undermined most efforts up to now. Addressing these pathologies will not solve this monumental problem completely, but not addressing them all but guarantees catastrophe. With the urgency of the problem in mind, Part III of the book identifies and outlines prescriptions for the pathologies identified in Part II, points to a number of associated policies and briefly considers what the prospects for climate governance might be in the future.

Chapter 8 reconsiders climate governance in some detail as a way to identify potential therapies for its pathologies. Starting with the pathologies of international relations, the chapter considers alternatives for climate governance that aim to temper narrowly defined national interests with the wider interests of citizens and the global community. States presumably seek to promote their national interests, but in the context of climate change it is often unclear precisely what is considered to be worth securing, and how it might be secured. Chapter 8 points to a different kind of diplomacy that is focused less on states and their supposed interests per se and more on people's interests, in essence taking national governments at their word that they exist to protect the interests and rights of their citizens. The chapter also briefly considers potential therapies for the pathologies of national politics. It affirms the identities of those actors that are responsible for climate change: not just countries, but also other actors operating and residing within them, including individuals. The chapter proposes merging the common but differentiated responsibilities of individuals – responsibilities that are not widely acknowledged and accepted in the context of climate governance by most countries or indeed by most individuals, if their behavior is any indication – with the common but differentiated responsibilities of countries, which have been officially accepted internationally for decades, albeit practiced mostly in the breech (Harris, 2016c: 172–6). Therapies for the pathologies of national politics are found in recognizing and acting upon global responsibilities while facilitating the environmental citizenship that will make doing so politically palatable. Finally, Chapter 8 looks at some of remedies for the pathologies of human nature. It advocates a campaign to enhance human well-being and address climate change more effectively by recalculating the value and meaning of modern-day economic life in general and material consumption in particular. To secure human well-being it will be necessary to transition rapidly from the current focus on growing personal consumption toward sufficiency and long-term happiness.

Building on the remedial diagnoses in Chapter 8, Chapter 9 lists some specific international, national and human prescriptions that could be administered to alleviate the pathologies of climate governance that are described in Chapters 3–7. These prescriptions are formulated as indicative solutions to the persistent and pervasive pathologies of climate governance. Ultimately, to address those pathologies involves bringing all of the resources of the international community, national governments, individuals and other actors together to achieve what they can unanimously support for themselves and others: a good life for everyone (not to mention a healthy environment). Chapter 10 describes a number of climate-related policies that are implied by the prescriptions. It also starts to paint a picture of what the world might look like if those polices were to be implemented, considers the prospects for climate governance and briefly contemplates whether the future is more likely to be one of prospering amidst climate change or merely coping with it.

Theory and the Analysis of Climate Governance

The ebb and flow of climate governance is nigh impossible for anyone to measure comprehensively. Innumerable, often unknowable, national, international, global, economic, ecologic, even geologic (e.g., the influence of an earthquake on Japan's climate-related energy policies; see Chapter 4) and other forces influence it. Complex, nationally unique, political and policy institutions and processes shape it. Variable human, cultural and social characteristics affect it in countless ways. As should become clear in the next chapter, climate change is the most complex political problem in history. However, complex problems are not unique; there are ways of getting our heads around them, at least partially, through the utilization of theories. Theories are, in effect, ways of simplifying the world and explaining the relationship among actors and other variables. Theories of international relations and foreign policy can often help to explain the behavior of states. Theories of domestic politics may help to explain national affairs. Social and psychological theories often help to explain the behaviors of people.

Theory has been deployed to explain every facet of life, and analysts interested in climate governance (also known as climate politics, climate policy, the international politics of climate change, etc.) have been among those to do so. However, there is no *single* theory of climate governance; there are almost as many theories as there are scholarly disciplines – political science, sociology, geography, law, economics and so forth – trying to explain it. The study of climate governance owes much to scholars of international relations, a subfield of political science (Backstrand and Lovbrand, 2015: xix), and most particularly to the international relations subfield of global environmental politics (Stevenson, 2016; Vogler, 2016). Theories of international relations germane to climate governance include, but are certainly not limited to, classical theories of realism and idealism; more recent liberal institutionalist and regime theories; critical cognitive and constructivist theories; theories of transnationalism, the world system and global governance; and increasingly prevalent, and arguably increasingly important, "radical" theories, sometimes variants of neo-Marxist theory (see Vogler, 2018).

It would be wrong to overstate the ability of theories to capture fully, or even adequately, the climate *problematique* (Dyer, 2017). Indeed, there is a danger that by adopting particular theories (least of all a single one), attempts at explaining, understanding and improving climate governance may be inadequate. Consequently, this book does not adopt a particular theory. It attempts to comprehend major aspects of the climate *problematique* and to draw conclusions from them about the way forward. While it is far from a theory, one overarching issue does emerge – which, not coincidentally, is consistent with a number of theoretical approaches to international relations, domestic politics and citizen behavior – namely, that *perceived self-interest* (not to be confused with selfishness as often conceived) is a vitally important force in climate governance. States seek to promote their perceived self-interests – their perceived national interests – when negotiating pathways for climate governance with other states, consistent with major "realist" theories of international relations and foreign policy (see, e.g., Vogler, 2015; Purdon, 2017). Within countries, governments and domestic actors seek to promote their own interests – to resist policy action on climate change that might harm their perceived interests and to garner benefit, insofar as they can, from the climate-related policies that are implemented – consistent with some theories of domestic politics (see, e.g., Michaelowa, 1998; Harrison and Sundstrom, 2010). Intentionally or not, and seldom to cause harm to others, individuals, families and other groups act to promote their perceived (often unknowingly misconceived) interests, and thereby exacerbate the climate crisis, through billions of tiny steps taken every day, in ways that are more often than not invisible to those taking them – consistent with some theories of human and social behavior (see, e.g., Shove, 2010; Swim, Clayton and Howard, 2011).

Another way of simplifying the world, notably the political world, is to use different levels of analysis. While there is debate among scholars as to how many levels of analysis there ought to be (e.g., whether bureaucracy and class constitute levels in their own right), there seems to be substantial agreement on the particular importance of three of them: the international, the national and the individual (cf. Waltz, 2001). These three levels of analysis help to focus our attention on, among other things, the attributes of the international system and the effect that they have on the behaviors of states and other actors; the characteristics of states, such as their political and economic systems, bureau-cracies and the like, and whether these characteristics influence how states behave; and individuals, not least those individuals who play a role in formu-lating and implementing policy, and the psychological and other factors that motivate them to think and act in the ways that they do. As will be apparent, the three pathologies of climate governance examined in this book fall rather neatly into these levels of analysis. That said, it is always important to bear in mind that reality is never so neatly stratified. The levels that are being analyzed, and in this case the pathologies being described, overlap and interact in the real world. They do so in countless and complicated ways. Thus, the real world is seldom as neat or as simple as levels of analysis and theories might tempt one to assume. This is especially true with respect to climate change.

Triage in Climate Governance

There is now an enormous amount of literature on almost every aspect of climate change, including thousands of books. Most readers of this book will have immediate access, via Internet websites and myriad news and media platforms, to most details of climate science, politics, policy, diplomacy, economics and the like. If anything, there is too much information for any normal person to digest. Because the climate change *problematique* is so complex, one important aim of this book is to help readers sift through all of the available information – to help them see the forest for the trees, and thereby to understand better the fundamental forces shaping climate change and associated governance. The goal is to cut through much of the (admittedly important) chaff to get at the (most important) wheat, so to speak. This is done by identifying and explaining the most important and powerful pathologies that have permeated and shaped climate governance up to now – and will likely continue do so well into the future if they are not confronted squarely very soon. The focus is then on remedying those particular pathologies.

This book is for readers who are frustrated with – or perplexed by – the chronically slow action by governments and other actors to stem climate-changing pollution and to deal effectively with its manifestations and future consequences. And it is for those who are looking for ways to address this incredibly vexing problem more quickly, more efficiently and more justly. An analogy for what is done in this book is that of an extremely sick person in triage. Much as a physician trying to diagnose a patient with multiple diseases would aim to treat the most life-threatening pathologies before moving on to lesser problems, the focus here is on the *most important* pathologies of climate governance – those that are vital to understanding and identifying palliative therapies. (As we will see, much of climate governance up to now has focused on many significant but lesser pathologies, thereby allowing the most pressing ones to fester.) A few of the prescriptions for climate governance that are proposed here may at first appear to border on the idealistic. However, they are practicable because they are premised on promoting the interests of the actors involved. They will not harm the interests of states or their citizens; to the contrary, they will promote their long-term security and well-being. To be sure, promotion of self-interest is not the only thing that motivates govern-ments, corporations or individuals to do the right thing. But it helps.

It will not be easy to address climate change effectively; that has been patently demonstrated by the tortuous process of climate diplomacy and policymaking over the past several decades. Addressing climate change fairly and equitably will be that much more challenging. Much as one cannot bring a chronically sick body to health by taking a single pill, and much as a healthy lifestyle requires many individual actions over a lifetime, reviving the health of Earth's climate system – or at least permanently arresting its decline – will take a variety of new actions, or ending current actions, right away, and then sustaining them far into the future. Some of those actions are more important, more urgent and will have more lasting effects than others. This book aims to focus on the more urgent ones, to describe why they are important and to suggest the ways in which they can actually promote the interests of almost every actor that has so far resisted doing enough up to now. Because the focus is on the most important pathologies, by definition there is much that is left unsaid here. But that is true of any book on climate change. The problem is just too big.

Before exploring the pathologies of climate governance, it is first important to highlight what we know about the dastardly problem of climate change. What have scientists told us about it? How have their findings affected climate-related policies? Why have those findings not had a much bigger impact? These are some of the questions addressed in the next chapter.

2

The Worsening Climate Crisis

Climate change is the most complex and difficult problem ever facing humanity. Because climate change is a manifest danger to people, other species and the biosphere upon which all life depends, it is a governance challenge that cannot be avoided. Increasingly it is being described as a crisis (Sobczyk, 2019) and, even officially, as an emergency (see, e.g., BBC, 2019b). However, due in no small measure to the incredible scientific complexity of the problem, involving as it does the living and non-living features of the entire Earth system over centuries, climate change was for decades slow to capture the full attention of policy makers and publics. What is more, for most people, and for most governments, until recently it was perceived – when it was perceived – as a prosaic problem, something caused by ordinary, everyday human and industrial activities, many of which, especially the burning of fossil fuels to produce the bulk of the world's energy, have been commonplace for centuries. Yet, even as the causes of climate change were ignored by some governments, corporations and individuals, its consequences were becoming all too real around the world.

As scientific understanding and associated predictions about the impacts on human societies and the natural world have evolved, climate change has become more prominent in the media and public discourse. Climate change is now a significant concern for almost every government, many major international organizations, industries of every variety, thousands of NGOs and indeed many millions of people around the world. Since the 1980s, climate change has moved from being a minor scientific issue in international relations, national politics and human affairs to being, as we move through the 2020s, one of the most high-profile political issues globally. New scientific findings about climate change are now routinely front-page news. Interactions with governance have followed. Indeed, climate change has already influenced who wins elections (in Australia, for example; see Chapter 5), and it will determine the fate of the most powerful global industries, not least those whose long-term value is a function of their assumed ability to control and exploit fossil fuels still in the ground. In short, climate change is now high politics.

Governments have negotiated agreements to study climate change and to put in place policies that limit the GHG pollution that causes it (see Chapter 3). All of this has been driven to a great extent by climate science. However, despite the high profile of climate change and actions around the world to address it, the responses of countries and other actors, including businesses and individuals, have failed to keep up with the increasing pace of change. While policies to address climate change are many and varied, and increasingly these policies are starting to slow GHG pollution, they are grossly inadequate. They come at the tail end of decades of virtual inaction – of failed governance. The problem is becoming so serious that the only avenues for averting the dangerous climate change that scientists and even most governments agree must be avoided may be radical action at all levels of global society (Barkdull and Harris, 2015). Inevitably, effective efforts to avert the worst effects of climate change will challenge very powerful vested interests. Those efforts will involve substantial changes to the status quo and to business as usual – changes to which actors will continue to wield political influence and how they will do so; changes to which actors will control economic resources and what they will do with them; changes to the way that most people, including in the most economically developed world, will live their lives; and transformational change to the world's energy systems so that they all but eliminate the burning of fossil fuels.

All of these attributes make climate change a Herculean governance challenge. Indeed, this challenge is so formidable, and has been so for decades, that the problem has defied control. Even if every country and every industry and every person were to suddenly change their ways, dangerous climate change would still be unavoidable for millions of people at least. In short, the world has already failed the climate-governance challenge. The governance challenge going forward is to stop making things worse – to admit that mistakes have been made and to change course toward global environmental sustainability as quickly as possible. Governance will have to hew quite closely to what the scientists tell us is required.

Why have we found ourselves in this position globally? What explains the failure of climate governance? To start answering that question, this chapter aims to illuminate more of the complexities of climate change while also shedding light on some important attributes of the problem. It briefly describes the emergence of climate science and points to how that science has been politicized in ways that have made a difficult governance problem vastly more difficult than it needs to be – precisely the intent of those actors that have sought to politicize it. And it shows how climate change continues to grow worse, both in its causes and, consequently, its impacts (cf. Harris, 2018).

The Emergence of Climate Science

The idea that actions by humanity could bring about major changes to Earth's climate system is not new. Hypotheses about a "greenhouse effect" precipitated by the accumulation of CO_2 in the atmosphere were proposed in the nineteenth century. Much more recently, particularly since the mid-twentieth century, and especially in recent decades as observed climatic conditions have become more noticeably abnormal, climate change has grown in prominence among scientists and governments. Carbon dioxide, produced in massive quantities through the burning of fossil fuels – coal, oil and natural gas – and by the cutting and burning of forests, along with other land-use changes, is the most influential greenhouse gas in aggregate. Other important anthropogenic (human-induced) greenhouse gases include methane and nitrous oxide. Human activities have added carbon to the environment at unprecedented rates, resulting in a number of profound ecological changes. The most prominent manifestation of climate change is warming of the atmosphere and oceans – global warming – from which many of the worst impacts of climate change follow. For example, warming of the oceans and atmosphere leads to rising sea levels as seawater expands and glaciers recede, sending their meltwater into the sea. Ocean acidification and the cumulative effects of other forms of pollution and environmental degradation are among many other ramifications of climate change arising from GHG emissions (IPCC, 2013).

Anthropogenic global warming was, until quite recently, viewed as an issue for future generations, future governments and future citizens to address. That is no longer the case. It is now evident to scientists, and indeed to many laypersons, that ongoing environmental changes, such as widespread droughts, more intense storms, extreme warming of the Arctic and widespread bleaching of coral reefs, are consequences of global warming and manifestations of contemporaneous climate change. The impacts of climate change on natural ecosystems and on human societies will be increasingly severe, particularly in parts of the world where geographic vulnerability and poverty make adaptation to changes difficult or impossible. Importantly for understanding the global governance of climate change, the problem is intimately connected to nearly all economic activity. It is particularly wrapped up with modern lifestyles and consumption habits (discussed at some length in Chapter 7), thereby connecting the science of climate change to how people live and work, and to what governments, industries and people care about the most.

Over the past half-century, scientists have greatly improved their knowledge of climate change. They have developed a nuanced understanding of how GHG pollution is affecting the environment on land, in the oceans and in the atmosphere. Very importantly, debates among scientists about climate change are now about the details of the problem; there is no longer significant *scientific* doubt that human activities are to blame for global warming and the myriad manifestations of climate change (Cook *et al.*, 2016). Indeed, the Intergovernmental Panel on Climate Change (IPCC) declared in its fifth assessment report that that it is *"extremely likely* that human influence has been the dominant cause of the observed warming since the mid-20th century" (IPCC, 2013: 17). The IPCC defines "extremely likely" as 95–100 percent probability (IPCC, 2013: 142; IPCC, 2014b: 37), which is about as certain as the scientific community can be when reaching a consensus about such a monumentally complex environmental issue. (As discussed later in this chapter, this certainty among scientists contrasts with persistent doubt, cultivated by certain politicians and industries, within some populations.)

Climatological and related research now involves many thousands of researchers around the world. Consequently, sources of scientific information on climate change are flourishing, in the process producing detailed and refined understandings of the processes causing climate change and the resulting impacts on environment and societies. (Online media sites that spread false information about climate change have also proliferated, although these have in turn stimulated sites that collect and correct the many falsehoods [see, e.g., Cook, 2020].) The most authoritative official reports on the causes and consequences of climate change come from the IPCC, which is an official international body of experts that was created by and for governments in 1988 as concerns about climate change gained prominence among policymakers. Because the IPCC is an official international institution whose membership is made up of persons appointed by governments, it tends to reach its conclusions based on consensus. Consequently, its findings have routinely tended to *under*estimate the pace and scale of global warming and other features of climate change, as well as the resulting adverse impacts (Oreskes, Oppenheimer and Jamieson, 2019). Generally speaking, based on reports from the panel over the better part of three decades, whatever conclusions the panel reaches and warnings it may give about future climate change, things are likely to be worse, possibly very much worse (see Spratt and Dunlop, 2018). Consequently, the panel's forecasts are best viewed as a relatively optimistic baseline for understanding the problem and formulating responses to it.

The basic science of climate change is straightforward. Observational research confirms scientists' hypotheses, and computer models are now quite accurate regarding general trends, such as that of overall global warming. We know this because scientists use their models to go back in time to predict subsequent environmental conditions that have been confirmed by field observations and measurements. This does not mean that uncertainties are gone; climate change is so complex that details will *always* be the subject of analysis. For example, there is uncertainty about the impacts of "positive feedback" loops, such as the potential for runaway global warming that could occur due to CO_2 and methane emissions released by melting tundra (and, worryingly, possibly by melting methane hydrates beneath the sea). Recent research suggests that such an outcome – tipping points leading to irreversible and abrupt climate change – may be near at hand (Lenton *et al.*, 2019), and that without "coordinated, deliberate effort" that far exceeds any action so far, humanity may find itself living on "Hothouse Earth" (Steffen *et al.*, 2018: 6). If that were to happen, the climate crisis would certainly become an overwhelming climate catastrophe.

What is very clear from the science is that, at minimum, the consequences of many uncertain impacts will be extraordinarily bad. Thus, the scientific uncertainty that we need to be concerned about is not whether climate change is happening or whether it will be the cause of future hardships, but instead that scientists have not yet determined fully how bad the many bad impacts will be – whether those impacts will be very bad or utterly catastrophic. In short, the reality of climate change and its basic causes and consequences are very firmly established. Questions for scientists are now about the worrying details.

The Momentum of Climate Change: From Bad to Worse

What have climate scientists been revealing? They have revealed that the governance of climate change is not keeping up with reality. As scientists have quite rapidly increased their understanding of climate change in recent decades, diplomats have gradually crafted agreements to coordinate international action to mitigate the problem. Most governments have by now formulated policies of various sorts to address climate change, countless NGOs have pushed for action, many businesses have started to respond and, increasingly, individuals around the world have become more aware of the issue, with many of them trying to live more sustainably and to support policies for climate protection. However, despite these and many more instances of climate governance, *the problem is growing much worse.*

Indeed, the GHG pollution that is causing climate change is *still increasing* globally (IPCC, 2018; WMO, 2020).

Trends in Greenhouse Gas Emissions

After 1970, global GHG emissions increased by 70 percent, with CO_2 in particular increasing by 80 percent, especially after 1995 (IPCC, 2007: 37; IPCC, 2013). Despite expanding use of renewable, carbon-free forms of energy, particularly wind and solar, fossil fuels remain by far the main sources of energy around the world. As the use of fossil fuels has increased globally, CO_2 emissions have risen accordingly (see Figure 2.1). In 2017, coal burning grew by 1 percent, petroleum use went up by nearly 2 percent and the use of natural gas increased by about 3 percent (BP, 2018: 2). In 2018, coal use increased even faster – by 1.4 percent – while oil and natural gas increased by 1.5 percent and 5.3 percent, respectively (BP, 2019: 2). In 2018, global energy use grew by 2.3 percent (IEA, 2019a), while total global carbon emissions increased by 2 percent, their fastest increase in seven years (BP, 2019: 2). Coal burning is to blame for one-third of human-caused global warming, and it is still the source of one-third of energy use worldwide (IEA, 2019a). While the growth in coal use moderated in 2019, global carbon emissions increased due to the persistent popularity of other fossil fuels, notably natural gas and oil (Friedlingstein *et al.*, 2019). Even a small increase in coal burning is problematic because scientists tell us that its consumption must *drop by two-thirds in*

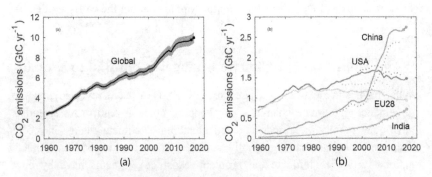

Figure 2.1 Fossil CO_2 emissions.
Source: Friedlingstein *et al.* (2019: 1806). Black-and-white reproduction under Creative Commons Attribution 4.0 License (https://creativecommons.org/licenses/by/4.0/).
Note: Graph (a) depicts global emissions, with an uncertainty range of ±5 percent; graph (b) depicts territorial emissions (solid lines) and consumption emissions (dotted lines) for highest emitters.

the next decade, and coal needs to fall to 7 percent or less of world energy *within 20 years*, if global warming is to be limited to 1.5°C (IPCC, 2018).

According to the World Bank's latest statistics, fossil fuels provide nearly 80 percent of the global energy supply, about the same as they did in the mid-1980s (World Bank, 2019). By one forecast, wind and solar power will supply almost half of global electricity demand by 2050, meaning that (if the projection is correct) the other half will still be supplied by coal and other traditional sources (BloombergNEF, 2019). The International Energy Agency (IEA) forecasts that carbon emissions will continue to rise until 2040, with that prediction assuming implementation of existing plans for limiting those emissions (IEA, 2019b). Governments have plans in place to produce 50 percent more fossil fuels by 2030 than would be compatible with limiting global warming to 2°C, and 120 percent more than would be compatible with limiting it to 1.5°C (SEI, 2019). These levels of warming are important because staying beneath them is the objective of the Paris Agreement on climate change (see Chapter 3), and even these levels will result in extremely dire climatic impacts. This persistence in the use of carbon-based fuels is explained by growing global energy demand, which is outpacing the rise in renewable sources (IEA, 2019a; Jackson, *et al.*, 2019). Without very substantial changes to existing energy policies around the world, GHG emissions could continue rising for decades (IEA, 2019c).

Not surprisingly, the concentration of CO_2 in Earth's atmosphere is increasing. At the start of the Industrial Revolution, the concentration was 280 parts per million (ppm) (NOAA, 2013). In 1958, when continuous measurements of atmospheric CO_2 began, it was still only 315 ppm (Kahn, 2017), a rise of 35 ppm over two centuries. The concentration of CO_2 in the atmosphere surpassed 400 ppm around 2013 (NASA, 2013), and it has remained above that level ever since (NOAA, 2020). In 2019, the concentration of CO_2 peaked at 415 ppm, the highest in at least *three million years* (Monroe, 2019). Put another way, that is a rise of 100 ppm in barely more than half a century. The amount of CO_2 in the atmosphere is set to go even higher in coming years. After a brief hiatus in 2017, in 2019 CO_2 concentrations returned to a decades-long growth trend of about 3 ppm per year (see Figure 2.2) (YaleEnvironment360, 2019; NOAA, 2020). The carbon dioxide that is in the atmosphere will continue contributing to global warming for centuries. If all of this were not bad enough, other greenhouse gases have also reached record highs – in 2018 methane reached 259 percent of pre-industrial levels and nitrous oxide rose to 123 percent of pre-industrial levels – and they continue to increase (WMO, 2019c). These trends may change for the better in future decades as climate policies are implemented, but it is difficult to imagine that they will do so at anything near the rate and scale needed to mitigate climate change markedly anytime soon.

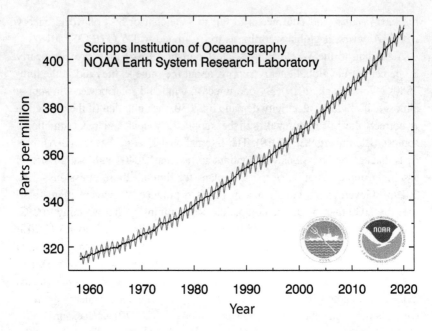

Figure 2.2 Atmospheric CO_2 at Mauna Loa Observatory.
Source: NOAA (2020). Reproduced with permission of the NOAA Global Monitoring
Division.
Note: The steady line in the figure indicates average annual concentrations of CO_2,
while the wavy line shows seasonal variations from which the averages are derived.

The coronavirus pandemic of 2020 resulted in a substantial fall in global
CO_2 emissions – with early predictions putting it on the order of 8 percent
compared to 2019 – as economic activity declined around the world (IEA,
2020b). The fall was largely attributable to the substantial decline in fossil-fuel
burning; the use of renewable energy remained strong during the crisis. But the
fall in GHG pollution during the pandemic highlighted the extent of the
problem: to limit global warming to 2°C would require that emissions fall
almost 8 percent *every year* from 2020 to 2030 (Plumer, 2020). It was all but
certain that emissions would instead rise once economies began returning to
normal. The question was not whether this would happen but rather how
quickly it would do so. Indeed, the economic crises associated with the
pandemic resulted in some governments relaxing enforcement of environmental standards, meaning that emissions in many countries would likely increase
when economic activity returned to normal, possibly exceeding emissions
levels before the pandemic (which is exactly what happened after previous

global economic slowdowns, including the recession that began in 2008). To put the predicted decline in emissions during the 2020 pandemic into perspective, it was forecast to reach the level last seen a decade earlier (IEA, 2020b). But those emissions were gargantuan, rapidly driving up carbon concentrations in the atmosphere. Consequently, the pandemic's direct impact on long-term atmospheric concentrations of GHGs will probably turn out to be negligible. Global warming will continue, short of major changes in how energy is produced globally.

Global Warming and Impacts of Climate Change

Given that the pollution causing global warming is still increasing and that the concentration of greenhouse gases in the atmosphere is the highest for millions of years, it should come as no surprise that Earth is warming at unprecedented rates. The average global temperature is now more than 1°C above what it was at the start of the Industrial Revolution; in 2019, it reached 1.1°C above the historical average (WMO, 2020: 6). This extent of global warming may not seem like much until one realizes that it is more than two-thirds of the way to a level – 1.5°C – that will have dire consequences globally, and that it masks far higher average temperatures in many vulnerable regions, not least the Arctic (IPCC, 2018). Of the 19 warmest years since recordkeeping began in the mid-nineteenth century, 18 have occurred since 2001 (Schwartz and Popovich, 2019). The five warmest years recorded were 2015–2019, with 2016 being the warmest year, and 2019 the second-warmest year, *ever recorded* (WMO, 2019a). In 2019, a temperature of 18.3°C was recorded in the Antarctic, the highest ever detected and further sign that temperatures there are increasing much faster than the global average (Readfearn, 2020). Atmospheric warming has become especially pronounced in recent decades: each of the past three decades has been warmer than the last, consistently and repeatedly exceeding historical averages (IPCC, 2013: 5; Fountain, 2020). True to this trend, 2019 ended the warmest decade ever recorded (WMO, 2019d). Records for extreme heat will likely continue to be set for many decades to come (Power and Delage, 2019).

As atmospheric temperatures rise globally, so do the temperatures of the oceans: they are warming rapidly, and they are doing so at an increasing rate. Incredibly, the oceans have absorbed more than 90 percent of the heat arising from humanity's GHG emissions (Wijffels *et al.*, 2016). Atmospheric and terrestrial warming, and the impacts of it that have already been experienced worldwide, would be much worse were it not for the oceans' ability to do this (IPCC, 2013). What is more, the oceans have absorbed roughly one-third of the CO_2 emitted by societies since the Industrial Revolution began (Khatiwala et al., 2013). This ability of the oceans to absorb CO_2 and heat is not inexhaustible (see Tollefson, 2016), and they are likely to eventually release heat back into the atmosphere, with potentially monumental consequences for humanity. Meanwhile, even as the oceans buffer global warming, higher levels of carbon in seawater are making it more acidic and thus less hospitable to marine life, with potentially catastrophic consequences for marine food chains (Harris, 2019c: 4–7).

Furthermore, as the atmosphere and oceans warm, sea levels are rising. The melting glaciers of Greenland are sending dramatic quantities of meltwater into the North Atlantic Ocean – at a rate seven times faster than in the 1990s (Shepherd et al., 2019). In 2018, scientists confirmed what some of them had been fearing: the Antarctic ice sheet is melting as well, and it is doing so at an accelerating rate (Shepherd, Fricker and Farrell, 2018; Shepherd et al., 2018). Combined with expansion of the oceans as they warm, not to mention melting of nearly all of the earth's other glaciers, melting of the Antarctic and Greenland ice sheets is contributing greatly to sea-level rise (Pattyn et al., 2018). The rise in sea levels will in turn translate into severe and widespread adverse impacts along coastlines – both for human settlements and coastal ecosystems. Indeed, it is already doing so in many places. What is more, Arctic sea ice has been markedly reduced, as has snow cover in many places, allowing the sun to warm those areas and thereby adding to yet further warming of land and sea (IPCC, 2013: 9).

According to the IPCC's fifth assessment report, every part of the natural world has been affected by climate change (IPCC, 2013: 4–13). Water systems have been particularly impacted – for example, with diminished snowfall that has reduced runoff in some locations even as melting glaciers in other areas have increased it. Species on land and in the sea are shifting their ranges, with, for example, some land animals moving toward higher elevations and fish moving away from areas of the oceans that are becoming too warm for them. Climate change has already contributed to the extinction of species, and a great many more are very likely to become so within decades if GHG emissions are not reduced (Trisos, Merow and Pigot, 2020). Very worryingly, worldwide crop yields are being affected by climate change, mostly adversely, thereby reducing global food security. Human health is also being undermined directly by climate change (Marsa, 2013), with children being especially vulnerable due to their physiology (Watts et al., 2019). More people are dying from heat stress and more are being affected by diseases spread by pathogens, such as mosquitoes, that benefit from warming. Extreme weather events have become more common. Increased heat waves, wildfires, droughts, severe storms and floods are causing suffering to humans and other species. These and other climate-related changes are multiplying the dangers posed by existing risks for communities and individuals. In the case of risks to people, they are especially high for those individuals and communities that have limited ability to cope – namely, the poor (Singer, 2018). People in areas of conflict face added vulnerability due to the impacts of climate change. These and similar changes will continue to increase in the future.

The most recent major scientific assessment from the IPCC was its 2018 report on limiting global warming to 1.5°C, the ultimate aspiration of the 2015 Paris Agreement on climate change (see Chapter 3) (IPCC, 2018). The report contrasts the impacts of warming of 1.5°C with that of 2°C, the nominal internationally agreed limit to global warming that scientists and policymakers have for many years agreed ought not be surpassed to avoid the worst effects of climate change. According to the IPCC's report, global warming is likely to reach 1.5°C as soon as 2030 if the current rate of warming is not halted. Impacts would be less severe than at 2°C. For example, global mean sea-level rise would be about 0.1 meter less at 1.5°C than at 2°C, allowing affected communities and ecological systems more time to adapt. Global warming of 1.5°C instead of 2°C would also have less severe impacts on marine biodiversity and ecosystems. Similarly, on land the lower level of warming would result in adverse impacts on ecosystems and loss of species, but those effects would be less serious than at 2°C. Global warming of 1.5°C will harm human health, undermine food security, endanger water supplies, undermine livelihoods and hinder economic growth, and these impacts will be even more severe at 2°C. Adapting to the impacts of climate change at 1.5°C will be difficult, with limited options. Not surprisingly, however, adaptation will be much easier if global warming is limited to 1.5°C than if it is allowed to increase further.

Limiting global warming to 1.5°C may be possible if the growth in world-wide emissions of CO_2 is halted no later than 2020 – which is likely to have happened due to the global economic slowdown arising from the coronavirus pandemic – *and* reduced by 45 percent by 2030. They must fall to zero (unless there are equivalent means to remove carbon from the environment) by 2050. This compares to what would be required to limit global warming to 2°C: cutting CO_2 by 25 percent by 2030 and reaching net zero emissions by about 2070. According to the IPCC, limiting global warming to 1.5°C will require "rapid and far-reaching transitions in energy, land, urban and infrastructure (including transport and buildings), and industrial systems. … These systems transitions are unprecedented in terms of scale, but not necessarily in terms of speed, and imply deep emissions reductions in all sectors…" (IPCC, 2018: 17).

Very importantly, and very worryingly, the IPCC's predictions for limiting warming to 1.5°C all assume major implementation of CO_2 removal measures (e.g., carbon capture and storage [CCS] technologies). Ominously, the IPCC reports that the only way to avoid the need for "large-scale deployment" of CO_2 removal would be to realize a decline in CO_2 emissions "well before 2030" (IPCC, 2018: 20).

The IPCC's report on 1.5°C of global warming demonstrates the importance of taking aggressive action to mitigate climate change. However, this must be contrasted with harsh realities. Without limits on GHG emissions that go far beyond those pledged by governments and industries, GHG emissions are unlikely to fall substantially anytime soon (WMO, 2019c) (short of persistent global economic decline). Even if fully implemented, pledges by governments to implement international agreements on climate change – the Paris Agreement in particular (see Chapter 3) – will result in global warming of more than 3°C before the end of this century (UNEP, 2019: 8). Indeed, in late 2019 the Secretary-General of the World Meteorological Organization (WMO) observed that "[t]here is no sign of a slowdown, let alone a decline, in greenhouse gases concentration in the atmosphere despite all the commitments under the Paris Agreement on Climate Change" (WMO, 2019b).

This trend reveals a tragic dilemma: up to now, there has been a near-total inability of climate governance to keep pace with climate science. *Already*, a "climate crisis disaster" is happening at a rate of once per week somewhere around the world (Harvey, 2019). The frequency of these events will only increase in the future (see Wallace-Wells, 2020). The trends of worsening climate change driven by still-increasing GHG pollution are tragic because the consequences will include great human suffering and environmental catastrophes – all from activities that were not intended to cause harm. They are, collectively, a historic dilemma because they result from humanity's pathological unwillingness, at a global scale, to choose between two desirable behaviors – enjoying the short-term benefits of polluting and consuming as if Earth's climate system were unaffected, on one hand, and behaving in ways that protect that climate system for perpetuity, on the other (see Chapters 3–7).

Denying the Crisis: The Politicization of Climate Science

Climate change is the most complicated and important scientific problem ever encountered. Why have governments (and other actors) been so slow to act on scientists' warnings about it? Part of the answer is found in the politicization of climate science. Despite the IPCC's tendency to be restrained in its dire predictions, for decades its findings have been routinely challenged by groups and individuals – generally labeled as "climate skeptics" or, more recently, "climate denialists" – as overstating the problem (Washington and Cook, 2011). Initially, large industries that profit from heavy use of fossil fuels, such as oil producers, major manufacturers and automobile companies, joined together to aggressively lobby governments to prevent international agreements and national policy action on the climate science. They used public relations and media campaigns to confuse the public about the realities of climate change. By politicizing climate science, and specifically be creating doubt about its reality and effects, they clouded understanding of otherwise clear reports from the IPCC and other scientific bodies. This cultivated sense of doubt has been made worse by "balanced" media coverage, which until recently reported the skeptics' views alongside the assessments of the scientists, and by "fake news" spread via online social media platforms. Over more than two decades, enough people and politicians were confused by this campaign to greatly restrain action on climate change. Skepticism and doubt about climate change has been especially influential in the United States, including within Congress and inside the federal government when it has been administered by Republicans (see Chapter 4). Even some US presidents have publicly expressed doubt about climate change, most recently Donald Trump, who apparently believed that it was a hoax of some kind (Baker, 2017).

However, as the science of climate change has become clearer, as the evidence has accumulated to demonstrate the accuracy of scientific predictions and as the realities of actual global warming and felt impacts of climate change have become more apparent around the world, publics have become more worried about the problem. It has become difficult for most politicians to remain climate skeptics, and many former skeptics now accept the science. That said, a hard core of climate denialists still exists, particularly in the United States, apparently including the Trump administration's heads of the US Environmental Protection Agency (EPA), not to mention numerous other officials appointed by President Trump.

Consequently, despite being in a minority, climate skeptics and denialists have been disproportionately influential in policy debates about climate change. To be sure, nearly all governments and the vast majority of people globally do not doubt climate science. That said, many people who believe the basic science still do not accept that things will be as bad in the future as scientists are predicting. These people might be referred to as "lukewarmers." They believe that global warming is happening, but that temperature rises and all that they portend will not be catastrophic. They believe that action is needed, but not major action and certainly not urgent action. They believe that global warming is manageable with modest effort. The danger of such views is that they help to hold back the bold policy actions that are needed to address both the causes and consequences of climate change.

Manufactured climate skepticism and denial inevitably affected the reporting of the IPCC. However, compared to its early assessments, in its most recent reports the panel has been more forthright in pronouncing the consensus among climatologists. In its fifth assessment report, the IPCC declared that "[w]arming of the climate system is unequivocal, and since the 1950s, many of the observed changes are unprecedented over decades to millennia. The atmosphere and ocean have warmed, the amounts of snow and ice have diminished, sea level has risen, and the concentrations of greenhouse gases have increased" (IPCC, 2013: 4). In its preceding assessment, the IPCC declared that "discernible human influences extend beyond average temperature to other aspects of climate, including temperature extremes and wind patterns" (IPCC, 2007: 40). These forthright findings are accepted by most governments, and they have informed international negotiations on climate change and related national policies in most countries. But they were long in coming, partly because the science is so complex, but also partly because the climate skeptics and their ilk created an environment in which many climatologists were afraid to express their true concerns for fear of being criticized by powerful interests.

What comes from this story is that climate science is definitely not just about science per se; it is also very much about politics. It demonstrates profoundly how climate change and power politics are intimately linked. This helps to explain why effective climate governance has been, and remains, such a monumentally difficult undertaking.

The Climate Change Dilemma

As the adverse impacts of climate change have been felt with greater frequency and intensity around the world, and as understanding of the problem has permeated the public imagination, especially among young people, climate skepticism and denial have lost their appeal in most places. Climate change is now on the front burner of global governance, and it seems only a matter of time before outliers (e.g., politicians, political parties and interest groups in Australia and the United States) openly accept the scientific consensus and the associated implications for climate governance. Yet, despite much progress, we cannot escape the reality that everything being done at present around the world to mitigate and adapt to climate change, and indeed everything that is likely to be done in coming years, will not be enough to avert extremely painful, and at least occasionally disastrous, impacts. As we have seen, the global pollution that is causing climate change continues to *increase*. The problem of climate change – increasingly referred to by world leaders as a climate emergency (Guterres, 2019b) – has reached the point where growing numbers of scientists are calling for global-scale efforts to engineer Earth's climate to prevent catastrophe arising from past, present and future GHG pollution (Pearce, 2019). The choice now is between holding on to behaviors and institutions that have prevailed for decades and centuries, and which have resulted in the worsening climate crisis, and finding new ways of thinking and behaving so as to avert disaster and cope effectively with a changing planet.

Ultimately, the climate dilemma and solutions to it arise from politics, specifically the way that those with power dominate certain resources and use them to promote their perceived interests. Most actors – national governments, subnational jurisdictions (such as municipalities and provinces), businesses, families and individuals – seek to promote and protect their own perceived interests. They are especially eager to protect their most vital interests, however discerned. For states' relations with one another, their most vital interest is perceived to be national security, which in normal times often involves seeking economic advantage vis-à-vis other countries. At the human level, individuals likewise seek to maintain their personal security and, when that seems assured, they routinely seek to promote their economic well-being in accordance with prevailing fashions of living. In the context of climate change, despite the mountain of evidence on the dangers of climate change (or perhaps due to its complexity), for many actors it is not clear where their interests lie – whether they involve continuing with the status quo further into the future or instead taking aggressive action today to combat climate change.

Why is the world still faced with this choice? Why has the governance of climate change failed to keep up with the science of climate change? Why have policy responses to climate change been so inadequate over a number of decades, and why do they remain inadequate? The next chapter begins to answer these questions by focusing on pathologies of *international* climate governance. Might something about the international system itself, the nature of the actors – states – that comprise it, and the manner in which they routinely behave help to explain the predicament of climate change?

PART II

Pathologies

3

Pathologies of International Relations

This chapter describes the basic features and lasting influence on climate governance of the international system of states. For centuries, and especially since World War II, countries have sought collective solutions to many problems through international collaboration of one sort or another. This is how issues as varied as trade, human rights and indeed other environmental problems have been addressed, often with great success. When the problem of climate change became apparent, countries responded to it in the same way: through diplomacy leading to international agreements for collective action. This chapter chronicles major aspects of this process. It summarizes how countries have negotiated a regime of international agreements and institutions intended to address climate change collectively and individually. A quarter-century was devoted to top-down measures – *internationally* agreed conventions and protocols setting out allowable GHG emissions for individual countries. More recently, the focus has been on bottom-up measures – *nationally* determined contributions to wider global efforts to govern climate change. While these efforts have resulted in a wide array of actions around the world to address climate change, and indeed they continue to do so, they demonstrate concretely the ways in which the international system, and the states operating within it, have precluded aggressive collective action.

The work of scientists has stimulated the global governance of climate change. However, the international system in which that governance has been formulated and implemented has resulted in a climate regime that is too febrile to address climate change effectively, hence the continued growth in GHG emissions described in the previous chapter. This brings us to the first of the pathologies of climate governance: the pathologies of international relations. These pathologies are rooted in the very idea of relations among states and even the notion of the state itself – its raison d'être and its fundamental motivations and behaviors. The pathologies of international relations arise from national interests and the system of states in which those interests intersect. That system encourages, and indeed is premised upon, a self-serving worldview whereby states inordinately focus on their individual short-term interests at the expense of the collective and long-term interests of humanity and the global ecosystem.

The pathologies of international relations have their roots in modern history, but they are older than the problem of human-caused climate change. They have permeated almost every aspect of climate governance – not just at the international level but also at the levels of national policy and individual behavior. These pathologies are so longstanding and tenacious that they cannot be cut out, as a tumor might be removed from a patient suffering from cancer. Yet, much like most bodily pathologies, ignoring them and failing to treat them will only make things worse. Addressing them is likely to bring substantial relief.

Roots of a Governance Pathology: The International System

Sovereign states have been the primary actors in climate governance, and it has been collective action by them that has largely determined the world's responses to climate change, notwithstanding myriad actions by non-state actors around the world. The stage upon which the global regime for governing climate change has been built is the international system of states. The international system is largely defined by interactions between and among the states that comprise it, much as a computer system is defined by inter-actions among its components, such as hardware and software. This system, and the behaviors of the states that populate it, have deep, widespread and persistent impacts on climate governance. Consequently, climate governance cannot be explained without knowledge of this system, and it cannot be made more effective if the system's inducements for states are not modified.

International History, Sovereignty and the National Interest

The world is largely governed by sovereign states. States have for centuries responded to collective action problems by trying to cooperate among them-selves. Consistent with this pattern, they have for several decades turned to diplomacy, routinely under the auspices of the United Nations, to negotiate potential solutions to climate change. These solutions have come in the form of international agreements (see below). This behavior is a logical outgrowth of the state system's historical evolution. It would have been unusual, even revolutionary, if global climate governance had been approached in a different way. For centuries many international and global problems, such as those relating to security, trade and human rights, were dealt with, or at least managed, quite effectively through diplomacy. Other transboundary environmental problems, such as dangers to migratory birds, pollution of rivers, regional air pollution, overfishing and the like, had been addressed through international diplomacy (Dorsey, 2014). Indeed, just as efforts to govern climate change were gaining in prominence in the 1980s, countries were able to negotiate a relatively effective set of agreements to eliminate pollutants destroying Earth's stratospheric ozone layer: the 1985 Vienna Convention and the 1987 Montreal Protocol (see Benedict, 1998).

Importantly for our understanding of potential alternatives to prevailing climate governance, the international system is not necessarily the only method for governing human affairs globally. The dominance of the international system, and the behavior it encourages among its member states, is not intrinsically natural. It is instead an outgrowth of the historical evolution of relations among political communities. It was sculpted and constituted by political leaders and their diplomats over centuries. The modern international system is putatively dated to the Peace of Westphalia of 1648, which ended the European Thirty Years' War of religion. (Hence, the modern international system is sometimes referred to as the Westphalian system.) The Peace of Westphalia was significant, and remains so today, because it codified (or is at least perceived to have done) the criteria that have since defined the global order: political communities that were party to the agreement were recognized as being their own masters rather than being the subjects of foreign religious or imperial powers. Each political community was recognized as being equally legitimate in the eyes of international law, and each agreed to accept, at least in principle, that what happened within another state would not be reason for war. Wars in Europe and elsewhere continued, to be sure, but following the Peace of Westphalia diplomacy and international law among mutually recognized states became norms that would dominate affairs among them (cf. Harris, 2013: 34–41).

Central to the international system are the principles of sovereignty and non-interference. The government of each state is recognized as having sovereignty – independent and supreme legal and political authority – within its territorial boundaries and over the people living there. In principle, sovereignty is inviolable unless relinquished by treaty or, in recent times, by extreme violation of international norms, such as by the commission of genocide. Accordingly, the internal affairs of a state are legally the concerns of that state and no other. Each state's government has the sole right to conduct its own domestic affairs and its relations with other countries – to have its own independent foreign policy. In principle, states are not entitled to intervene in the internal affairs of other states.

In reality, these fundamental precepts of the international system have been and are breached frequently. States regularly concern themselves with what is happening in other states, and it is not at all unusual for them to intervene in one another's affairs in many different ways, ranging from official criticisms (which most countries ignore, while others, such as China, find to be intolerable) to armed invasions, sometimes for concocted reasons (as was the case with the US invasion of Iraq in 2003). However, the fundamental principles of the international system have been self-sustaining for the simple and powerful reason that states themselves have a very fundamental interest in maintaining them. The international system creates and reinforces an obsession with protecting the interests of the state from external threats. Protecting the state's perceived interests – the "national interest" – becomes the primary purpose of governance.

For better or worse, each state aims to promote its perceived national interests as discerned by the powerful actors in that state. Foremost is the protection of the state's territorial integrity – without which there can be no state, a particularly vexing issue for some small-island states that will eventually be submerged due to climate change – and its continued existence as a sovereign entity. In addition to protecting the state's territory, other important national interests are (or are perceived to be) economic vitality, including a strong national economy, jobs, financial prosperity and connections with the world through profitable trade, as well as what can be characterized simply as the state's (or, even more precisely, the nation's) way of life, including preserving attributes such as the language, culture, religion, political system and other features that define a particular country and its population's sense of collective identity and purpose. From this prevailing perspective, national governments are seen to be legitimate if they defend these vital national interests. This is true to varying degrees in both democratic and non-democratic states.

States are not always focused solely on their own national interests. Both their governments and their citizens routinely show concern for the interests of other countries. This is evidenced by bilateral and especially multilateral international development assistance and even the occasional willingness of countries to use military force to aid other countries (and even people) for humanitarian reasons. That said, nearly all governments are very heavily inclined to promote the perceived interests of their own countries, whether those are the perceived interests of their citizens in democracies or the interests of the ruling party or elites in authoritarian countries. In times of crisis, such as during economic downturns and when threatened with military aggression, the interests of other countries become relatively or completely irrelevant unless connected to the crisis at hand. As scholars of political "realism" might argue, it is every state for itself much of the time, and every state for itself all of the time when the going gets tough.

This has significant implications for climate governance. National policies intended to mitigate climate change have the potential to adversely affect economic conditions in the short term, and they can be perceived as such even when they might be likely to do the opposite. Of equal or greater importance, those policies may adversely affect powerful interest groups. In both cases, the consequence is political resistance to climate action. In contrast, it is now clear that the effects of climate change will bring hardship to most countries, undermining long-term economic development and human health, and even pose an existential threat to some island countries. Naturally, this pushes the latter countries to support more assertive and impactful climate governance (see Chapter 6).

Collective Action and Globalization

Where countries often find common ground is in the need to work together to protect and promote their own interests. For centuries states have sought to solve collective action problems – that is, those that simply cannot be solved by acting individually – through international cooperation. History is replete with examples where acting in this way was vital to the survival of states. For example, a balance of power often arises in international relations when weaker countries ally together to defend themselves against more powerful actual or potential adversaries. Prominent examples of this include US interventions in Europe during the two world wars of the twentieth century. Joining together also happens in other issue areas, for example, when developing countries allied together in the 1970s to form the G-77 bloc as part of their efforts to win a greater share of the global economic pie from Western industrialized countries. A balance of power of sorts has also been manifested in international negotiations on climate change. Groups of countries have worked together in blocs (including the G-77) to enhance their bargaining power. This has often been seen when groups of relatively poor or vulnerable countries have allied together to push for action on climate change by rich or larger countries.

Since World War II, international cooperation has often been brokered by the United Nations and other international organizations. An outgrowth of this cooperation is a proliferation of international regimes, which can be defined as "principles, norms, rules and decision-making procedures around which actor expectations converge in a given issue-area" of international relations

(Krasner, 1982: 185). For example, in the postwar period, countries regularly negotiated norms and rules for international trade through institutions of the General Agreement on Tariffs and Trade and its successor, the World Trade Organization (WTO). Similarly, countries have responded to climate change by negotiating agreements and by trying to develop norms of behavior intended to address the problem. By definition, this cooperation has been consistent with the fundamental underlying norms of the international system, specifically those norms that assume the importance of assuring each country's self-perceived national interests. But this is precisely the problem – the pathology – of the system that makes truly effective collective action so difficult: these international norms are frequently stronger than the desire to protect Earth's climate system and to help those countries that are most affected by climate change (which often means poor countries) adapt to the consequences.

The basic assumption of the international system – that states' individual sovereignty and interests are all but inviolable – has always faced challenges, most profoundly when countries have gone to war. In recent decades, since about the 1970s, states' autonomy and sovereignty have been challenged by the forces of globalization. Globalization can be defined broadly as the erosion of governments' control over what happens within and across their borders. Manifestations of globalization include the increasing integration of national economies through transnational trade, production and finance, and a speeding up and deepening of connections among economies and people. Globalization has for decades been encouraged by governments and other actors that support global free-market capitalism and the economic integration of the entire world. It has enabled people to share information and interact easily regardless of national borders. Much of this has been accelerated by technologies of the microelectronic revolution, manifested in things such as "smart" telephones (e.g., the Apple iPhone), the World Wide Web, Internet-video applications (e.g., Skype and Zoom) and so forth. Globalization has arguably helped many countries economically – the remarkable expansion of China's economy and its newfound global influence would be hard to imagine without globalized trade – but it has hurt others in various ways, resulting, for example, in the effective export of jobs and even entire industries (arguably helping to explain the rise of populist leaders around the world, including in some EU countries and the United States).

Economic globalization has received most of the world's attention; for most people, the word "globalization" may evoke notions of mostly unrestricted international trade and of global economic winners and losers. To be sure, globalization has limited the ability of most countries to manage autonomously their own national economies, thereby affecting economic development.

But the most profound manifestation of globalization is arguably not economic; it is instead *environmental*. This is because globalization has been fueled by decades of massive extraction, transport and consumption of natural resources needed to stoke the material economic growth for which globalization received so much praise in the West, at least until relatively recently. This environmental globalization, manifested most profoundly in climate change, is challenging the sovereignty of states like nothing else. Put simply, governments cannot stop climate change from affecting what happens within their territories; often they cannot even mitigate its impacts without relying on the cooperation and collective action of other countries.

For some countries, the impacts of climate change, such as sea-level rise, present existential threats: those impacts might wipe them off the map. For such countries, climate change is the ultimate erosion of sovereignty. Collective action on climate change is clearly in their national interests. A big problem is that many other countries, including those that are the largest sources of the GHG pollution that ultimately threatens the existence of some countries, have not yet perceived their own national interests as being best served by joining in the collective action that is required. Thus, governing climate change effectively will require an expansion of what is perceived to be in the latter countries' national interests. It will have to include preservation of Earth's climate system.

Top-Down Governance: The Emergence of a Framework

One cannot understate the power of the principles of the international system in the context of climate governance. While many scientists, activists and, increasingly, citizens view climate change as a global problem requiring collective global action, for most national governments, politicians and diplomats, climate change is customarily defined in terms of "state-centric territorialization" (O'Lear, 2010: 34). From this dominant perspective, and according to the prevailing arguments of many, perhaps still most, governments, climate change is foremost a problem *for states*, GHG emissions are measured in terms *of states*, climate negotiations are of course *among states*, obligations and interests are held *by states*, the problem is perceived to create security challenges *for states*, the scientists in the IPCC are nominated by the governments *of states* and so on. This "territorial trap" has constrained how climate change is perceived and thereby narrowed the preferred policy options (Patterson and Stripple, 2007: 156). For example, the overarching question of how to allocate GHG-emissions entitlements globally has become "unambiguously a statist project, which starts from, and reinforces, the conception that it is states that have both rights and responsibilities in relation to the rest of the world," with the "logical" governance options therefore focusing on those which diplomats can negotiate while assuming the sovereign equality of states (Patterson and Stripple, 2007: 157).

Some countries have taken the sovereignty principles underlying the international system to extremes. For example, at the 2009 Copenhagen conference of the parties to the climate change convention (discussed below), China refused to accept outside monitoring of even its voluntary pledges to improve energy efficiency. It justified this refusal on the grounds that attempts by international secretariats or other states to verify implementation of its voluntary pledges would constitute interference in its internal affairs and thus would be serious violations of its national sovereignty. It must be assumed that other countries were suspicious of China's pledges if, when making them, it simultaneously refused to allow verification of their implementation. The reasonable consequence of such suspicion is for many of those other countries to similarly reject international verification and standardization of pledges and actions through a negotiated "rulebook" of common international standards, something that sank the 2019 international negotiations on how to implement the 2015 Paris Agreement (also discussed below).

Whether the lack of trust in China's or other countries' pledges is justified is not the point. (As it happens, there are reasons to be suspicious, as noted in the next chapter.) The point is that the principles and norms of the international system that emerged from seventeenth-century Europe have been very powerful at the level of diplomatic negotiations on climate change, thereby affecting the outcomes of those negotiations. The longstanding principles of the international system, most powerfully the inviolability of individual countries' rights and interests, have contributed to weak climate change agreements year after year, decade after decade. This is a chronic pathology of international relations at work, something that is reflected in negotiations to craft the climate regime. A summary of that process follows (cf. Harris, 2018: 129–36).

Negotiating International Governance: The Framework Convention on Climate Change

Due to increasing scientific knowledge of the potential dangers of climate change, in December 1990 the UN General Assembly established the Intergovernmental Negotiating Committee for a Framework Convention on Climate Change. The goal of that committee was to negotiate a "framework" convention, much as happened in negotiations in Vienna in 1985 to address stratospheric ozone depletion (Benedict, 1998). The framework convention would form the foundation of subsequent "protocol" agreements to deal with the problem of climate change. Diplomats from more than 150 countries negotiated the UN Framework Convention on Climate Change (UNFCCC), which was signed at the 1992 UN Conference on Environment and Development, popularly known as the "Earth Summit." The declared objective of the framework convention was, and remains, the "stabilization of greenhouse gas concentrations in the atmosphere at a level that would prevent dangerous anthropogenic interference with the climate system" (UN, 1992: article 2). While the precise definition of "dangerous" was not specified (quite a normal thing for international agreements), the convention did make clear that the level of acceptable GHG emissions would be one allowing "ecosystems to adapt naturally to climate change, to ensure that food production is not threatened and to enable economic development to proceed in a sustainable manner" (UN, 1992: article 2). The convention, which came into force in 1994, called on the economically developed countries to reduce voluntarily their GHG emissions to 1990 levels by 2000. In addition to agreeing to reduce their GHG pollution, which, it turned out, they failed to do, developed countries also agreed to provide "new and additional" resources to developing countries to help them address climate change. This pledge to provide aid did not come easily. The United States, for example, was very much opposed to taking on new obligations to provide assistance to developing countries.

Negotiations for the framework convention were fraught in other ways, with major disagreements between economically developed and developing countries in particular. (Throughout this book, "developed" countries refers to the more industrialized and economically prosperous states of the Global North, including those parties listed in Annex I of the UNFCCC. "Developing" countries here are the less economically developed and poor states of the Global South. The UNFCCC officially lists some highly developed and middle-income countries, for example, South Korea and China, as "non-Annex I" parties that are not required to reduce emissions [see UNFCCC, 2020]. As used here, the latter types of countries are not considered to be actually "developing.") These disagreements between developed and developing countries set a precedent for subsequent negotiations toward a protocol and other agreements intended to realize the declared aims of the framework convention. Indeed, the struggle between the most-affluent and most-polluting countries, on one hand, and the relatively poor and highly vulnerable countries, on the other, have waxed and waned for several decades, reflected prominently even in the most recent climate negotiations, which were held in December 2019 (see below).

International negotiations leading to the Framework Convention on Climate Change were a harbinger of things to come. During the 1990s, negotiations among countries to devise means for addressing climate change effectively become regularized and recurring. In 1995 the Conference of the Parties to the framework convention was established. The meetings of this conference of states, referred to as "COPs," quickly became more-or-less annual events (the planned 2020 conference – COP26 – was rescheduled to November 2021 due to the global coronavirus pandemic), often with interim meetings held to prepare the way for more prominent annual gatherings, the latter sometimes including high-level officials and, occasionally, heads of state and government. The COPs would become the overriding authority of the framework convention, with the objective of negotiating the details of how GHG limitations and other aspects of the framework convention would be achieved.

At the first Conference of the Parties – COP1 – held in Berlin in 1995, developed countries acknowledged that they had a greater share of the responsibility for causing climate change and should therefore act to address it first. This acknowledgment became known as the "Berlin Mandate," central to which was the recurring demand of developing countries that affluent countries take on greater commitments to reduce their GHG emissions and, very importantly, to assist the poor countries in achieving environmentally sustainable development and to cope with the impacts of climate change. The Berlin Mandate was an affirmation of common but differentiated responsibility (CBDR), an important key principle of climate governance that had been formalized in the UNFCCC (UN, 1992: article 3). According to this concept, all countries have *common* responsibility to address climate change, but the economically developed countries have *differentiated* – that is, much greater – obligation to do so.

Implementing International Governance:
Two Decades of Trying from the Top Down

At COP2 in Geneva in 1996, diplomats called for a legally binding protocol to the UNFCCC that would have specific targets and timetables for limiting GHG emissions from developed countries. That conference culminated in the Geneva Ministerial Declaration, which would become the foundation for the first formal protocol to the UNFCCC: the Kyoto Protocol (UN 1996: 71–4). The protocol was negotiated in December 1997 at COP3 in Kyoto. It required most developed countries collectively to reduce their GHG emissions by 5.2 percent below 1990 levels by 2012 (UNFCCC, 1998: article 3). Importantly, and in keeping with the CBDR principle, the Kyoto Protocol did not require developing countries to limit their GHG emissions at all. This partly explains why not all developed countries agreed to be bound by the protocol. As for those that did agree, much as developed countries failed to do what they promised in the UNFCCC, collectively they also did not actually do what the Kyoto Protocol required of them. This happened despite a range of methodologies used to make implementation more palatable and easier for states that were party to the protocol.

While the Kyoto Protocol was a "top-down" instrument – that is, by agreement it imposed negotiated GHG limitations on countries – it was designed to provide flexibility in implementing its objectives. This flexibility was to be achieved through three related market-based mechanisms: emissions trading (the "carbon market"), joint implementation and the Clean Development Mechanism (CDM). Emissions trading enabled developed countries to barter emissions credits among themselves. If a country could limit its emissions more than required by the protocol, it would have unused emissions reductions that it could sell to other countries with reduction targets. The price of the unused emissions reductions was to be determined by market demand. One contentious issue among all countries was whether the use of carbon sinks, such as planting forests and other land-use changes that remove GHGs from the atmosphere, should be counted alongside concrete reductions in GHG emissions. The effectiveness of such an approach is a subject of enduring debate, in part because sinks might be reversed. For example, trees planted to sequester CO_2 might be cut down prematurely or lost to fire. Nevertheless, sinks would continue to be one of the means for trying to mitigate future GHG concentrations in the atmosphere.

Another market-based mechanism under the Kyoto Protocol was joint implementation. Under this scheme, developed countries could earn emissions credits when investing in one another's emissions-reduction projects. The aim was to allow developed countries to join forces to use the least expensive means of reducing their joint GHG pollution. The Clean Development Mechanism is similar in that it was designed to allow developed countries to achieve their emissions limitations, or to receive saleable emissions credits for use in the carbon market, by supporting emissions-reduction projects in developing countries that were not subject to emissions limitations themselves. (From a global climatic perspective, it makes little difference where GHG emissions cuts are made.) The CDM scheme quickly resulted in an expanding market for emissions credits from projects in China, India and other developing countries (although China took the vast bulk of the projects in the early years). The intent was for these countries to build less-polluting factories and other facilities than they might have done without assistance from the CDM, or to clean up existing factories that might not have been cleaned up otherwise.

The argument in favor of CDM projects was that they had the potential to be good for all of the countries involved: developed countries would be able to reduce their GHG pollution at lower cost by paying for projects in developing countries, and the latter countries that had suitable projects would benefit from new investment. Furthermore, cleaner facilities would reduce local air pollution. However, these projects were not without their problems. One concern was that many of them would go ahead even without CDM investment, meaning wasted funding and the counting of GHG cuts by developed countries that they arguably would not deserve. Another concern was that projects were created simply to profit from the CDM's financial transfers, not specifically to limit GHG emissions, for example, by constructing a polluting factory for the purpose of shutting it down in return for a CDM payment.

It was clear in the 1990s that addressing climate change effectively would require emissions limitations from both developed and larger developing countries – from all countries contributing substantially to GHG pollution. Yet, for some years much of the attention at COPs was focused on finding means for implementing the very limited objectives of the Kyoto Protocol. Some of these means were negotiated at COP4 held in Buenos Aires in 1998 (IISD, 1998). At COP5 in Bonn in 1999, a timetable for completing outstanding details of the Kyoto Protocol were agreed (UN, 1999). Two sessions were needed to complete COP6, starting in 2000 at The Hague (IISD, 2000) and concluding in Bonn in 2001 (IISD 2001). Around this time, ratification of the Kyoto Protocol by signatories was put into doubt with the election of Republican George W. Bush to the presidency of the United States (see Chapter 4). He subsequently withdrew US support for the protocol – much as his fellow Republican, Donald J. Trump, would move to withdraw the United States from the 2015 Paris Agreement two decades later (see below). Nevertheless, COP6 resulted in further discussions, albeit with much disagreement, on emissions trading, carbon sinks, compliance mechanisms and aid to developing countries.

Diplomats formulated the Marrakech Accords at COP7 in 2001 (UN, 2002). The accords were a complex set of proposals for implementing the Kyoto Protocol, largely designed to "buy" ratification from enough developing countries to allow the protocol to enter into force. Diplomats also agreed to increase funding for the UNFCCC's financial mechanism – the Global Environment Facility – and to create several new funds to help poor countries: the Least Developed Countries Fund, the Special Climate Change Fund and the Adaptation Fund. Creation of the Adaptation Fund served as formal recognition by states that efforts to mitigate climate change would not be enough to prevent painful impacts, notably in poor countries.

That idea was reinforced in 2002 at COP8 in New Delhi, where diplomats shifted focus away from the forlorn objective of cutting GHG emissions toward adapting to unavoidable climate change. At the conference, developed countries agreed to help developing countries do the latter (UNFCCC, 2002). This approach would enable developed countries to avoid having to undertake as many costly actions to reduce GHG emissions as would be required if mitigation of climate change were to remain the overriding priority. Because developing countries were expected to be hit by the effects of climate change anyway, the shift toward adaptation had some practical merits, specifically that those countries might benefit from additional assistance from richer parts of the world. Because GHG concentrations in the atmosphere had by then probably reached the point where very significant climate change had become inevitable, adaptation was an obvious near-term priority for those most affected.

At COP9, which met in Madrid in 2003, diplomats discussed ways to implement previous agreements, such as the Marrakech Accords, and to move toward ratification of the Kyoto Protocol, and there were calls for stronger and more urgent national action on climate change – essentially calls for countries to put common cause above narrow national interests, which have been repeated at every COP (IISD, 2003). In 2004 Russia ratified the Kyoto Protocol (see Chapter 5), thereby enabling it to enter into force the following year. At COP10, held in Buenos Aires in late 2004, negotiations once again focused more on adaptation to climate change than on the mitigation goals of the protocol – so much so that the conference was dubbed the "Adaptation COP" (IISD, 2004: 14). Reflecting what had been and remains a trend in climate negotiations, the Buenos Aires conference resulted in more pledges of additional assistance to aid the poor countries that were expected to be most affected by climate change. However, there were no clear commitments made to enable access to that funding.

COP11, which also met as "First Conference of the Parties Serving as the Meeting of the Parties" to the now-in-force Kyoto Protocol, convened in Montreal in 2005 (IISD, 2005). The conference began the process of formalizing implementation of the protocol through negotiation of rules for emissions trading, joint implementation, crediting of emissions sinks and penalties for non-compliance. Steps to strengthen the CDM and to establish guidelines for the Adaptation Fund were also discussed. Several developing countries expressed interest in undertaking *voluntary* measures to limit their national GHG emissions, likely realizing that doing so was needed to call the bluff of developed countries, not least the United States, which had been demanding action by them before it would agree to greater burdens itself. That said, those developing countries remained strongly opposed to *binding* obligations to limit their emissions. It would be another decade before a more universal approach to GHG limitations – whereby *all* countries would take some sort of action (thus satisfying persistent US demands) – was formally codified in the Paris Agreement (see below).

Subsequent climate negotiations resulted in incremental steps, at least in rhetorical terms, toward action on climate change, in the process highlighting recurring differences among countries about how best to achieve the objectives of both the UNFCCC and its Kyoto Protocol. The continued challenges and limited ambitions of most countries were revealed at COP12 in 2006, held in Nairobi, during which diplomats agreed that there would be no new commitments under the Kyoto Protocol anytime soon (IISD, 2006). Similar to other conferences before it, differences among countries were apparent at COP13 in Bali in 2007. At COP13, European countries argued for greater international commitments for GHG cuts, revealing their growing willingness to take more action to address climate change than the United States was willing to do. In contrast, the United States strongly opposed adding new commitments, even as developing countries argued that they ought to receive more financial and technological assistance. The discussions at Bali were pushed to a substantial degree by the IPCC's fourth assessment report (IPCC, 2007), which would have removed any remaining doubt about the main causes and consequences of climate change were it not for the lingering influence of climate skepticism, especially in the United States. One significant aspect of the Bali conference was widespread opposition to efforts by US diplomats to prevent negotiation of a new agreement that would require developed countries to go substantially further to reduce their GHG pollution and to provide much more assistance to developing countries to help them adapt to climate change. The conference resulted in the so-called Bali Roadmap, which was intended to guide negotiations toward more robust action and a related agreement to be finalized at COP15 two years later (IISD, 2007).

A tiny step in that direction was COP14, which met in Poznan, Poland, in 2008. The Poznan COP was noteworthy because even the European countries that had for a decade argued in favor of greater action to address climate change were less supportive of deeper GHG emissions cuts (IISD, 2008). This was perhaps not surprising given the global financial crisis that took hold the same year. Yet, by this point in the international negotiations on climate change – more than two decades since they had begun in earnest – there was realization that much more needed to be done if the objectives of the climate convention, including avoiding dangerous interference in Earth's climate system, were to be achieved. This realization, including at the highest levels of governments, was reflected in the extent to which countries, including a majority of their leaders, participated in the COP15 Copenhagen conference at the end of 2009: diplomats representing 192 states, and 119 state leaders, were in attendance (IISD, 2009). The most important outcome of COP15 was the Copenhagen Accord. The accord was agreed on the last day of the conference by a small number of diplomats and leaders, including US president Barack Obama, meeting behind closed doors. This "butting of heads" in private was necessary to reach an agreement, but it reflected the persistent influence of powerful countries not only to garner agreement but also to limit its impact on their perceived national interests.

The Copenhagen Accord reaffirmed the science of climate change, acknowledged the need to stop increasing GHG pollution globally and declared that global warming should be limited to not more than 2°C above the historical average. (The 2°C limit evolved as a political objective; it is not derived from science [Titley, 2017], as demonstrated by the more recent aspiration, codified in the Paris Agreement [see below], of limiting warming to 1.5°C.) The accord offered a fig leaf (at least a paper one) to developing countries by promising $100 billion in annual assistance from developed countries by 2020, and it established the Green Climate Fund to help those countries cope with the impacts of climate change (UN, 2009).

At first glance, the Copenhagen Accord was a significant step forward because it appeared to demonstrate commitment to the cause of addressing climate change by most of the world's governments, including those in the Global North. On closer inspection, however, the accord looked to be something less. That is because, just as happened with the original pledge by countries at the 1992 Earth Summit, the accord's provisions were *voluntary*. Countries had revealed a willingness to *pledge* action. However, in most cases they had also revealed, or rather reaffirmed, a continued unwillingness to accept and implement internationally mandated robust cuts to their GHG pollution. Indeed, the Copenhagen COP was so weak in its outcomes, especially compared to expectations and the realities of climate change, that it was routinely deemed to be a failure (see, e.g., Vidal, Stratton and Goldenberg, 2009). Consequently, at the Cancun COP16 in 2010, diplomats yet again concluded their negotiations by saying that more effort was needed, although they were unable to agree on what to do when the Kyoto Protocol was scheduled to expire in 2012 (IISD, 2010).

Bottom-Up Governance: National Pledges to Rein in Climate Change

The tortuous diplomatic process to negotiate the Kyoto Protocol and work toward its implementation revealed a fundamental problem with climate governance: like any collective action problem among countries, those that are called upon to act will often avoid doing so. The United States, which until about a decade ago was the largest national source of GHG pollution historically, has been a case in point. Over decades of international negotiations on climate change, the United States never really displayed a strong willingness to change its ways (see Chapter 4). It used its diplomatic muscle to water down the Kyoto Protocol. Nobody seriously thought that cutting GHG emissions of developed countries by about 5 percent, as required by the protocol, would do much to solve the problem. The United States also used its influence to see that the protocol remained weak in implementation. A big reason for US reticence could be found in the CBDR principle, which served as the foundation of the climate convention and the Kyoto Protocol: that developing countries ought not bear the burden before developed countries, most of all the United States, take on theirs. The "differentiated" aspect of CBDR was a core feature of top-down international climate governance, but the United States wanted emphasis on the "common" aspect of it.

Something had to give, or so many argued. Ultimately, it was becoming clear that, with too many countries unwilling to compromise their perceived national interests for the common interests of battling climate change, the top-down approach to climate governance – negotiations among diplomats leading to international regulations to be imposed on states – was not working. Diplomats from the United States and several other countries had for years advocated an alternative, bottom-up approach, one in which individual countries would set their own pollution-reduction targets based on their own capabilities and circumstances. Given the failure of the Kyoto process, the Americans got their way. This bottom-up approach would guide the next major stage in international climate governance.

The Withering of Top-Down Governance: Moving beyond the Kyoto Protocol

By the time that diplomats met in 2011 for COP17 in Durban, South Africa, it was clear that the top-down approach to climate governance would not result in policies that could achieve the objectives of the climate convention. Perhaps recognizing that more effort was needed, diplomats at the conference agreed to several measures, including the Durban Platform for Enhanced Action. This platform was new insofar as it charted out a path toward future GHG emissions limitations by developing countries, specifically "nationally appropriate mitigation actions" (UN, 2012: 8). Diplomats at Durban agreed to keep the Kyoto Protocol alive and committed their governments to negotiate an entirely new climate agreement – which would become the 2015 Paris Agreement – that would include pledges for GHG limitations by *all* countries. Diplomats from the European Union called for the new agreement to include legally binding emissions commitments from large developing countries, essentially making the same argument that the United States had been making for years. Meanwhile, China and India argued that developed countries should first implement past agreements. China's chief diplomat at the Durban conference suggested that China would consider accepting new commitments after 2020, but only if developed countries fulfilled the obligations that they had agreed to accept during earlier COPs.

Despite the title of COP17's platform suggesting that it was about additional action, its contents were mostly boilerplate pledges to implement previously negotiated agreements. For example, the platform called for implementing the Green Climate Fund and finding new sources of financing for developing countries, but it did not identify the actual sources of that funding (IISD, 2011). Importantly, the action plan agreed at COP17 reaffirmed the objective of keeping global warming below 2°C. At the same time, negotiators acknowledged that twice that level of global warming was likely without new national commitments to cut global emissions of GHG pollution much more aggressively. At the conclusion of COP17, there was little prospect that governments would agree to those essential cuts.

The Durban conference once again exposed a basic flaw in climate change governance: states are congenitally inclined to put their own perceived short-term interests before common long-term environmental objectives. Nevertheless, efforts to move toward the latter continued, manifested in negotiations at COP18, held in 2012 in Doha, and at COP19, held in Warsaw in 2013 (IISD, 2012; IISD, 2013). The outcomes of these conferences were consistent with past conferences: agreement to continue negotiations and to work toward resolving the perennial problem of developed countries (most prominently the United States) failing to meet their obligations and developing countries (most ominously China) quickly becoming major sources of global GHG pollution.

In late 2014, shortly before COP20 in Lima, Peru, the IPCC released new assessment reports reaffirming that climate change would have ruinous environmental and social impacts (see, e.g., IPCC, 2014a; IPCC, 2014b). The reports pointed to the urgent need for both GHG cuts and preparations to adapt to unavoidable climate change. In a separate report, the UN Environment Program argued that urgent action would be required to stem the growth in GHG emissions, specifically halving them very quickly and eliminating them completely later in the century (UNEP, 2014). At COP20, several developed countries offered to contribute substantial new money to the Green Climate

Fund (IISD, 2014). This was probably intended, at least in part, to nudge developing countries to take on GHG emissions limitations of their own. Indeed, at a China-US summit that nearly coincided with the Lima conference, Chinese president Xi Jinping said that China's carbon emissions would level off no later than 2030, and US president Barrack Obama pledged that US emissions would fall by a quarter or more by 2025 (White House, 2014). Significantly, both Xi and Obama used 2005 as the base year for their pledges. This meant that their proposed limits on GHG pollution were not nearly as impressive as they might have been had both presidents used the 1990 base year that had been the norm since the Earth Summit in 1992.

The agreement that emanated from COP20 – the Lima Accord (UN, 2014) – was significant in that, for better or worse, it was a clear shift away from the traditional differentiation between developed and developing countries that had permeated the climate regime for decades. Lima was at least a partial repudiation of the original premise of CBDR principle: it emphasized the common responsibility of *all* countries to act on climate change, albeit still expecting historical polluters of the Global North to take on greater responsibility for climate change and to provide aid to developing countries affected by it. Developing countries would not be expected necessarily to promise future *cuts* in their GHG emissions – although that is what the science suggested was needed from the largest polluters among them – but they would be expected to pledge future emissions *limitations* (i.e., at least taking steps to restrain increases in future emissions relative to what they might be without acting on such pledges). However, the Lima Accord did not include any concrete new pledges from countries to cut their contributions to growing global GHG pollution. That was to come the following year in the run-up to COP21.

Embarking on Bottom-Up Governance: The Paris Agreement and Beyond

The COP21 conference, held in Paris in late 2015, was the culmination of efforts to move international climate governance away from top-down collective mandates to bottom-up national pledges. The conference resulted in the Paris Agreement, which, for the first time in the decades-long history of international negotiations on climate change, required developing countries, in addition to developed countries, to limit their GHG pollution (UN, 2015a). The requirements of the agreement – what each country would be required to do by way of limiting its GHG emissions – were to be *self*-declared in the form of Nationally Determined Contributions (NDCs) to the collective Paris Agreement objectives. This bottom-up approach to climate regulation – essentially self-regulation – for the first time openly put the sovereign autonomy of states foremost, albeit in the cause of achieving a common, global objective to govern climate change more effectively. Whatever one thinks of the utility and fairness of such an approach, it is clear that it hews much more closely to the underlying principles of the international system than did many earlier agreements. One great advantage of this approach is that it garnered nearly universal participation; almost every state in the world joined. An associated disadvantage is that this bottom-up, nationally determined approach does not necessarily go far beyond what countries would do anyway.

Importantly, COP21 went beyond previous conferences by affirming that all countries would pledge to take action to contribute to the common goal of limiting global warming to less than 2°C *and* to work toward action that would prevent global warming from surpassing 1.5°C (IISD, 2015). In addition to pledges by developed countries to be more forthright with financial assistance to help developing countries, the latter aspiration of limiting warming to 1.5°C was a concession to those countries that were most vulnerable to climate change. Significantly, each country pledged to limit its national emissions in some way, although not necessarily to *reduce* them. The idea was that these pledges (the NDCs) would become baselines for more robust action in the future. However, it was quickly apparent that the national pledges to implement the Paris Agreement would not be nearly enough. Even if all of them were to be fully implemented by almost every country, global warming would likely surpass 3°C (UNEP, 2016). That warming, which would be double the warming aspired to by the agreement, was a recipe for dangerous climate change, precisely what the foundational climate convention (the UNFCCC) was designed to avoid.

All of the conferences of the parties to the climate convention that followed COP21 dedicated much of their attention to reaching agreement on implementation of the Paris Agreement – which entered into force in November 2016 – and finding ways to increase the "ambition" of countries' NDC pledges so that they would limit their GHG pollution enough to have hope of realizing the agreement's objectives. Meeting in Marrakech in mid-November 2016, COP22 resulted in the Marrakech Action Proclamation for Our Climate and Sustainable Development. The proclamation was, in effect, a laundry list of familiar steps to be taken to address climate change. It devoted much attention to the priorities of developing countries, such as mobilization of new financing, capacity building in the developing world and otherwise increasing support for affected countries (IISD, 2016). The COP faced new doubt about the role of the United States when, just before the conference commenced, Donald Trump won the presidential election there.

The next conference of the parties, COP23, was hosted by Fiji and held in Bonn in 2017 (IISD, 2017). Like many of its predecessors, COP23 was a "procedural" meeting, focusing mostly on technical issues and operationalization of the Paris Agreement. Naturally, diplomats sought to ensure that such technicalities would not undermine their own countries' perceived national interests. This was reflected once again in debates over finance, with developing countries calling for more effort by developed countries to produce it, and developed countries often working to avoid doing just that. In the end, they agreed in principle that the Adaptation Fund would serve the Paris Agreement. In addition to negotiating aspects of the so-called Paris Rules for implementation of the Paris Agreement, COP23 agreed to terms of the Talanoa Dialogue for Climate Ambition, which was intended to be a facilitative dialogue (i.e., sharing of ideas and information) among countries and other actors between COP23 and COP24 (Fiji, 2017).

The contrast between COP23, which was hosted by a small-island developing country highly vulnerable to climate change, and COP24, which was held in 2018 in Poland, one of the most polluting countries in Europe and one that was highly reliant for energy upon, and was politically wedded to, its large coal industry, was revealing. The populist host government of Poland was in no mood for pushing action that would threaten its bedrock of support among coal miners. (It was no coincidence that the host city, Katowice, was in the heart of Poland's coal-mining region.) Consequently, like its predecessor, COP24 focused substantially on technical matters, notably progress on drafting the rulebook for implementing the Paris Agreement. Once more, the question of common versus differentiated responsibilities was prominent, with developing countries again arguing for their differentiated, flexible commitments to action and developed countries generally arguing for equal accountability by all countries (IISD, 2018). In the end, as in previous conferences, pledges by developed countries to assist developing countries with climate finance overcame some differences, as did the fact that many of the most contentious issues were, also once again, pushed to the next COP.

At the time of writing, the most recent conference of the parties to the climate convention was COP25 held in Madrid at the end of 2019. (The COP was initially planned for Brazil, but it was moved, first to Chile after the right-wing politician – and vocal climate-denialist – Jair Bolsonaro was elected president and withdrew Brazil's support for the conference. The COP was then moved from Chile, the formal state host of the conference, to Madrid due to civil unrest in Chile.) The scale of the conference, involving tens of thousands of participants, was indicative of the interest among all actors – state, substate and nonstate – in the international approach to climate governance. Important focal points of the conference included whether developing countries would be compensated for loss and damage from climate change and, as always, questions of climate finance. There was some modest progress on these points, albeit largely pointing to what countries believed that they ought to do sometime in the future. There was little clarity on where the finance, specifically the developed countries' longstanding – and unfulfilled – promise of providing $100 billion annually to vulnerable developing countries by 2020, would come from (Ives, 2018). A major area of negotiation included a recurring sticking point from previous COPs: the use of market mechanisms, and specifically the rules for when and how countries would be allowed to use them to implement the NDC pledges that they had given at Paris four years earlier (IISD, 2019). Questions of ambition – how to strengthen NDCs so that they might, if implemented, actually achieve the Paris goal of limiting global warming to no more than 2°C, and ideally 1.5°C – remained largely unresolved.

The COP25 meeting ended without new emissions pledges, despite a months-long full-court press by Antonio Guterres, the UN Secretary General (Farand, 2019a). He had convened the Climate Action Summit at the United Nations a few months before COP25. During that summit, diplomats reaffirmed the need to limit global warming to 1.5°C, and 70 of them informally pledged their countries to achieve net-zero GHG emissions by 2050 – although none of the world's largest polluters was among them, and together those 70 countries produced only one-tenth of global GHG emissions (UN, 2019). The Madrid COP was also preceded by a deluge of scientific reports warning of the dire consequences of climate change if aggressive cuts in GHG emissions were not forthcoming (see, e.g., IPCC, 2019). Diplomats at the COP faced historically overwhelming pressure from NGOs and activists, not least Greta Thunberg, the Swedish student who mobilized hundreds of thousands of young people around the world to "strike" for climate action.

Those calling for more action viewed COP25 as an opportunity for countries to greatly increase their NDC pledges. However, many of the diplomats involved in the negotiations saw things differently. Tensions between countries (or at least their governments) with perceived interests in slowing action on climate change, ranging from Australia (see Chapter 5) to Saudi Arabia (see Chapter 6), and those that wanted greater action, including some European countries (see Chapter 5) and of course the most vulnerable countries on the frontline of climate change (e.g., small-island states; see Chapter 6), were very much in evidence. As at previous COPs, the question was which developed countries would make big cuts in their GHG pollution; whether some of the large developing countries, not least China, would take greater action; how national GHG limitations would be measured; and which countries would pay, and how much, the poorest countries most vulnerable to, and harmed by, climate change.

The twenty-fifth COP was indicative of the continued power of countries' perceived national interests relative to the growing pleas of activists, and increasingly climatologists, to take much more aggressive action to stop global GHG pollution. It showed, much as COP21 in Copenhagen had done, that growing concerns about climate change, including among many countries' leaders, do not necessarily translate into concerted action on climate change. If anything, the pattern seems to be something akin to the opposite. Experienced observers of COPs over decades identified the fundamental source of failure at COP25: "Under the Paris Agreement, the level of countries' ambition is determined nationally. There are primarily only soft levers, based on moral suasion, that can convince parties to do more. For COP 25, these limitations were in the agenda, defined by parties themselves. The modest mandates for COP 25 were set years ago, through states' self-interested negotiations" (IISD, 2019: 26). A number of participants in the Madrid COP "pointed to a 'lost decade' of action by developed countries in terms of mitigation and support provided to developing countries" (IISD, 2019: 26). There was that, to be sure, but in truth they might have more accurately pointed to lost *decades*. A very big explanation for those lost decades is found in the pathologies that are inherent to the international system.

Both top-down and bottom-up approaches to international climate governance (summarized in Table 3.1) have resulted in progress toward addressing climate change. They have been reflected in new policies on climate change in a number of countries. However, aggressive action to reverse climate pollution in major ways, and indeed to deal with the impacts of climate change, have been severely lacking globally. One might argue that it is early days to assess the effectiveness of the bottom-up approach. Whether the Paris Agreement has any chance of being successful will be determined by whether it is a catalyst for countries to take far more aggressive action in the very near future to reduce enormously their collective GHG pollution and to end their economies' dependence on fossil fuels.

Initial indications have been mixed at best. The United States has been schizophrenic on the Paris Agreement (see Chapter 4). It was embraced by President Barrack Obama, who put in place national policies to help nudge the United States away from heavy reliance on coal, although even his efforts would not have been enough. In contrast, his successor, Donald Trump, declared US withdrawal from the agreement. The Trump administration worked to undo alternative-energy policies of the Obama administration and

Table 3.1 *International climate governance: top-down and bottom-up*

	Top-down international governance	Bottom-up international governance
Major international agreement under the 1992 UN Framework Convention on Climate Change	1997 Kyoto Protocol	2015 Paris Agreement
Emissions mitigation expectations for developed countries	Reduce collective GHG emissions 5.2% by 2012	Reduce national GHG emissions as nationally determined toward international objective of limiting global warming to <2°C (ideally 1.5°C)
Emissions mitigation expectations for developing countries	No obligation to reduce emissions	Limit national GHG emissions as nationally determined toward international objective of limiting global warming to <2°C (ideally 1.5°C)
Support for implementation and adaptation	Joint implementation, Clean Development Mechanism, Global Environment Facility, etc.	Green Climate Fund to increase assistance to developing countries to $100 billion per year using voluntary contributions from developed countries, etc.
Nominal achievements	GHG emissions of developed countries in the Kyoto Protocol fell by <2% (IISD, 2019: 25) Financial pledges of developed countries to developing countries not met	All national pledges up to 2020 likely to result in global warming of >3°C (UNEP, 2019: 8) Financial pledges of developed countries to developing countries not met

actively promoted the continued use of coal, even when that dirtiest of fuels was unable to compete with less-polluting alternatives. Nevertheless, other major countries, such as members of the European Union and major developing countries, notably China and India, have variously pledged to limit their GHG emissions in the future, although not enough to prevent dangerous climate change (see Chapters 5 and 6). More often than not, the pledges and actions of countries to implement the Paris Agreement can be explained by their governments' concerns about their perceived national interests. These are largely determined by national politics and the attractiveness for powerful actors of the status quo: those actors that enjoy it do not want to change the way that they behave, and those actors that profit from it have worked hard to protect the rules and institutions that have benefited them.

Sovereignty, the National Interest and Climate Change

Governing climate change internationally, as the first order of business when awareness of the problem emerged in the 1980s, made perfect sense from the standpoint of world history. Climate change was perceived and acted upon as a problem requiring collaboration among sovereign states because that is the way that other transboundary problems were dealt with historically. Greenhouse gas pollution from one country affects every other country indirectly through global warming and other manifestations of climate change. It is impossible for any individual country, regardless of its power resources, whether economic or military, to stop climate change alone. In the context of climate change, practical sovereignty is now a fiction; it is an anachronism. Most countries seem to recognize this, reinforcing the desire to deal with the problem collectively. In the context of the history of the international system and the priorities of its constituent states, creating an international climate regime was therefore the normal approach to the climate crisis.

Unfortunately, three decades of negotiations to address climate change have been characterized by two contrasting themes: growing awareness of the rapidly increasing dangers of climate change (as described in Chapter 2) and much-too-gradual movement toward agreement on responding to those dangers in ways that are effective and timely. Scientists have called for GHG emissions to be reduced very rapidly and eliminated as soon as possible (IPCC, 2018). Yet, the best that most developed countries were able to achieve collectively was a meager 1.8 percent reduction (comparing 2017 to 1990; IISD, 2019: 25) – despite three decades of effort. Top-down efforts to govern climate change, while producing many results, failed to produce the one result that is essential: action to cut global GHG pollution substantially.

The bottom-up approach to climate governance is still relatively new, and some have argued that it will be more successful than the top-down approach. Some scholars have characterized the Paris Agreement's bottom-up approach as "fundamentally novel" (the view of an anonymous reviewer of this book). However, it may be more realistic to portray the bottom-up approach as evidence of a chronic pathology of climate governance: the powerful influence of the system of legally separate sovereign states vying to protect, and whenever possible to promote, their individual national interests as perceived by those actors with power or influence at any given time. The United States pushed for a bottom-up approach for many years, which is highly suggestive given its record on climate change (see Chapter 4). This approach garnered widespread participation by countries because it allowed them to set their own *nationally* determined GHG emissions limitations instead of having to implement policies and regulations for achieving internationally agreed targets. In other words, the Paris Agreement and related bottom-up efforts at international climate governance are anachronistic *affirmations* of the national interests that have consistently held back more effective governance of climate change. These interests are routinely a function of the sorts of policies and actions that have created the problem of climate change to begin with. This is not to say that the Paris approach to climate governance is without value, but rather to suggest that it is a symptom of underlying pathologies of international governance more generally.

Looking at the lengthening history of efforts by states to govern climate change internationally, a pattern emerges. It is a pattern of glacial progress toward an objective – preventing dangerous climate change – even as that objective moves further away at an accelerating pace. To be sure, the international climate negotiations are striking in their complexity and comprehensiveness. They have been – they continue to be – the most sweeping international negotiations in history, demonstrating the seriousness with which the problem of climate change is viewed by the world's governments. And the international approach has arguably had results. For example, some European countries have been taking action to reduce their GHG pollution, and several have pledged to become carbon neutral by mid-century (see Chapter 5). Even when national governments have sought to thwart international governance of climate change, as in the case of the United States under President Trump, subnational governments (e.g., US cities and states) and other actors have pointed to the Paris Agreement's objectives as goals that they take seriously when making policies (see, e.g., We Are Still In, 2017). That said, such actions are the many exceptions that seem to prove the larger rule: looked at in global terms, the actions of most countries (and other actors) are still going in the wrong direction.

The inability for national and global common interests to dovetail to the extent required to prevent dangerous climate change arises from the pathologies of international relations: states in an international system with inviolable sovereignty as the guiding principle. In short, it is the very nature of the international system and the states from which it is made that explains why both top-down and bottom-up efforts to govern climate change have failed so far and seem very unlikely to engender sufficiently strong policy responses in the near- and medium-term (and possibly longer). By definition, the international system divides the world into nominally sovereign states whose legitimacy and meaning derive from acting upon their individual, separate interests as perceived at any given time. In such a system, the universal interests of Earth's climate system are subjugated to the perceived interests of states – to the perceived interests of the actors within states that have the most influence over policies, whether those actors be monarchs, as in some petroleum-exporting nations, party officials or oligarchs, as in China and Russia, industry and its lobbyists, as in Japan and many European countries, or captured political parties and unctuous politicians, as in Australia and the United States.

Importantly, the pathologies of international relations have not been impediments to international cooperation on climate change. Quite the opposite: they explain why international negotiations have been the preferred means by which to approach climate governance for decades. But they are also a very big explanation for the weakness of the agreements resulting from that process. The international approach to climate governance seems to reveal the limits of diplomacy when perceived national interests are at stake. As William Marsden (2012: 287) notes, the climate agreements are negotiated by "armies of diplomats who are themselves hardwired in the narrow diplomatic traditions of defending their country's self-interest." Indeed, there is a case to be made that the very process of governing climate change internationally has been intended, at least by some countries, to prevent more aggressive action. There is an impression that many of the agreements reached during COP negotiations were "empty," actually designed to give the impression of progress when none had been realized, in the process legitimizing the lack of collective action and, in effect, preventing more effective climate governance (Dimitrov, 2019). That is, international negotiations and the resulting agreements divert attention enough to allow countries to continue, more or less, with business as usual.

It is hard to describe this as anything other than normal behavior in the international system; diplomats are doing what their governments believe to be in the national interest. The international response to climate change has revealed a fundamental clash between the global interest of addressing climate change effectively through major cuts in GHG pollution, among other actions, and states that perceive their interests as being best served by continuing with the status quo. This history of international climate governance suggests that something will have to change if the climate crisis is to be addressed much more effectively. Somehow, the raison d'être of states must move away from protecting and promoting national interests, *as currently conceived*, toward something else. What that something else might look like is explored in the chapters of Part III. But first, the next four chapters describe more pathologies of climate governance. Those pathologies are associated with national politics and human nature.

4

Pathologies of National Politics
in the United States and China

The international system of sovereign states has shaped – or misshaped – the world's responses to climate change. The system itself encourages countries to maximize their perceived national interests while discouraging them from maximizing collective international and global interests, including those associated with climate change. But how are countries' national interests conceived? Where do they come from? And how does this process in turn manifest itself in both domestic and foreign policies related to climate change? To help in answering these questions, and particularly to understand how the processes of formulating and implementing climate-related polices differ – or do not differ – around the world, we need to look *within* countries. Doing that reveals additional pathologies of climate governance, specifically those engendered in national politics. These national pathologies are explored in this chapter and the two that follow.

This chapter describes how the pathologies of national politics have manifested themselves in the United States and China (cf. Harris, 2013: 64–92). These two countries are examined in some detail here because they are the largest national sources of GHG pollution, together accounting for about 40 percent of the global total (in 2018; Crippa *et al.*, 2019: 12). For this and many other reasons they have an outsize role in influencing global climate governance. These countries' experiences tell us much of what we need to know about the pathologies of national politics and how those pathologies interact with the pathologies of international relations. Chapters 5 and 6 survey the terrain in a number of other countries in both the industrialized Global North and the developing Global South to demonstrate the degree to which the pathologies of national politics have infected climate governance around the world.

The Limits of Perception: National Interests and National Politics

Before looking at national climate politics, it is important to note that not all national interests derive primarily from domestic considerations. For example, if a country faces an existential threat, such as imminent invasion and occupation by an enemy state's armed forces, the default national interest is, all things being equal, to maximize national defense to repel those forces. In such a case, national politics is normally highly simplified – all, or nearly all, domestic actors agree on the threat to the national interest and more or less how to respond to it, at least in the short term. But if the threat is not imminent, indeed if it is perceived to be relatively distant in the future, national politics take on a much more complex role from the outset. In such an instance, domestic actors will compete to set the narrative, to define the threat and to make the case for how to respond. Often, they do this to maximize their own interests, for example, by extracting economic gain from the process. If there is no clear and present threat to the national interest, or there is much dispute over whether there is a threat at all, national politics can completely dictate or define the national interest. The national interest becomes a function of politics, and little else.

This process largely applies in the case of climate change. Some countries do face a clear existential threat, or nearly so, from climate change, a few of them even in the short to medium term. For example, some small-island states (described in Chapter 6) may become practically unhabitable quite soon due to sea-level rise, and in the long term their territories may become submerged (creating a new field of international law around rights of states that no longer have the key defining feature of a state: territory). States in these circumstances perceive the effective governance of climate change as a first-order national priority; it is in their vital interests that climate change is addressed effectively through both adaptation (their short- and medium-term interests) and mitigation (their long-term interests). In contrast, for a few countries, such as Australia (see Chapter 5) and the United States, climate denial retains influence, at least among some political leaders. For them, action on climate change is itself often perceived to be a threat to national interests, especially the interest of economic growth. Similarly, for countries whose economies are heavily reliant on fossil fuels, such as Saudi Arabia (see Chapter 6), climate action is also viewed as a threat to vital national interests. For some countries, climate change may even be perceived as an economic opportunity. Russia, for example, sees benefits in the opening of Arctic sea routes due to global warming, not to mention that it relies heavily on exports of oil and gas to prop up its economy (see Chapter 5). For most other countries, climate change falls somewhere in the middle: it is viewed as a long-term threat worthy of action, but other national interests, most notably short- and medium-term economic interests, also factor into determining overall national interests, and the latter considerations often weigh heavily on politicians and policymakers.

National politics will determine which among these interests is given priority. More often than not, climate action never makes it to the top of the list, and at the very least is watered down. For most countries, then, climate governance is very largely a function of domestic political considerations.

Much as the behavior of states in international climate governance has been quite normal in historical terms, it is also quite normal, albeit ultimately harmful to humanity and the environment, for them to rely so much on national politics for shaping climate governance. This is because states are, to draw upon a diagnosis made by Amitav Acharya and Barry Buzan (2019: 270), "autistic." By this characterization they mean that a state's "reaction to external inputs is based much more on internal processes of the state – its domestic political bargains, party rivalries, pandering to public opinion (whether it be nationalist or isolationist) and suchlike – than rational, fact-based assessment of and engagement with the other states and societies that constitute international society" (Acharya and Buzan, 2019: 270). Acharya and Buzan argue that this autistic response is "a normal feature of states. It is built into their political structure that domestic factors generally take first priority, whether because that is necessary for regime survival, or because the government is designed in such a way as to represent its citizens' interests" (Acharya and Buzan, 2019: 270). As a consequence of their autism, each state "sees only their own interests, concerns and 'rightness,' and is blind to the interests, concerns and 'rightness' of others" (Acharya and Buzan, 2019: 270). This pathology exists in every country to varying degrees, as becomes clear when we look at climate politics – and resulting policies – around the world. Taking that look is the task of the remainder of this chapter and the two that follow.

American Politics: Climate Governance in a Pluralistic State

The CO_2 emissions of the United States in 2018 were 14 percent of the global total, making it the second-largest polluter after China (producing 30 percent of global emissions), which took the top spot around 2006 (Friedlingstein, 2019) (see Figure 2.1). Per capita CO_2 emissions in the United States, at

16 tons (CO_2 equivalent in 2018), are among the highest in the world (Crippa *et al.*, 2019: 11). In historical terms, the United States remains the largest polluter, accounting for 25 percent of global CO_2 emissions since the mid-eighteenth century (although China will very likely take that mantle eventually) (Ritchie and Roser, 2019). In addition to its total contribution to causing the problem, the United States is outsize for its influence over the international governance of climate change, whether directly in climate negotiations or indirectly through regulatory and trade policies that affect other countries. It is also especially influential insofar as it has the ability to provide the financial and other resources that have been demanded by developing countries for decades and which will be essential for effective climate governance in the future.

Arguably, the United States has been the single biggest obstacle to effective global governance of climate change – but many other countries, indeed most of them, have played along. It did not have to be this way. Every US president since John F. Kennedy was given warnings from experts about climate change (Hulac, 2018). Most of them, with the exception of Donald Trump, recognized such warnings, if sometimes belatedly. For example, in 1965, President Lyndon Johnson (1965) forewarned the US Congress about the danger of CO_2 emissions. Over the decades, many members of Congress have echoed such warnings and introduced legislation to act upon them. But decades of alarm about climate change have not translated into robust policies. Presidents and Congress have been afraid to challenge the American way of doing business, and the American way of life.

Climate Change versus the American Way of Life

Alongside most other countries, at the 1992 Earth Summit in Rio de Janeiro, the United States joined the climate convention (the UNFCCC). In so doing, it pledged to reduce its GHG emissions. However, US delegates at the summit insisted that "the American life-style is not up for negotiation" (Elmer-Dewitt, 2019: 9). This declaration, which was indicative of official US sentiments leading up to agreement on the convention, reflected the importance that domestic considerations would have in guiding US climate diplomacy in subsequent years. It also reflected what would be a persistent contradiction in US climate policies in the decades since: eventual acknowledgment, sometimes very grudgingly and sometimes eagerly, that climate change is a serious global threat in need of effective governance, on one hand, and the unwillingness to formulate and implement policies that would make such governance successful, on the other.

This phenomenon was reflected in US policies during the Republican administration of President George H. W. Bush (1989–1993), which was populated with climate skeptics – who were also found in Congress at the time – and which strongly opposed any international agreement that would *require* the United States to reduce its GHG emissions. Indeed, the Bush administration was so opposed to mandatory GHG reductions that it sent the message that President Bush would not participate in the Earth Summit at all if the climate convention to be signed there included them. The administration feared, as did many members of Congress, that mandatory GHG cuts would reduce American economic competitiveness internationally (Park, 2016: 80–2). This concern would become a persistent theme in American climate politics. Reflecting another theme that would emerge, the Bush administration responded to climate change primarily by calling for more research, which had the practical effect of delaying concrete policies to reduce Americans' GHG pollution.

Under the Democratic administration of President Bill Clinton (1993–2001), climate change was seen as a much more serious issue. This was manifested in efforts by the vice-president, Al Gore – who had for some years as a legislator and author advocated action on climate change – to bring the United States into line with improving scientific understanding and growing global concerns about climate change. Gore's personal interest extended to diplomacy; he attended the negotiations in Japan that resulted in the Kyoto Protocol of 1997. While it seems that both Clinton and Gore wanted the United States to be a leader on climate governance, they faced intense domestic opposition, both from members of Congress and from politically powerful industries with vested interests in continued extraction and burning of fossil fuels. Shortly before the Kyoto conference, the Senate debated and overwhelmingly passed the Byrd-Hagel Resolution (US Senate, 1997). The resolution declared the Senate's opposition to any international agreement on climate change if it would harm the US economy or require the United States to reduce its GHG emissions without simultaneously requiring developing countries to take on emissions commitments (see Harris, 2001a: 106–10). A coalition of American fossil-fuel-dependent corporations, notably petroleum producers and automobile manufacturers that were opposed to any action to address climate change, had successfully lobbied senators (Betsill, 2016: 215).

The Kyoto Protocol passed neither test of the Byrd-Hagel Resolution because it was interpreted by numerous members of Congress as a threat to US businesses and because it would, by design, require the United States to reduce its GHG emissions – albeit by only 7 percent from the 1990 level by 2012 – without requiring developing countries to take on emissions limitations. Because ratification by the Senate is required before an international agreement can pass into US law, the Byrd-Hagel Resolution made the Kyoto Protocol a non-starter for the United States. Knowing that the protocol would not be ratified, the Clinton administration never submitted it to the Senate. While the administration did undertake modest attempts to rein in US GHG emissions, it faced too much domestic opposition to make significant progress.

Republican control of the presidency returned in 2001 with the advent of President George W. Bush (2001–2009). His administration was skeptical of climate science and very much opposed to US domestic action and international agreements to address climate change, so much so that President Bush – a former Texas "oil man" – quickly withdrew the US signature on the Kyoto Protocol. (That move foreshadowed an even more significant declaration a decade and a half later by his Republican successor, Donald Trump, to remove the United States from the Paris Agreement.) Mirroring post-1970s Republican administrations' strong dislike of any kind of environmental regulation, the Bush administration opposed all restraints on energy use, most notably the burning of fossil fuels (also a foretaste of what would come during the Trump administration). This anti-regulatory policy was actively promoted by President Bush's powerful vice-president, Dick Cheney, who shared the president's close relationship with the oil industry (Austin and Phoenix, 2005). The administration joined with industrial lobbies to attack, manipulate and suppress climate science as a way to sow doubt among the public and politicians (Bradley, 2011).

However, as the science of climate change improved, such blatant disregard for it became more difficult to support. By his second term in office, President Bush acknowledged the essential reality of climate change. However, his change of mind came too late, and was shared by far too few of his fellow Republicans, to bring about policies toward climate action. Throughout Bush's tenure, US diplomats actively opposed international efforts to govern climate change more effectively, often facing open derision from other diplomats, as happened prominently at the Bali COP in 2007 (see Chapter 3). The Bush administration will be remembered for its efforts to prevent national or international regulation of the fossil-fuel industry, or indeed regulation of Americans' profligate use of fossil fuels. During the Bush administration's eight years in office, US GHG pollution continued to increase, as did emissions globally.

From Deliberate Action to Fiery Obstruction

By the time that Democratic president Barack Obama (2009–2017) took office, it seemed that the United States was ripe for action on climate change (cf. Harris, 2009a). The science was clear, public support for action had increased and even respected members of the national security establishment were pointing to the threats to US interests posed by climate change. However, despite the willingness of the president and his vice-president, Joe Biden – who had, two decades earlier as a new senator, unsuccessfully sponsored the first climate legislation in the Senate – to take action on climate change, opposition persisted in Congress, including among Democratic senators from US states with substantial fossil-fuel and automobile industries (Brewer, 2015: 169–70). The most prominent legislative attempt to govern climate change more effectively during the Obama administration was the American Clean Energy and Security Act, which included provisions for a nationwide cap-and-trade system to bring down carbon emissions. Legislation for the act passed the House of Representatives in 2009, albeit barely, but in 2010 it was abandoned due to opposition in the Senate. (Due to Senate voting rules, a minority of senators can block passage of bills that have support from the great majority of their colleagues [see Brewer, 2015: 161–8].) Consequently, not long into its first term, the Obama administration began to focus on taking steps that would not require new legislation in Congress. Its strategy was to use existing laws and regulations, and the powers of the presidency insofar as possible, to regulate GHG pollution in the United States.

At the domestic level, the Obama administration acted on the Supreme Court's 2007 ruling that greenhouse gases were pollutants and thus could be regulated under the Clean Air Act by the EPA – a ruling that the Bush administration had chosen not to implement. This resulted in new regulations on coal-fired power plants, notably the Clean Power Plan (EPA, 2015), which had the effect, alongside falling prices for natural gas and renewable energy (solar and wind), of sounding the death knell for many coal-burning electricity plants. These regulations were promptly challenged in court, but in 2012 a federal appeals court upheld the right of the administration to regulate GHG emissions in this way. Additional regulations were put in place, such as those requiring substantially higher fuel efficiency for automobiles, which was a major step given the enormous GHG pollution coming from this source, and those for reducing methane and other emissions from natural gas production and its transportation, which was also an important step given the rapid growth in the American gas-extraction industry and the fact that methane is one of the most potent GHG pollutants. At each step, the Obama administration faced opposition from Congress, many US states and the fossil-fuel industry – all of which had the familiar effect of watering down the administration's efforts to regulate climate change more effectively within US borders.

The change of presidential administration from Republican to Democratic also had a substantial impact on the foreign climate policy of the United States. The Obama administration was far more sympathetic to international governance of climate change. President Obama attended the Copenhagen COP15 in 2009 (see Chapter 3). He was personally involved in negotiations that resulted in the Copenhagen Accord. However, the COP was held amidst the palpable effects of a global economic recession, which no doubt affected what Obama and other leaders of developed countries were willing to accept. In the event, the accord did little to advance efforts to reduce US GHG emissions, or indeed those of most other developed countries, nor did it clarify when and whether the United States would actually be more forthcoming in providing financial assistance to developing countries. Had the accord required major cuts in US emissions or new foreign assistance spending for this purpose, it is all but certain that Congress would have been ready to block it.

The Obama administration had an equally big impact on negotiations for COP21's Paris Agreement. It was somewhat consistent with previous administrations in seeking to temper, if not prevent outright, international regulation of US actions. Because the Paris Agreement called for *nationally determined* contributions to international efforts to limit global warming, it met this criterion (although Obama's successor would clearly disagree with this fact). Very important, because the Paris Agreement was a voluntary instrument under the legal rubric of the UNFCCC, which had been ratified by the Senate in 1992, Obama did not need Senate approval to put the agreement into force domestically. The NDC pledge made by the United States at the Paris conference was to reduce US GHG emissions by 26 percent below 2005 levels by 2025 (US, 2015). Because the base year used in this pledge was 2005, not the 1990 base year used for most calculations in the climate regime, the proposed emissions cuts were less than they appeared to be. That made them less impactful on US economic sectors and therefore less likely to engender domestic political opposition. But it also meant that they were far below what was required of the United States for the Paris objective of limiting global warming to 2°C, let alone 1.5°C, to be realized (Climate Action Tracker, 2020).

But even the Paris Agreement's voluntary nature was too much for Obama's successor. President Donald Trump came into office in 2017 by riding a wave of nationalist populism that included opposition to action on climate change (Jotzo, Depledge and Winkler, 2018). He behaved as though he had one overriding objective with respect to climate change (and apparently every other issue): to dismantle absolutely everything done by President Obama. The Trump administration's efforts to reverse US policies for reducing the country's GHG pollution were breathtaking. Almost immediately, it went to work reversing environmental regulations generally and limits on fossil-fuel production and consumption specifically (Drollette, 2020). In addition to declaring US withdrawal from the Paris Agreement, Trump lifted regulations on methane leaks from oil and gas production, opened public lands and offshore fields to new oil and gas drilling, weakened fuel-efficiency standards, replaced the Clean Power Plan with an alternative intended to keep coal-burning plants open longer and weakened implementation of the Endangered Species Act to allow oil and gas production in protected areas (Schwartz, 2019). Indeed, in every way conceivable, the Trump administration went in exactly the opposite direction of the Obama administration.

Trump and his administration utterly ignored the findings of congressionally mandated scientific reports showing the threats that climate change posed to the United States (USGCRP, 2018). Climate denial, which was vanquished within the federal government (if not Congress) by the Obama administration, returned with the advent of President Trump (Davenport and Landler, 2019). Climate denialists, who were quickly appointed to influential positions in every agency even remotely connected to climate governance, systematically imprinted climate denial on the scientific reporting of the federal government (see, e.g., Tabuchi, 2020a). A climate denialist became the most senior science advisor in the US government. There was a systematic expurgation of climate change from the federal government's policy objectives, with the president himself attacking US automakers because they opposed his rollbacks in automobile efficiency standards, which they feared would result in costly regulatory requirements in different US states (Colman, 2019).

The Trump administration's climate denial also greatly influenced US foreign climate policy. Even before taking office, Trump declared that he would withdraw the United States from the Paris Agreement. (Provisions of the agreement meant that formal withdrawal could not occur until November 2020.) American diplomats continued to attend COP meetings because the United States remained a member of the UNFCCC. They became spoilers (alongside other like-minded countries, variously including Australia, Russia and Saudi Arabia) in negotiations to reduce global GHG emissions. Under Trump, the United States joined with other climate-denying countries, especially Saudi Arabia, in refusing to recognize the international policy implications of the IPCC's 1.5-degree report and in blocking negotiation of the Paris rulebook for emissions trading and the like (Chemnic, 2018). The Trump administration's opposition to climate governance extended beyond the COPs; for example, it was alone in opposing a declaration on climate change at the 2019 G7 and G20 meetings.

American opposition to the international governance of climate change during the Trump administration was an extension of the longstanding US desire for unhindered sovereignty, vividly reflecting the power of the pathologies described in Chapter 3. By way of evidence, in a speech to the UN General Assembly, Trump (2018) declared that "responsible nations must defend against threats to sovereignty . . . from global governance" before adding: "we must protect our sovereignty and our cherished independence above all." Overall, the Trump presidency greatly exacerbated adverse trends in global climate governance, including inadequate GHG-reduction targets and policies, insufficient climate finance, growing populist conservatism opposed to climate action and continued production and consumption of fossil fuels (Selby, 2018).

All of this happened despite strident calls in Congress – specifically in the House of Representatives, which flipped to a Democratic majority after elections in 2018 – for a Green New Deal (GND). The objective of the GND was to make governance of climate change a national priority while also solving a host of economic and social ills (Galvin and Healy, 2020). The GND was subject to much debate among politicians, including among Democrats vying for their party's nomination in the run-up to Congressional and presidential elections in 2020. However, it had little chance of shaping policy at the federal level while Republicans retained control of the Senate. Indeed, even the Democratic-controlled House of Representatives had other legislative priorities. Representative Alexandria Ocasio-Cortez, a left-wing Democratic member of the House, characterized them this way: "If you really want to understand what Congress's true priorities are, you look at must-pass legislation – you look at what they give up and what they double down on. And if you look at must-pass legislation, this Congress is engaged in climate denial" (quoted in Cochrane and Friedman, 2020).

Three decades of climate governance – or opposition to it – in the United States reveals some important attributes of the country's national politics. Issues that are considered to be of vital importance to the United States by one presidential administration might well be viewed very differently, even in an opposite way, by another administration. Congress may agree or disagree, often shifting its position every two years as the makeup of the House of Representatives changes. Lobbyists for the fossil-fuel industry are able to take advantage of these circumstances (Downie, 2017). Consequently, it may not be hyperbole to say that the unique national politics of the United States "will have changed the geological history of the earth" (McKibben, 2018).

Having said this, it would be wrong to conclude that Americans have done nothing to address climate change. As suggested already, agencies of the federal government, ranging from the EPA to the Department of Defense, are staffed by many people who understand the threats posed by climate change and have tried to implement policies to address those threats. These policies have certainly had an impact. For example, President Obama's automobile- and energy-efficiency standards, despite being undermined by President Trump, have mitigated CO_2 (and other) pollution. Support from the federal government for research on climate change has had a lasting impact, and some US diplomatic efforts during Democratic administrations have arguably nudged international governance of climate change in a positive direction at times.

Where climate governance is happening in earnest in the United States is within and among some US states, initially the northeastern states and California but increasingly elsewhere. For example, several US states and municipalities, as well as many businesses and universities, have relatively ambitious GHG emissions targets, including many initiatives to fulfill the Obama administration's pledge under the Paris Agreement and in some cases to aim for net-zero, or near-zero, GHG emissions by 2050 (see America's Pledge, 2020; US Climate Alliance, 2020). A case in point may be the state of Virginia, a newly Democratic Party–controlled state, which in 2020 passed a law aimed at reaching carbon neutrality in power generation by 2045 (AP, 2020b). More than half of US states require that a portion of the electricity sold within their borders be generated in part by renewable sources. A number of them participate in regional emissions cap-and-trade programs that include parts of Canada and Mexico (efforts that faced challenges from the Trump administration).

These efforts to govern climate change are noteworthy and increasingly significant. They reflect growing worry among Americans about the effects of climate change (Goldberg *et al.*, 2020). That may be why the US fossil-fuel industry is fighting back, with substantial success, through sophisticated public-relations campaigns and lobbying of state and local officials to thwart more widespread climate governance across the United States (Meyer, 2020). Consequently, subnational endeavors are extremely unlikely to reduce US GHG pollution nearly enough to enable the United States to fulfill its necessary role in achieving the Paris Agreement's targets for limiting global warming.

Obstacles to American Climate Governance

Because the American political system affords access to all manner of actors, ranging from voters to powerful (and wealthy) industrial lobbies, policies that do not have overwhelming support from the former, while being opposed by the latter, almost invariably lack priority at the federal level. The fossil-fuel industry has been especially effective in lobbying members of Congress to oppose legislation that would require major changes to the status quo. This is vitally important because, unlike in many other countries, Congress must support US involvement in international agreements. The Senate must give its consent before the United States can join international treaties and the House of Representatives must join with the Senate in providing any funding that is needed to implement them. Members of Congress tend to vote in ways that enable them to get reelected, which normally means voting to protect or further the interests of their home states and constituents. Many senators represent states that rely on coal production for jobs, and some states still depend on coal for a significant portion of their electricity generation. Even the relatively new shift away from coal to natural gas as a primary source of energy in the United States presents obstacles because it, too, contributes greatly to national GHG emissions. As renewable energy grows in prominence and related industries lobby Congress, it may become easier for legislation to act on climate change to pass. Until that happens, this persistent political bias in favor of fossil fuels helps to explain why climate change has had so much trouble in rising to the level of a vital national interest in the United States.

Perceptions matter at least as much as reality in US politics. The extreme partisanship in American national politics, which has grown more intense over the decades that climate change has gained policy prominence (although political partisanship has substantial precedent in US history), makes almost every issue a political battleground. Due to the persistence of climate skepticism and denial among many politicians, and concerns among others about the political consequences for them of supporting climate action, anything related to climate change is certainly one of those battlegrounds. Although climate skepticism and denial are falling among Americans, more of them (13 percent) deny that climate change is being caused by humans than in any other developed country, and 17 percent of them believe that "the idea of manmade global warming is a hoax that was invented to deceive people" (Milman, 2019). The tenacity of climate skepticism among Republicans, including those in Congress, is nurtured by right-wing cable-television and online media. Climate science – and science in general – is anathema to the ultraconservative Christian nationalists that have been the most persistent supporters of the Republican Party and President Trump (Stewart, 2020). This helps to explain why the Republican Party is "the world's only major climate-denialist party" (Krugman, 2020).

Skepticism and denial are cultivated not only by fears that action on climate change might undermine aspects of the US economy. There is also fear that it might restrict the established freedoms of individuals and businesses. In this sense, climate governance is perceived by conservative politicians and corporations as a governmental threat to the power of their cherished free-market ideology, thus justifying their campaign to sow doubt about climate change (Oreskes and Conway, 2010: 169–215). This cultivated American doubt about climate change as a serious threat to US national interests helps to maintain business as usual, and specifically continued dependence on fossil-fuel energy, as the default national interest in the minds of enough politicians to stop, delay, dilute and, under the Trump administration, reverse US governance of the problem. As one scholar has put it, "Only one thing matters between now and 2030: climate change. Strange, then, that [the United States] will do nothing about it – for reasons of politics. The Republicans are denialists whose main constituencies are in states whose business model is carbon heavy. The Democrats are Green New Deal-ers at the grass-roots level, but the money people inside the party fear and distrust their base" (Blyth, 2019: 10).

While concerns about domestic economic growth and personal freedoms, among other considerations, have motivated US opposition to international action on climate change, outward concerns, quite unrelated to climate change itself, also influence American climate politics. Among these are growing concerns about the role of China in the world. China is increasingly viewed as a competitor, economically and politically, and even a real threat to US vital national security interests. American politicians, supported by some industries and growing public concern about China, do not want climate governance to weaken the United States relative to China nor to strengthen China relative to the United States. Furthermore, US opposition to international attempts to govern climate change, in particular the top-down approaches described in Chapter 3, is a reflection of "deeper opposition to international constraints on US sovereignty," an opposition so strongly felt that the United States resists joining international agreements "even when they otherwise enjoy very wide-spread support" (Bodansky, 2007: 62). This suspicion of international treaties has deep roots in US history. Opposition to international agreements on climate change is therefore par for the course in US politics.

Opposition to international governance of climate change that would regulate US behavior is also a practical consequence of the US political system and its co-equal branches of government. Like all treaties, international climate agreements ratified by the Senate become binding on the US government. Failure of the government to implement them is likely to result in lawsuits from citizens, NGOs or US states (unlike in some other countries, such as China, where governments need not concern themselves with judicial oversight).

American opposition to the international governance of climate change, or at least a failure to garner sufficient support for it, arises from domestic political processes that favor the status quo and business as usual, exacerbated by historical opposition to international regulation. Climate change has not risen to the point in the minds of American citizens or politicians where it can push aside the forces that have shaped US responses over the past several decades. This may be starting to change as awareness of climate change grows and concern about it increases, particularly among young people. In a 2020 survey, more than half of Americans polled said that climate change should be the top priority of the president and Congress, a substantial increase over previous years (Pew Research Center, 2020). The survey revealed an extreme partisan divide, with more than three-quarters of self-identified Democrats saying this compared to barely one-fifth of Republicans. However, among younger Republican respondents (aged 38 and below), more than half believed that the federal government was not doing enough to reduce the effects of climate change (Popovich, 2020). Furthermore, more industries now seek to capitalize on the inevitable shift away from fossil fuels, and more businesses see it as in their interest to reduce their reliance on them as soon as possible.

Despite extreme opposition to climate action by President Trump and the Republican Party, a time will come when the United States has no choice but to embrace a path toward the decarbonization of its economy. That will require effective climate governance at all levels of government – federal, state and local. It is tempting to say that this time will come soon. Joe Biden, the Democratic candidate for president in 2020, made climate change a theme in his bid for the White House. The great hope among many Americans was that he would win office and sweep away the enormous damage to climate governance that had been done by Trump and the Republicans. However, the precedent of decades of climate politics in the United States, under both Democratic and Republican administrations, suggested that very much optimism for the kind of concerted, even radical, action that was needed in the United States to help the world avert dangerous climate change might not be vindicated.

Chinese Politics: Climate Governance in an Authoritarian State

China is the largest national source of CO_2 pollution, having replaced the United States around 2006 (Netherlands Environmental Assessment Agency, 2007). Its emissions quadrupled in the 25 years after 1990 (Joint Research Centre, 2017), and as of 2018 it produced 30 percent of the global CO_2 emissions, double those of the United States and three times those of the European Union (Friedlingstein et al., 2019) (see Figure 2.1). At about 8 tons in 2018 (Crippa et al., 2019: 11), China's per capita CO_2 emissions are now among the highest in the world, having increased by more than three and one-half times between 1990 and 2018 (Global Carbon Project, 2020).

Although per capita emissions in China are half those in the United States, they are 18 percent above those of the European Union and far above those of most developing countries (Crippa *et al.*, 2019). Judith Shapiro (2018: 145) has captured the importance of these statistics succinctly: "We cannot separate China's carbon from the carbon that is driving temperatures up across the globe."

In addition to being the top national source of GHG pollution, China also has preferences and interests that have an outsized role in the international governance of climate change. Over the decades of international climate negotiations, it has intermittently been a diplomatic champion of developing countries, arguing strongly that they, along with China itself, ought to be full beneficiaries of the CBDR principle and its full implementation. As such, China has opposed mandatory GHG emissions limitations, let alone cuts, for developing countries, and it has joined them in repeatedly demanding financial assistance from the developed world. However, over about the past decade China has drifted away from the poorest and most vulnerable developing countries as they have started to view it as more of a climate threat than a climate ally.

China's Role in Climate Governance

The process by which China formulates and implements policies related to climate change is complex, reflecting the enormity of the Chinese state and the multifaceted policymaking apparatus of the Chinese government and the ruling Chinese Communist Party (CCP). Climate governance in China involves a large number of ministries and agencies, all with competing interests. Despite China having a centralized authoritarian political system, these competing interests, particularly those related to economic development and growth, prevent climate change from becoming the top priority of the government. That said, climate change is a significant issue for China and the government's perception of national interests in terms of domestic and international affairs. At the domestic level, China will be greatly affected by climate change, and actions to address GHG emissions have the benefit of reducing one of the major scourges of modern China: air pollution. At the international level, climate change affords an opportunity for China to assert great-power status. At the same time, however, its status as the world's largest source of GHG pollution places it under increasing pressure from environmentalists and other countries, developed and developing, to take the issue seriously.

The importance of climate change for the government has been evident for several decades, but it has gained salience this century. For example, the

National Coordination Committee on Climate Change was created in 2003, and in 2007 the Leading Committee on Climate Change, chaired by the Chinese premier, was formed alongside release of a national climate change program. Less than a decade later, climate change was even more prominent, garnering direct attention from the highest-level economic agencies and playing a central part in the personal diplomacy of the Chinese president, Xi Jinping, at the Paris COP in 2015 and in his meetings with President Obama (Sandalow, 2019).

Although China has always maintained that it has no *obligation* to limit its GHG emissions, it has taken steps nationwide to do so, thus mitigating the increase in emissions that would have occurred without such steps. For example, it has shut down many of its dirtiest coal-fired power stations and factories, and reduced construction of new ones; promulgated regulations to increase automobile and energy efficiency; used subsidies to encourage development of renewable energy sources, notably solar, wind and hydro power, and constructed related infrastructure; and experimented with emissions trading schemes regionally, promising to take them nationwide. These and other policies are part of the Chinese leadership's declared objective to transform China into an "ecological civilization" (Li and Shapiro, 2020).

However, despite these and other domestic policies to curb emissions, GHG pollution from China has continued to increase. Energy demand from factories and transport, not least the country's massive and growing fleet of private cars, has outstripped regulations and policies to limit pollution coming from it. Coal still provides three-quarters of China's energy, a figure that would likely be larger had the government not chosen to cancel a number of planned coal-fired power plants and push targets for alternative energy to the point where solar and wind energy supply reached one-tenth of the country's electricity (Dessler and Parson, 2020: 182–3). However, there are signs that coal use will continue, and might even increase, in coming years, with closed coal plants being restarted, new plants being built and many coal mines operating to help provinces cope with economic slowdown (Global Energy Monitor, 2020).

Internationally, China's positions on climate change have reflected its national priorities, especially economic development and growth, as well as its desire to join the ranks of great powers and to be treated accordingly (Kopra, 2019). Initially, climate change was viewed as a largely scientific issue, requiring stepped-up research domestically and research cooperation internationally. However, by the 1990s climate change had become a matter of importance for the country's economic development, in part because international climate action might harm the economy or, in contrast, bring financial and other aid. To promote the latter, China cooperated diplomatically with developing countries during international negotiations leading to agreement on the UNFCCC and the Kyoto Protocol. China and its developing-country allies were especially focused on negotiating and codifying the CBDR principle in the climate convention (see Chapter 3). Although the United States and a number of other developed countries wanted China to take on more responsibility given its growing economic status, neither the UNFCCC nor the Kyoto Protocol placed any legally binding limits on its GHG emissions because, for the purposes of climate change, it was classified as a developing country. And just as China desired, the Kyoto Protocol's CDM became an opportunity for it to garner billions of dollars from developed countries, with little apparent restraint on its GHG emissions, and even some indications that its CDM projects actually increased them (Schapiro, 2010).

As China's economy expanded and its GHG emissions exploded, starting in the 1980s, demands for it to take action on climate change – that is, to limit its own GHG pollution – increased gradually and, in recent years, have become more strident. It became increasingly difficult for China to maintain that it was just another developing-country victim of climate change caused by developed countries, not least because, by the advent of President Xi Jinping in 2012, one of its paramount foreign policy objectives was to be perceived as a responsible great power (Kato, 2019). While China was not – and still is not, just like the United States – willing to accept internationally prescribed requirements for restrictions on its GHG emissions, it seemed to recognize that it could package its domestic efforts to mitigate pollution as action on climate change. This contrivance was grafted onto Chinese foreign policy in 2009 when, not long before COP15 in Copenhagen, it was announced that China would, no later than 2020, reduce its carbon intensity (i.e., its CO_2 emissions per unit of output) by 40–45 percent compared to what it was in 2005 (Black, 2009). The Chinese made it very clear that their carbon-intensity pledge was strictly voluntary, and that it could not be monitored by any outside actors. From the Chinese perspective, to allow outsiders to verify implementation of its pledge would be tantamount to a violation of its most-cherished value: unhindered, and unquestioned, national sovereignty (Christoff, 2010: 644). But there may have been much less to the pledge than many had hoped: it was unlikely to be very difficult to implement because it amounted to, more or less, business as usual. By way of indication of what was likely to happen anyway, between 1991 and 2006 China's carbon intensity declined by 44 percent even as its CO_2 emissions grew by more than 100 percent (Lewis and Gallagher, 2011: 273; cf. Harris, 2013: 74). Even if fully implemented, China's Copenhagen pledge meant that its own GHG pollution, and thus the world's, would continue to increase.

China's motives at the Copenhagen COP became more apparent when it opposed calls by many of the world's most climate-vulnerable countries for international agreement to limit global warming to 1.5°C. It seems that Chinese officials wanted to avoid an international target that could only be achieved if China reduced its own GHG emissions substantially (due to its large share of global emissions). China was championing its own national interests, and specifically its domestic economic and political priorities, despite the costs of doing so for the developing countries whose cause it claimed to champion (Christoff, 2010: 647–8). Thus, as demands for it to reduce its emissions grew, the top-down approach to international climate governance increasingly challenged China's perceived national interests. This may help to explain why it came to support the bottom-up approach to international climate governance, codified in the Paris Agreement, which had been championed for so long by the United States.

Indeed, for the Paris Agreement, China made an NDC pledge that enabled it to continue to prioritize its own economic development. China pledged that it would "increase the share of non-fossil fuels in primary energy to around 20%," reduce CO_2 intensity 60–65 percent below what it was in 2005 (without saying by when) and stop the growth in its CO_2 emissions by "around 2030" (NDRC, 2015: 5). Like its Copenhagen pledge, China's Paris pledge amounted to little more than what was likely to happen anyway (Harris, 2017; Dessler and Parson, 2020: 183). The energy-intensity target mirrored improvements in energy efficiency that had already been happening in China and other developing economies (Vivid Economics 2013). The pledge to reach a peak in CO_2 emissions by around 2030 was a reflection of business as usual, with experts predicting that it would happen even sooner with modest effort (Gallagher *et al.*, 2019).

Over several decades of climate governance, China has tried to have it both ways. From the outset, it has sought to demonstrate solidarity with developing countries. Doing so fit with its role as a leading developing country and brought domestic benefits from climate-related international assistance. More recently, it has also tried to enhance its international reputation and "soft" power (Askar, 2018), all the while continuing to develop its own economy free of external limits. The former objective was evident at recent COPs. For example, at COP25 in 2019, China sided with developing countries, reiterating the need for developed countries to implement CBDR and specifically to provide financial and other assistance to poor countries (Kaneti, 2020). But China did this only up to a point; it sidestepped demands from some of the countries that were most vulnerable to sea-level rise to cut its own GHG emissions, a reminder of its behavior at COP15. This shows that a top-down approach to climate governance, in which *developed* countries – defined officially in the context of the UNFCCC as not including China – are required to reduce their GHG emissions and assist developing countries with finance, has merits for China. However, the more recent bottom-up approach has obvious appeal as well because it allows China to take on a bigger role in climate governance while doing so on its own terms through its domestically generated NDC toward the Paris Agreement's goals.

China's ambivalence toward global GHG mitigation has been reinforced by other aspects of its foreign policy. A major example is its so-called Belt and Road Initiative, which was conceived to fund and build infrastructure abroad, especially in developing Asian countries, and to connect them – some might say to make them dependent upon – China. The initiative was dear to President Xi, who called for it to promote environmental protection and be "green" (Hilton, 2019). Yet, 85 percent of the projects in the Belt and Road Initiative involved high GHG emissions (Bradsher, 2020). Even as China was closing its own coal-fired plants to reduce local air pollution, and nominally to limit GHG pollution, as part of the Belt and Road Initiative it funded construction of at least 63 such facilities abroad, mostly by Chinese companies that had lost business at home. What is more, one-quarter of all coal plants being planned or under construction around the world beyond China are financed by China's state-owned financial institutions (Shearer, Brown and Buckley, 2019). Thus, China has used its external policies to lock many developing countries into the same high-polluting development model that resulted in so much GHG pollution from China itself (Hilton, 2019).

Forces Shaping Chinese Climate Governance

China is an authoritarian state, so the national politics shaping its climate-related policies are *relatively* straightforward compared to the United States and other, more pluralistic, countries. That said, it would be wrong to describe China's national politics as lacking complexity or many of the political machinations that are evident in democracies. The process of distilling China's national interests in the context of climate change involves inputs from multiple agencies and substate actors, such as provincial and municipal governments, and is weighed alongside more immediate and higher priorities of the CCP. As in other countries, domestic economic considerations weigh very heavily when determining the direction of climate governance, as do concerns about local pollution. However, in China something comes even before such issues when defining the national interest: protecting sovereignty. Indeed, one cannot overstate the importance that China attaches to traditional – one might say anachronistic – conceptions of sovereignty. The Chinese government is obsessed with preventing all forms of interference in its domestic affairs, which includes anything that could conceivably be construed by Chinese officials as threatening the integrity of the state or its absolute rule by the CCP. *Any* perceived interference in China's affairs, including relatively mild verbal criticism from foreign officials, is interpreted as an affront and routinely elicits a strident response from the government. The most obvious example is criticism of China's human rights record, but its obsessive opposition to any kind "intervention" extends to all issues, including climate change (Drexhage and Murphy, 2009: 3).

The intensity of the Chinese government's extreme preoccupation with the state's sovereignty may seem out of place in the modern world, especially given China's current wealth and power. After all, most other countries of stature routinely ignore criticisms of their domestic and foreign policies and actions. But China's focus on sovereignty – its relatively intense affliction with this pathology of international relations (Chapter 3) – has strong historical roots. Its relationship with other countries, particularly its deep feelings of grievance (cultivated for many decades by the government through education and propaganda) toward several Western countries and Japan for interventions in China's affairs from the mid-nineteenth to mid-twentieth centuries – a period that is cursed in China as its "century of humiliation" – sets the tone for its domestic and international responses to climate change (and most other issues) (Zhang, 2003; Kaufman, 2010). Any climate-related demand from other countries that might conceivably restrain China's development is perceived through this historical lens.

This explains why China has been so vociferous in opposing international monitoring of its GHG emissions and pledges related to agreements arising from, for example, the COP15 negotiations in Copenhagen and the COP21 negotiations in Paris. In the former case, a global mitigation target that would effectively require China to reduce its GHG pollution was perceived as a Western threat to China's development – as the West once again trying to hold China back. The associated need to know whether China would actually implement GHG reductions presented it with the prospect of direct "intervention" by foreign accountants and inspectors, something that the government could not countenance. Consequently, despite its Paris pledge being nationally determined in such a way as to avoid any threats to the country's economic development, China was not willing to accept the intervention in its affairs that outside monitoring of the pledge would require (not least because there was widespread skepticism internationally of official statistics coming out of China).

Beyond magnified concerns about its sovereignty, China defines its national interests in terms of economic growth, much like the United States. Economic growth is essential for realization of the government's policy objectives, including becoming a "middle-sized" economy as soon as possible and building up its military strength, thereby enabling it to protect the integrity of declared Chinese territory, which includes not only the Chinese mainland but also Taiwan and nearly all of the South China Sea. Furthermore, economic growth is viewed by the CCP as vital to both political stability across China and, perhaps foremost, a key to the party's hold on power (Shirk, 2007). Consequently, economic growth has greatly influenced its approach to climate governance domestically and internationally. The threat of economic stagnation is viewed as a far bigger threat than is climate change. That said, the party and government do recognize the importance of environmental issues, not least because public concerns about pollution, including air pollution, have grown markedly in recent decades. One reason that China has seen such growth in alternative energy, and the shutting of many coal-fired facilities, is the desire to reduce local air pollution. When a factory powered by coal is shut down to reduce air pollution in a nearby city, China's GHG pollution also falls. But it would be inaccurate to ascribe such actions to a top-down international mandate or a bottom-up drive by the Chinese government to prevent global warming. Those actions are not motivated by an official desire to govern climate change effectively (Schreurs, 2011).

The Chinese government is not naive; the threats to China's medium- and long-term interests posed by climate change are real, and thus climate change must be taken seriously by the government. However, to a very great extent, China's climate-related policies, both domestic and foreign, are incidental to *other* national priorities and interests. If climate governance, including mitigation of GHG pollution from China and policies for adaptation to the impacts of climate change, is consistent with other national priorities, action will be taken. This is especially the case if benefits for the national economy arise from climate governance – such as receiving Western financial assistance to clean up or close polluting factories, or as has occurred with national investment in solar-energy technology. But if climate governance conflicts with national interests that are perceived to be dearer by the Chinese government, including the CCP, action on climate change will not be taken. Climate governance by China is hostage to other perceived national interests. This contrasts with the United States, where climate change per se has *sometimes* motivated policy action. However, the overall effect over several decades has been the same in both countries: some efforts to govern climate change, but vastly less than what the science dictates, and indeed far short of what other countries have demanded.

5

Pathologies of National Politics
in the Global North

A picture that emerges from the previous chapter's descriptions of climate governance in China and the United States is one of national interests being perceived, for reasons arising almost exclusively from their respective national politics, in ways that effectively discount the threat of climate change. Climate change has been on the national agenda for decades in both countries, but national politics has repeatedly prevented it from being interpreted as a vital national interest in either. In particular, both countries still perceive the risk of acting to address climate effectively as being a threat to their economies, or at least to powerful economic actors. This does not necessarily cause them to ignore climate change – although that is exactly what President Trump ordered to happen at the federal level in the United States – but it does result, at best, in watered-down climate governance.

A question is whether this picture of national politics holding back climate governance is typical of most countries – whether it reveals widespread pathologies of climate governance. This chapter aims to start answering this question by going beyond the United States to look at the governance of climate change in more of the world's industrialized countries, starting in Europe. This sample of countries, along with those presented in the preceding and subsequent chapters, while only scratching the surface of events around the world, gives a picture of how pathologies of national politics influence climate governance globally. Regardless of the country, climate change is perceived to be a national interest to the extent that national politics determine it to be so.

Europe: Diluted Leadership

Europe is the birthplace of the Industrial Revolution that ignited the carbon-fueled global energy system that has resulted in climate change. Europe is also, potentially, the first place where carbon will be extinguished as a significant source of energy for major national economies. Although Europe is home to some of the most polluting, carbon-reliant countries in the world, it is also home to those that have pledged to all but eliminate their GHG pollution by mid-century. Most European countries are now members of the European Union, which has since at least 1990 sought to be the global leader on climate action (Harris, 2007b: 361–5; Parker and Karlsson, 2015: 195; Schreurs and Axelrod, 2020: 209). It has done this by nudging member countries to limit their GHG emissions and by pushing for stronger international agreements to encourage non-European countries to do likewise. The EU's CO_2 emissions fell 22 percent between 1990 and 2018 (Crippa et al., 2019: 5). This fall masked enormous variation among member states, ranging from a one-third fall in the United Kingdom (which was helped in this reduction by shifting to natural gas for electricity production – and which withdrew from the European Union in 2020) to a one-fifth *increase* in Portugal and Spain (Dessler and Parson, 2020: 183). In 2018, the EU's CO_2 emissions were 9 percent of global total (Friedlingstein et al., 2019), and per capita emissions, at about 7 tons, were far lower than those of the United States and even lower than those of China (Crippa et al., 2019: 11) (see Figure 2.1).

Ambition and Action in the European Union

The GHG emissions-reduction targets of the European Union have increased over time. For the Kyoto COP3 in 1997, the Union proposed GHG reductions by developed countries of 15 percent by 2010, ultimately agreeing to an 8 percent cut in its members' collective emissions by 2012 under the Kyoto Protocol (Dupont and Oberthur, 2015: 225). Importantly, as it normally does, the European Union was using 1990 as the base year for its reductions, something that a number of non-EU countries have stopped doing. (By using more recent base years, the latter countries mask the relative paucity of their emissions pledges.) Following a decision the previous year by the European Council (the arm of the European Union that defines overall political and policy priorities), in 2008 the Union proposed reducing EU-wide GHG pollution 20 percent by 2020, with a pledge to cut it 30 percent if other major economies made similar pledges – which they did not do – and to increase the Union's share of renewable energy to 20 percent and to improve energy efficiency by the same percentage. By 2009 the European Council had set the goal of reducing EU GHG emissions by 80–95 percent by 2050, essentially declaring that most of the European economy should aim for near-total decarbonization. Toward that end, in 2015 the European Union pledged to reduce its joint GHG emissions at least 40 percent from the 1990 level, improve energy efficiency by 27 percent and increase the share of renewables by the same percentage, all by 2030 (Latvian Presidency, 2015). In 2019 the European Commission (the executive arm of the European Union) promulgated an ambitious European Green Deal (EGD) for reaching carbon neutrality by 2050, with a new interim emissions-reduction target of 55 percent by 2030. It also proposed a European Climate Law to create legal obligations for reaching carbon neutrality (European Commission, 2019b).

Emissions pledges and objectives of the European Union have been implemented through a climate policy framework that is intended to guide action by member states. The framework has comprised measures such as energy-efficiency standards, renewable-energy infrastructure and emissions trading. The EU-wide Emissions Trading Scheme (ETS) was initiated in 2003 to create a market for reducing GHG emissions. The ETS faced obstacles from the outset, including initial prices of emissions permits that were set much too low to incentivize the desired emissions reductions, and failed attempts to have all airlines using EU airspace join the scheme (Jevnaker and Wettestad, 2017). Presumably these and other efforts will be strengthened and supported in coming years through the EGD and will in turn be reflected in more robust national climate governance within EU members' borders.

Several individual EU member countries already have their own relatively ambitious plans to reduce GHG emissions by mid-century. For example, the United Kingdom, while still an EU member, set a target for reductions of 80 percent, Sweden pledged 85 percent, the Netherlands committed itself to 95 percent and Denmark has aimed to be carbon neutral by 2050, facilitated by a national law to cut carbon emissions 70 percent by 2030 (Timperley, 2019; Dessler and Parson, 2020: 185). Other EU countries have even more ambitious plans to reduce their GHG pollution. One case is Finland, where in 2019 a new left-leaning government made the ambitious pledge to achieve net carbon neutrality by 2035 (Henly, 2019). These and other emissions-reduction pledges across the European Union have been accompanied by policies and regulations aimed at achieving their objectives, although it ought to be noted that governments making progressive pledges have tended to leave the policies that are most difficult to achieve for future governments to implement. It must also be noted that, in contrast to the ambitious pledges of some EU member countries, several other members have done relatively little to reduce their GHG emissions, and specifically their dependence on fossil fuels. Some of them have repeatedly held back more ambitious EU-wide policies (see below).

European Union policy on climate change (and nearly everything else) involves negotiations and compromises between EU institutions, notably the

European Commission, the European Parliament and member states. The EU's overarching objectives with respect to climate governance are normally first agreed by heads of government and state in the European Council. Fiscal matters related to climate change normally require unanimous agreement in the Council. This need for unanimity helps to explain the failure of proposals for an EU-wide carbon tax in the early 1990s, and it has plagued EU climate governance ever since. It means that ambitious targets preferred by the Commission, members of the European Parliament and member states can be undermined by the least ambitious members (Skjaerseth, 2017). Some Eastern and Central European members that are heavily reliant on coal for energy have vetoed several plans to rein in the EU's collective GHG pollution. For example, in 2009 Poland blocked a "roadmap" for a low-carbon economy that was proposed by the European Commission to help realize the Union's target of reducing GHG emissions by 80–95 percent by 2050 (Dupont and Oberthur, 2015: 228). It did the same thing a decade later when it blocked a plan by the Commission to tighten the Union's 2030 emissions cuts from 40 percent to 50 percent (Schulz, 2020).

It is one thing for the Council to call for near-decarbonization of European economies; it is quite another for each member state to take the necessary steps to realize that objective. The skepticism among some members regarding taking difficult policy choices suggests that the Commission will have no choice but to give them substantial concessions and incentives if climate action and the EGD are to be implemented effectively. If EU institutions and the wealthiest members are able to muster subsidies for renewable energy infrastructure and financial support for businesses and communities affected by the transition away from fossil fuels, it will be easier for skeptical governments to comport with the Commission's aspirations – in short, to see that effective climate governance is in their national interests. Much as in the United States, "all politics is local" (an adage attributed to former speaker of the US House of Representatives, Tip O'Neal) – or, in the context of the European Union, at least national.

From National Politics to EU Leadership on Climate Change?

Those member states that are inclined to be leaders within the European Union on climate governance invariably face their own internal obstacles to defining climate change as a vital national interest requiring action to reduce GHG pollution. That Poland and other countries heavily reliant on coal face such obstacles is understandable, but this phenomenon applies widely. Events in Germany demonstrate how national politics affect climate governance even in the Union's wealthiest member country. For decades, Germany has been relatively proactive in implementing policies to reduce its GHG pollution. It has had one of the most ambitious policies for installing solar panels, for instance. However, it has faced many political obstacles to more aggressive emissions cuts. It still relies on coal for one-quarter of its electricity, with some German states being relatively more dependent on coal for power and jobs (Sengupta and Eddy, 2020). Those German states are consequently much less willing to support deeper and faster cuts in coal than those not so reliant on it.

Germany's ambitions were complicated in 2011 when, in response to the Fukushima nuclear disaster in Japan (see below), the government decided that all German nuclear power plants would be closed by 2022. As the process of doing so began, Germany's use of coal actually increased because enough alternative sources of energy were not yet in place to replace nuclear power (Dessler and Parson, 2020: 184). Perhaps as a consequence, Germany's own contribution to EU emissions reductions suffered; it was unable to fulfill its plan to reduce its GHG emissions 40 percent from the 1990 level by 2020. Recognizing that more needed to be done, and as protesters demanding more action took to the streets of 500 German municipalities, in 2019 the parties making up Germany's coalition federal government agreed on a new target of reducing emissions 55 percent by 2030. The plan, which met with criticism from protestors for not going far enough, was to be facilitated by increasing the cost of carbon fuels and subsidizing alternatives (BBC, 2019a).

The German case demonstrates how the European Union has been unable to fulfill consistently its desire to be the leader of global climate governance due to political dynamics and varying levels of political commitment among member states (Dupont and Oberthur, 2015: 231). Just as in China and the United States, economic considerations have weighed heavily. The decade-long global economic crisis, starting in 2008, pushed climate change down the list of national priorities for all EU countries. Concerns about employment, economic growth, national debt and immigration (the latter due to external factors, such as the civil war in Syria) have dominated national political agendas, not least because those issues can determine the outcome of elections. Central and Eastern European members have repeatedly blocked robust climate governance measures for reasons more directly related to the problem: they feared the substantial impacts on their economies that emissions reductions might engender.

To be sure, more EU governments – and industries within them – have come to see action on climate change as an opportunity for economic growth and European economic leadership globally in the future. However, because most decisions by the European Council require consensus, those countries that wish to thwart Union-wide action on climate change have disproportionate ability to do so. What is more, top-down initiatives by the European Union have become more difficult to formulate and implement as Euro-skepticism among publics in some member countries has increased (although this sentiment seemed to have abated, at least somewhat, by the political chaos and economic uncertainties experienced by the United Kingdom as it withdrew from the European Union).

Members of the European Union face other pressures around climate governance, making it difficult for them to clearly ascertain their related national interests. Several European countries have experienced strong opposition to action on climate change by right-wing and populist political parties that have, much as in the United States and Australia (see below), portrayed environmentalists generally, and action to address climate change in particular, as threats to jobs, freedoms and ways of life. While these parties have seldom dominated national climate policy, at least in Western Europe, their growing popularity at least gives pause to governments wishing to implement more aggressive policies for climate governance. At the same time, environmentalist Green parties are seeing a rise in their popularity as the political middle in Europe has been eroded, meaning that these parties' advocacy for climate action has substantial influence in some EU member countries.

International forces simultaneously influence the EU's climate governance: if the Union's major economic competitors, not least the United States, continue to do less than is required, there is reduced pressure on Europe to take action on climate change and indeed substantial continued pressure to delay action in order to maintain short-term economic competitiveness, notwithstanding the argument that the process of shifting away from fossil fuels will, in the long run, make Europe much more competitive than the United States and will help it to compete with China. There is also the argument that continued emissions from other parts of the world, especially China and India (see Chapter 6), mean that Europe's cuts will not be enough to prevent dangerous climate change, thus raising doubts about the environmental efficacy of EU climate governance.

The European Commission's EGD proposal in 2019 was clearly designed to overcome political opposition and to consolidate support for more robust climate governance across the European Union. The EGD was promoted more as an economic and industrial policy than an environmental one, with Commission ministers emphasizing its potential to benefit both EU citizens and industries through better employment, improved social justice and higher investment in research and innovation (European Commission, 2019a). All of these things factor into member states' calculations of their national interests.

What is more, climate change governance is directly related to national security. One strong incentive for EU countries to reduce their CO_2 emissions is to increase their energy security. Several member countries are highly reliant on energy imports, especially natural gas from Russia. Russia's coercive restriction of gas supplies to Ukraine in 2014 "underpinned" the European Council's support for the Union's 2030 climate policy framework (Dupont and Oberthur, 2015: 233). At the same time, citizens of EU countries are, overall, increasingly concerned about climate change, with nearly all of them – 97 percent according to the European Union itself – viewing climate change as a serious problem (European Commission, 2019b). European students and activist organizations have spawned widespread protests for action that have been especially significant in raising awareness in recent years, alongside increasing media coverage of the impacts of climate change across Europe and around the world.

Overall, there is general agreement within the European Union that governing climate change effectively is in the interest of member countries (cf. Harris, 2015: 571–2). Generally speaking, the European Commission and EU member governments have chosen to make reduction in GHG pollution a major policy objective. They are willing to do more than China and the United States. The European Union is most easily distinguished from the United States by the extent to which it is willing to accept and act upon the CBDR principle, and specifically the Union's collective differentiated responsibility for climate change, first agreed at the Berlin COP in 1995. Most European countries recognize that they have disproportionate historical responsibility for causing climate change and disproportionate capability to take action to govern the problem effectively.

Consequently, when looked at holistically and globally, EU countries have, despite the outliers, done more to address climate change than other major countries. They have done the most to reduce GHG emissions and the most to assist vulnerable and poor countries to adapt to climate change. However, much as in China and especially the United States, forces within Europe opposed to more effective climate governance, often to protect powerful domestic economic actors, have prevented the European Union and its members from doing more.

Thus, while one cannot argue that the European Union, least of all every one of its members, has done enough to meet the Union's apparent aim to decarbonize by mid-century, nor to do its full share of the work to fulfill the objectives of the UNFCCC – avoiding dangerous climate change – or of the Paris Agreement – limiting global warming to 1.5°–2°C – if there is currently a world leader in climate governance, it would have to be the European Union.

Indeed, being the global leader on climate change may become a political raison d'être for the European Union, a way to bind the Union together as it is buffeted by internal and external forces and events (Lombrana and Krukowska, 2020). Insofar as the pathologies of national politics persist globally, it appears likely that the European Union will retain this relative leadership role.

Russia: Committed to Carbon

As noted earlier, Russia has been a factor in the climate governance of the European Union and some of its member states due to their reliance on its energy exports. Reducing their dependence on fossil fuels could reduce their vulnerability to potential cuts in the flow of Russian natural gas. Russia's climate change policies are substantially motivated by its own economic reliance on those same exports. Nearly 5 percent of global CO_2 emissions in 2018 came from Russia, making it the fifth-largest national polluter, having been overtaken by India (see Chapter 6) in 2009 (Crippa et al., 2019: 12, 14). Per capita carbon emissions in Russia stand at about 12 tons, double those of China but below those of the United States (Crippa et al., 2019: 14). Total CO_2 emissions from Russia fell by a quarter between 1990 and 2015 due to economic stagnation after the dissolution of the Soviet Union. Its emissions initially fell rapidly in the early 1990s before more or less leveling off for nearly two decades at below what they were during the Soviet period. In recent years, Russian emissions have risen somewhat as domestic use of coal, natural gas and oil has increased (Crippa et al., 2019: 14, 17). The country is highly dependent on these fuels for electricity, heating, industry and export. Leading Russian officials recognize that the economy is overly dependent on fossil-fuel exports, but they do not see this as an imminent threat. They expect that the global energy sector will be heavily skewed toward fossil fuels at least until the 2040s (Kokorin and Korppoo, 2017: 7).

Given Russia's great size, including its vast Arctic and sub-Arctic territory, it may be more widely affected by climate change than any other country. It is already experiencing the impacts. Its territory is warming more than twice as fast as the rest of the earth, with parts of the Russian Arctic already 6°–7°C warmer than the 1961–1990 average (Davydova, 2017). Arctic warming is having substantial adverse effects, such as forest fires and damage to infrastructure from melting of the permafrost that covers 60 percent of Russian territory (MacFarquhar, 2019). Other impacts across the country include heat waves and floods, and there are likely to be substantial adverse impacts on human health (Davydova, 2017). These and other impacts are starting to affect the Russian economy. According to one estimate, economic losses arising from climate change could equal 1–2 percent of GDP by 2030 (Davydova, 2017). These and other consequences of climate change do not translate directly into concerns about the national interest, let alone policies for climate governance. Much as in the United States, China and European countries, Russia's climate policies, and specifically its determination of where the national interest lies in this context, are a function of quite complicated national politics comprising "multiple and sometimes competing political interests and advisors who influence national policies" (Andonova, 2009: 37).

Russian Skepticism, Ambivalence and Unpredictability

The Russian leadership, including President Vladimir Putin himself, has questioned the anthropogenic causes of climate change, and thus "cutting GHG emissions is not a goal per se" for Russia (Kokorin and Korppoo, 2017: 7). Consequently, Russia has few strong domestic policies, and has taken relatively few steps, to rein in its GHG emissions. Most of its efforts with respect to energy have involved business-as-usual improvements in efficiency, with regulation toward decarbonizing the economy not being considered for implementation before the late 2030s (Kokorin and Korppoo, 2017: 10). That said, the government has recognized the need to improve energy efficiency to make the economy more competitive internationally and to attract foreign investment. In 2009 it set a goal of lowering the energy intensity of the whole economy 40 percent below what it was in 2007 by 2020 (although it seems that these efficiencies were not realized), and it has a plan for 2035 to reduce energy intensity by one-third compared to 2015 (Kokorin and Korppoo, 2017: 4–5). In keeping with the leadership's apparent skepticism about whether humanity is causing the climate crisis, the country's 2016 Climate Action Plan, its 2017 Environmental Security Strategy and other related policy plans emphasize *adaptation* to the impacts of climate change rather than mitigation of the pollution causing it (Kokorin and Korppoo, 2017: 2–3). Accordingly, in 2020 the Russian government announced a plan for adaptation to climate change and to "use the advantages" of warming experienced across the country (AFP, 2020).

In international climate negotiations, Russia has played varying roles. Much as in other countries, but even more so than in other industrialized countries whose GHG emissions were regulated by the top-down phase of the climate regime, domestic economic concerns have been the primary consideration in Russian foreign policy on climate change. It was initially skeptical of the climate regime, questioning the science and joining with other fossil-fuel-exporting countries to block quantitative limits on CO_2 emissions, before taking a more moderate stance of advocating very limited emissions cuts for developed countries (Andonova, 2009: 34–5). The large decline in Russia's GHG emissions after 1990 insulated it from having to make cuts of its own if such limited objectives were agreed. This proved to be the case in the Kyoto Protocol, which accorded Russia "by far the most favorable terms of all industrialized states" (Andonova, 2009: 35). The emissions that it was allowed were set at what they had been in 1990, thereby allowing it to *increase* its emissions by up to one-third.

Russia was able to achieve this outcome in the negotiations due to recognition by other countries that its economy was in dire need of economic growth and due to its relatively large share of global emissions. The importance of the latter became apparent when Russia ratified the Kyoto Protocol in 2004. For the protocol to go into effect, 55 countries with a total of 55 percent of industrialized-country emissions in 1990 were required to ratify it. This made Russian ratification all but essential, not least because the United States had no intention of consenting to the protocol. This need for Russian involvement enabled it to extract concessions during post-Kyoto, pre-ratification international negotiations. For example, at COP7 in Marrakech in 2001, it was able to persuade other countries to increase its allowance for how much carbon could be officially absorbed by Russian forests (Andonova, 2009: 35). In recent years, Russian diplomats have jostled to limit international regulations that might require Russia to implement difficult GHG limitations or that would threaten its fossil-fuel-driven economy. They have allied with diplomats from like-minded countries – those that are skeptical of action on climate change or outright opposed to it – to water down the wording of agreements reached at COP meetings. For example, at COP24 in 2018, Russia joined with the United States, Saudi Arabia and Kuwait to block the conference from embracing the IPCC's special report on 1.5°C of warming (IISD, 2018).

Russia had self-interested reasons for supporting the bottom-up approach to international climate governance that emerged at COP21 in Paris. In its Paris NDC, Russia pledged that it "might" restrict its GHG emissions to no more than 70–75 percent of what they were in 1990 by 2030 (similar to a presidential declaration in 2013 to limit them to 75 percent of 1990 emissions by 2020), "subject to the maximum possible account of absorbing capacity of [its] forests" (Russian Federation, 2015). This "critically insufficient" standard was higher than its prevailing emissions and a recipe for 4°C of global warming (Climate Action Tracker, 2020). It reflected the same sort of business-as-usual scenario found in China's pledge: doing what the country was doing already, irrespective of the climate regime generally and the Paris Agreement's objectives specifically. Russia's NDC was therefore similar to that of some other countries' pledges: it did not require much effort, and there was little downside to making it. Doing so might bring potential economic benefits, keep other countries off Russia's back diplomatically and enable its diplomats to retain their seats at the table during international negotiations to write the official "rulebook" for implementing the Paris Agreement and to plan future international regulation of GHG emissions.

Russia's attitude toward climate change, and specifically its cooperation with other countries to address it, has at times seemed to be "wrapped in unpredictability" (Andonova, 2009: 29). This unpredictability arises not so much from the problem itself, but rather from national calculations about how the problem, and especially national and international responses to it, might affect the perceived interests of Russia and those with power and influence there. Russian concerns about the impacts of climate change *in Russia* have not motivated its involvement in related international cooperation, and "environmental benefits from climate mitigation *per se*, as understood in the West ... have not been recognized in the Russian debate" (Korppoo, Tynkkynen and Honneland, 2015: 49). Instead, Russia has been motivated by the benefits to its economy and foreign policy that it expects to accrue from being involved in climate governance. Like China, one purpose of Russia's involvement in international climate negotiations has been to affirm and exercise its diplomatic influence.

Unlike other countries greatly affected by climate change, in Russia the official perception seems to be that climate change is not a threat to vital interests of most people or the state. While the reality of climate change is widely recognized, skepticism, at least about the human causes, is reinforced by national media narratives and related public opinion. Public concern about climate change is growing, but Russians might be forgiven, at least during their long winters, for perceiving global warming as being potentially desirable – as more than a quarter of them did in one survey (Russian Public Opinion Research Center, 2017). The public has a limited role in government policy in Russia, but any skepticism about taking costly action on climate change helps to reinforce the leadership's choices.

Russian Politics and Russian Interests

Russian domestic politics have included significant debate about what form climate governance should take nationally and internationally. For example, there was domestic opposition to the Kyoto Protocol on the grounds that its provisions might, by restricting the use of fossil fuels, undermine President Putin's promises to double the size of the economy; that the benefits of the agreement (e.g., joint implementation) would bring limited benefits; that the agreement would be ineffective in addressing climate change; that it would be used by the European Union to unfairly capture the Russian market; that it was a conspiracy to gain access to Russian natural resources; and that it would undermine Russian sovereignty (Korppoo, Tynkkynen and Honneland, 2015: 28–30). Just as in China, the prospect of international scrutiny of Russia's GHG emissions, and necessarily its industries, "was seen as increasing [foreign] control over Russia" (Korppoo, Tynkkynen and Honneland, 2015: 29). In contrast, there were those who supported participation in the Kyoto Protocol because it was perceived to bring economic benefits, including significant foreign investment; it would be an opportunity to modernize ageing production technologies; Russia would be "compensated" for the ecological services provided by its huge forests; and joint-implementation projects would be under its full national control (Korppoo, Tynkkynen and Honneland, 2015: 31–40).

A number of Russian businesses, including in its energy sector, have supported Russian participation in the climate regime (Andonova, 2009: 44–5). For example, the Russian natural gas company Gazprom supported ratification of the Kyoto Protocol. Like other fossil-fuel companies, it could benefit from international assistance arising from the protocol, and it would be relatively easy for it to generate credit-worthy cuts in emissions from its antiquated infrastructure. What is more, because Russia's emissions were set from such a low baseline (i.e., 1990, the baseline year for the Kyoto Protocol), all of the climate agreements placed relatively few demands on the country. Some actors in Russia argued that the economic benefits justified joining the Kyoto Protocol even if the science of climate change was wrong, and others argued that doing so would boost Russia's international credentials, thereby increasing the likelihood that it would be allowed to join the WTO, which indeed was an assumed informal *quid pro quo* between Russia and the European Union (Korppoo, Tynkkynen and Honneland, 2015: 27–8). Given these realities, and the potential to benefit economically from joint implementation and other programs, it made sense for Russia to implement the protocol.

However, Russia was slow to ratify the agreement because President Putin wanted clear evidence that there would be more gains than losses, and to give his diplomats time to obtain concessions in other international negotiations from countries that were anxious to see the protocol enter into force (Henry and Sundstrom, 2007). The strategy for implementing the protocol – which continued with subsequent international climate agreements – was to maximize profits from the its mechanisms rather than to maximize reductions in emissions (Henry and Sundstrom, 2007). The protocol was so limited in its objectives that it would have little effect on global demand for Russia's energy exports. Furthermore, the fall in Russian GHG emissions from 1990 allowed Russia to sell surplus emissions quotas through the protocol's joint-implementation provisions (Korppoo, Tynkkynen and Honneland, 2015: 25–6). It also benefited from financial aid programs from the European Union for climate-related capacity building. In addition, the protocol was perceived to bolster in Russia "an image of itself as a good member of the club of advanced industrialized states" (Henry and Sundstrom, 2007: 1). These and other economic benefits from the Kyoto Protocol contributed to the decision to support ratification and to give responsibility for the management of climate change policies to the Ministry of Economic Development and Trade – apparently demonstrating that climate change was viewed as an economic issue rather than an environmental one (Andonova, 2009: 41–2).

Just as with the Kyoto Protocol, Russia was also slow to ratify the Paris Agreement. It was only in 2019 that it did so – the last industrialized country to formally accept the agreement – and then only after years of lobbying by European governments in favor of ratification and some domestic industries opposed to it (Gershkovich, 2019; Sauer, 2019). This reticence to formally ratify the Paris Agreement made sense for Russia because the leadership viewed it as "part of the global economic low-carbon trend, which entails risks to a national economy based on the export of oil, gas, metals and mineral resources" (Kokorin and Korppoo, 2017: 4). The last thing that the Russian government wants to see is an end to the world's reliance on fossil fuels. This calculation helps to explain Russia's ongoing role in international climate negotiations, and specifically its perpetual resistance to attempts to burden Russia itself with significant emissions obligations or to decarbonize the global economy anytime soon. From the official Russian perspective, aggressive global governance to address climate change is not in the country's national interest. After all, many, if not most, of the adverse impacts of climate change for Russia are unavoidable, thus limiting interest in shifting substantially away from fossil fuels.

What is more, any substantial Russian efforts to mitigate its own GHG pollution are complicated by a perception within the leadership that, for Russia, climate change is not entirely a bad thing. Due to Arctic warming, the Northern Sea Route between Asia and Europe, which traverses waters along Russia's coastline, is anticipated to be economically practicable by 2040 (Hansen *et al.*, 2016: 7). Several ships have already demonstrated the feasibility of the route, which has the potential to produce revenue and increase

Russian political influence. Arctic warming has the added benefit of opening access to oil and gas deposits there, potentially increasing export earnings. It will also make it easier for the Russian fishing industry to access more of the Arctic Ocean, into which more fish species are migrating as waters farther south become too warm for them. Russia is reopening Arctic military bases to protect the potentially lucrative new sea route and newly accessible ocean resources, as well as to increase its presence in the region relative to other littoral powers, especially the United States.

Much as in China, there seems to be no evidence that the threats that climate change poses to national territory have directly affected Russia's choices regarding climate governance. Whether Russia will be harmed by climate change or benefit from it has been a subject of domestic debate, including among the country's scientists, but the overall conclusion seems to have been that the potential benefits (e.g., increased access to the Russian Arctic, longer growing seasons) mostly outweigh the potential drawbacks (e.g., melting of permafrost, impacts on infrastructure), at least in the near future (Andonova, 2009: 37–8). For Russia, in the short and medium term, the perceived national interest is about economic vitality and political considerations. Continued (perhaps willful, even cynical) skepticism in Russia about the causes of climate change, and more realistic realization of its inevitability, may combine with concerns about near-term economic development and recognition of potential advantages of global warming to encourage the Russian government to continue doing what it can to slow global efforts to end the use of fossil fuels.

Given that the impacts of climate change that are likely to affect Russia in coming decades are quite severe, the Russian case highlights vividly how future climate change per se is rarely enough to motivate changes to the perceived national interest. This demonstrates, once again, how the pathologies of national politics can greatly dilute the kind of governance that is essential if dangerous climate change is to be mitigated and managed effectively.

Other Northern Countries: Politics and the Persistence of Fossil Fuels

It is important to pay extra attention to how the United States, China, EU countries and Russia have approached climate governance. Together they account for well over half of global GHG emissions. It is impossible to avoid dangerous climate change if those emissions are not cut drastically as soon as possible. What is more, most of these countries together account for the majority of GHG pollution that has entered the atmosphere since the Industrial Revolution. With this comes disproportionate – that is, much greater – responsibility to take action to address climate change – perhaps less so for China given its relatively recent emergence as a relatively developed country, although its responsibility is increasing rapidly. What is more, most of these countries are wealthy enough to provide the resources that are necessary to help other countries, notably those in the developing Global South, to respond to climate change more effectively themselves, including through adaptation.

Before looking at those developing countries, it is useful to take a brief look at a few more developed countries to ascertain whether they, too, are afflicted with the pathologies of national politics that undermine effective climate governance. To varying degrees, from moderate to extreme, indeed they are. They provide further evidence that national interests are still very much equated with the continued use of fossil fuels despite all of the efforts around the world to align those national interests with the collective global interest in mitigating the climate crisis.

Australia

Australia provides a fascinating real-world juxtaposition of severe climate impacts, on one side, and the capture of key political institutions by the fossil-fuel industry, on the other. It shows how the leadership of a country that is immediately and significantly vulnerable to climate change can nevertheless perceive that the national interest lies in contributing to the problem rather than to its solution. The dangers that climate change poses for Australia are indeed many. They range from severe drought and bushfires to cyclones, flooding, extreme stress on agricultural productivity, loss of species, coastal erosion, widespread bleaching of the Great Barrier Reef and adverse effects on human health and the economy, among other impacts (IPCC, 2014a: 1371–1438; Zhang *et al.*, 2018; Climate Council, 2019). Emphasizing its vulnerability, in 2019–2020 Australia experienced unprecedented wildfires. According to one expert on bushfires, those blazes were "the country's worst peacetime catastrophe precisely because of climate change" (quoted in Tarabay, 2020: 5). That assessment was backed up by attribution studies (which aim to ascertain the extent to which weather-related events can be attributed to climate change) showing that global warming likely contributed greatly to the fires (Oldenborgh *et al.*, 2020).

When looked at nationally, Australia is a relatively minor contributor to climate change; it accounts for 1 percent of global CO_2 emissions from the burning of fossil fuels (Crippa *et al.*, 2019: 12), although, unlike many other developed countries, its emissions continue to increase (Global Carbon Project, 2020). Its GHG pollution per capita, at nearly 17 tons in 2018 (down from more than 20 tons a decade earlier), exceed those of the United States and put Australians among the highest polluters of the atmosphere globally (Ritchie, 2019a). This very high level of emissions per person is partly attributable to the country's substantial reliance on coal for electricity and the heavy use of carbon-based fuels for commercial and private transport over long distances (Bradsher and Kwai, 2020).

Australia's national and international climate change policies are characterized by frequent change: as governments change, so do the policy objectives, sometimes radically, similar to what has happened in the United States. In 2011, under Labor prime minister Julia Gillard, the government won passage of legislation for a Carbon Pricing Mechanism, but that legislation was repealed in 2014 by the right-wing coalition government under Prime Minister Tony Abbott (Bailey, 2019: 53). Abbot had campaigned against Labor's "'economically devastating' carbon tax" (Bailey, 2019: 56). Gillard's predecessor and successor, Kevin Rudd, tried to get a Carbon Pollution Reduction Scheme through the legislature, but he was unable to overcome opposition from industry (Bailey, 2019: 55). For many years, Australian governments have been at the mercy of the country's economically and politically powerful coal lobby and its supporters in the media. Australian prime ministers have been ousted more than once over their positions on fossil fuels and climate change. Prime Minister Scott Morrison's party coalition won reelection (to some surprise) in 2019 with support from Queensland voters who favored continuation of coal mining over action on climate change (Cave, 2019). Queensland produces more coal than other Australian regions. This has special significance because, much as in the United States, where the Electoral College system gives inordinate political influence to smaller US states, in Australia some regions – including Queensland – have more influence than others (Bradsher and Kwai, 2020).

Morrison's government highlights the extent to which Australian national politics have resisted action on climate change. His government's national economic model was wedded to fossil fuels. Despite the most devastating wildfires in Australian history in 2020, and the majority of Australians supportive of action on climate change, Morrison minimized the connections between the fires and global warming, and he held tight to his government's policy of supporting coal as one of the country's primary sources of electricity and its second-largest export earner (Albeck-Ripka, Tarabay and Kwai, 2020). Morrison defended the mining industry, which employed 250,000 Australians, and he saw action on climate change as a threat to it (Bradsher and Kwai, 2020).

The government did not blatantly deny the reality of climate change, but it did mirror the Trump administration in the United States by reducing the input of climate science to government policy. It emphasized that, due to its size, Australia could not play a meaningful role in mitigating climate change. Instead, the government provided some assistance to Pacific small-island countries to help them adapt to climate change – perhaps displaying recognition of Australia's historical role in contributing to global warming and thus sea-level rise.

Australia's foreign policies on climate change have varied greatly over time. When the Labor Party has governed, Australia has arguably "played a leadership role" at times, as it did in the early negotiations for the Kyoto Protocol. In contrast, under coalition governments made up of right-of-center parties it has been a "laggard" (Nursey-Bray, 2009: 21), as demonstrated by its efforts at COP25 to use accounting methodology to avoid joining substantial efforts to implement the Paris Agreement. But even examples of Australian leadership have left much to be desired when considered in the context of the objectives of the various climate change agreements. For example, in COP negotiations leading up the Kyoto Protocol, Australia argued that it ought not be required to limit its emissions as much as other developed countries due to its economy's high dependence on coal (Chasek, Downie and Brown, 2014: 158). Consequently, under the protocol, it was allowed to *increase* its emissions by 8 percent, meaning that, even if it failed to reduce its GHG pollution, it could potentially take a credit toward its pledge under the Paris Agreement.

Australia's emissions pledge (NDC) in the run-up to the Paris COP in 2015 was to implement a national GHG-reduction target of 26–28 percent of 2005 levels by 2030 (Australia, 2015) – all but identical to the US pledge, thus allowing the government to claim that it was doing no worse than some other developed countries – a pledge that has been deemed "insufficient" for achieving the Paris Agreement's objectives (Climate Action Tracker, 2020). At COP25 in December 2019, Australia was instrumental in preventing consensus on the Paris Agreement's "rulebook" because it insisted on being allowed to carry over credits from its emissions limitations under the Kyoto Protocol. This was not the work of diplomats interested in effective climate governance; they seemed to be interested only in protecting the Australian economy, or parts of it.

Looked at without consideration of national politics, Australia appears to be a country that should want to race as quickly as possible to a carbon-free future – to set an example to the rest of the world of how a developed country can quickly shift from reliance on coal to universal use of renewable energy, and to use its role in international climate negotiations to push other countries to do likewise. However, in Australia, national politics, which determine climate governance almost exclusively, have resulted in the country doing the opposite: its government has so far been wedded to fossil fuels, especially coal, and it has used its diplomacy to undermine international efforts to divorce the world from them. It seems likely that Australia's government, most probably under the Labor Party, will eventually shift direction as public and international pressures mount. Australia is a test case of whether severe climate-related impacts will be enough to influence the public's voting behaviors, or whether, as happened in Australia and elsewhere in the past (and as the Morrison government no doubt hoped after the 2019–2020 wildfires), the public will move on to other livelihood issues instead.

Canada

Much as in Australia, in Canada domestic political considerations, rather than the threat of climate change per se, have shaped climate governance policies. Canada shares many of the same vulnerabilities to climate change as the United States, including adverse impacts to ecosystems, infrastructure, agriculture and human health. Like the US state of Alaska and much of Russia, Canada's vast sub-Arctic and Arctic regions, including its boreal forests, will experience – and are already experiencing – inordinate warming. Canada shares some of the responsibility for causing these impacts due to its historical pollution and its continued substantial reliance on fossil fuels for energy. The country's GHG emissions rose almost 19 percent between 1990 and 2017, with notable declines in some provinces (e.g., Ontario) and substantial increases in others (e.g., Alberta) (Environment and Climate Change Canada, 2019: 5). Although Canada accounts for only about 1.6 percent of global carbon emissions (Crippa *et al.*, 2019: 12), its per capita emissions, at about 15 tons, are similar to those of the United States and very high by global standards (Union of Concerned Scientists, 2020). However, relative to many other developed countries, including its neighbor to the south, Canada uses more non-fossil-fuel energy for its electricity – 82 percent (60 percent of which comes from hydroelectric dams and 15 percent from nuclear-power plants) – with solar and wind energy increasing 18 percent between 2010 and 2017 (Natural Resources Canada, 2019: 31).

Canada's policies for reducing its GHG pollution – "all weak and none fully implemented" (Dessler and Parson, 2020: 31) – have varied substantially from one federal government to another, and from national to regional and local levels, much as has been the case in the United States. The federal government under Prime Minister Justin Trudeau pushed for nationwide carbon taxes and a phaseout of coal. These policies have been resisted by some regional governments, including Alberta, which in 2018 had 143,000 people working in its fossil-fuel-heavy energy sector (Natural Resources Canada, 2019: 12, 21), and some other provinces have vociferously opposed carbon taxes (Herring, 2020). However, similar to what has happened in the United States, some regions and municipalities have taken more action to address climate change. For example, British Columbia has had a carbon tax, albeit a very modest one, since 2008.

Mirroring domestic governance, Canada's foreign policies on climate change have been uneven. Its Kyoto Protocol pledge in 1997 was to reduce its GHG emissions 6 percent from 1990 levels by 2012. A decade passed before it ratified the protocol, reflecting not only significant domestic opposition but also the reality that even such a modest cut in emissions would require more effort than was politically possible. Perhaps Canada should never have ratified the protocol; under a right-leaning, Conservative Party–led government, and with the support of Western oil-producing provinces, it withdrew from the protocol in 2011 (Dessler and Parson, 2020: 186). With a change to Trudeau's left-leaning Liberal Party–led government, by 2015 Canada's NDC pledge for the Paris Agreement was to reduce its 2005 GHG emissions 30 percent by 2030 – on the scale of the Australian and US pledges – and to aim for an 80 percent cut in emissions by 2050 (Canada, 2015). This pledge was "insufficient" for fulfilling Canada's responsibilities in achieving the Paris objectives (Climate Action Tracker, 2020), which would be the case especially if a future Conservative government were to repeat past behavior and withdraw from the Paris Agreement.

The twists and turns in Canada's climate policies are proximately caused by differing perceptions of the national interest by political parties and their leaderships, as well as the various interests, not least businesses, that lobby them. Consequently, as ruling parties change, so do the country's policies related to climate change. Canadian parties on the right of the political spectrum have tended to oppose substantial national and international action to reduce GHG emissions, least of all CO_2 emissions. Parties toward the left of the political spectrum have tended to support action to do so. Yet, even the left-leaning government that everyone assumed would be most likely to implement policies to address climate change – that of Justin Trudeau – hedged considerably, advocating action to reduce GHG emissions while simultaneously taking steps with exactly the opposite effect. Most notably, as the Trudeau government pushed for carbon taxes to be implemented across Canada, it facilitated major expansion of the Trans Mountain Pipeline from the Alberta tar sands to the British Columbia coast. The pipeline would triple the flow to export markets of perhaps the most carbon-intensive form of petroleum, in the process defying the wishes of the government of British Columbia and Indigenous peoples, not to mention Trudeau's erstwhile environmentalist supporters (AP, 2020a). Trudeau may have taken this action to weaken opposition in some regions to his climate-related policies. As in other developed countries, national politics, particularly national political economy, have been decisive in shaping Canada's approach to climate governance.

Japan

Australia and Canada, like other developed countries described above, further highlight the pathologies of national politics that often overwhelm efforts to address climate change. Japan does so as well. It especially shows how domestic concerns about energy security, which can change suddenly due to unforeseen circumstances, can result in a watering down of policies that might otherwise be more effective in reducing GHG pollution. In the long term, Japan certainly has an interest in seeing emissions reduced. It is vulnerable to climate change and has arguably already experienced the effects, whether from powerful typhoons or by way of adverse changes to marine ecosystems and fisheries. Human health in Japan is also vulnerable. For example, in 2018 more than 1,000 people died in a heat wave that "could not have happened without climate change" (Tabuchi, 2020b). Japan holds some responsibility for these impacts due to its historical and continuing GHG emissions. Between 1990 and 2018, those emissions increased 4–5 percent (Crippa *et al.*, 2019: 5–6). Japan produced 3.2 percent of global CO_2 emissions in 2018, when its per capita carbon emissions were 9.4 tons (Crippa *et al.*, 2019: 12, 14), very high for a country with a longstanding reputation for energy efficiency relative to most other countries.

Japan's policies and plans for GHG emissions reductions are both comprehensive and modest. In its 2012 Basic Environmental Plan, the government set a goal of reducing GHG emissions 80 percent by 2050, to be achieved through, among other measures, maximization of energy efficiency and use of renewable energy (Ministry of the Environment, 2014: 14). Mirroring the plans of some other developed countries, notably by changing the base year for measuring reductions (from 1990), not long thereafter it proposed reducing emissions 3.8 percent below the 2005 level by 2020 (Ministry of the Environment, 2014: 21). The government then crafted a plan of action to achieve this target through, among other measures, a new carbon-tax scheme and policies to promote low-carbon cities and energy-efficient appliances and transport, additional voluntary action by industry, and carbon capture and storage by coal-fired power plants (Ministry of the Environment, 2014). In 2016 the government released a Plan for Global Warming Countermeasures that envisioned continued reliance on coal and other fossil fuels. It was anticipated that Japan would obtain about 25 percent of its electricity from coal in 2030 (Tabuchi, 2020b), which conflicts with its GHG emissions pledge for the Paris Agreement (see below). The country's plans for coal are not restricted to its domestic affairs; after China, it is the largest source of funding for coal-plant construction internationally.

Japanese leaders have "consistently accepted the reality" of anthropogenic climate change (Aldrich, Lipscy and McCarthy, 2019), but Japan's "bureaucracy does not prioritize climate change mitigation" (NRDC, 2017: 2). The country's climate-related policies "are mainly driven by joint ministerial and business interests" (Andresen, 2015: 432). Energy policy is dominated by the economics bureaucracy, currently under the Ministry of Economy, Trade and Industry (METI), with the Ministry of the Environment – nominally in charge of climate policy – having far less sway in government, and both ministries are advised by influential committees dominated by corporate representatives, including members from energy-intensive industries (NRDC, 2017: 3). Public opinion, which has generally favored action on climate change for some decades, has not been a very strong force in shaping the country's climate-related policies, although the public's views buttressed pro-climate policies advocated by Japanese diplomats early in the international negotiations (Ohta, 2009: 40). The strong influence of pro-business ministries contrasted with the weak influence of climate-friendly public opinion helps to explain why efforts to reduce GHG emissions have been relatively weak when compared to the climate science and the nominal objectives of the climate regime, particularly the Paris Agreement.

Japan was relatively more favorable toward effective governance of climate change during the early COPs. At that time, combating climate change fit well with the country's "inflated self-image" as a "great" economic power with a "sense of 'responsibility'," including toward "betterment of the global environment" as a component of its "national quest for 'internationalization' and 'international contribution'" (Ohta, 2009: 40–2). Being an international leader on these issues was considered by the government to be "politically safe" (Ohta, 2009: 42). However, as negotiations for the Kyoto Protocol approached, Japan became reluctant to maintain this leadership role because the economic costs of implementing emissions cuts proposed by the European Union and the Alliance of Small Island States (AOSIS; see Chapter 6) were deemed to be too high (Ohta, 2009: 42). After the global oil shocks of the 1970s, Japan's economy became much more energy efficient. This made further efficiencies in the 1990s and beyond more costly than in most other countries, potentially threatening economic growth and international competitiveness.

Japan hosted the Kyoto COP in 1997 to assert its major-power status in technological and economic terms (Vogler, 2015: 17–18). Its emissions-reduction pledge for the Kyoto Protocol was the same as Canada's: to reduce its GHG pollution 6 percent from 1990 levels by 2012. However, Japan's efforts to reduce its emissions in the wake of the Kyoto conference were not up to meeting this objective. Emissions a decade later were 9 percent above what they were in 1990 (Dessler and Parson, 2020: 31), and by the end of the protocol's commitment period (2012) the country's emissions were still up about 6 percent (Ministry of the Environment, 2014: 9). (This may explain why Japan chose not to accept a second Kyoto Protocol commitment period proposed by other countries.) However, Japan was able to claim that it had met its Kyoto pledge because it used credits allowed under the protocol, particularly the counting of its forests as carbon sinks and credit for overseas joint-implementation projects (Ministry of the Environment, 2014: 9; Dessler and Parsons, 2020).

Japan naturally joined with other developed countries in supporting the bottom-up approach to international climate governance that resulted in the 2015 Paris Agreement. In doing so, it was "trying to tear down the 'firewall' between North and South" so that GHG pollution from large emitters, notably China, that had been excluded from the top-down Kyoto Protocol would finally be subject to limitations (Andresen, 2015: 430). Japan's 2015 NDC pledge to achieve the goals of the Paris Agreement was to reduce its GHG emissions 26 percent below what they were in 2013 by 2030, and toward that end to reduce its emissions 3.8 percent by 2020 (MOFA, 2016) – an objective that it achieved the same year the pledge was made. These pledges were "unambitious" (NRDC, 2017: 1) and "highly insufficient" for meeting the Paris objectives (Climate Action Tracker, 2020), not least because the unusual base year of 2013 concealed the modest limitations relative to the once-normal base year of 1990. What is more, much like it did with its Kyoto pledge, Japan intended to meet much of its Paris pledge by taking credit for its forest-management and other land-use practices, as well as through emissions reductions that it would support in other countries.

Japan's NDC pledge was akin to that of China: pledging to do what it would do anyway instead of demonstrating ambition to reduce GHG emissions as part of a global effort to mitigate climate change and keep global warming below $1.5°$–$2°C$. Japan's "minimal" NDC pledge reflected the priorities of Japanese policymakers who were "more concerned about energy security than climate change. In fact, members of Parliament – especially those from the ruling Liberal Democratic Party – do not include climate change in their agenda of priorities" (NRDC, 2017: 1).

Japanese policymakers' prioritization of energy security over climate governance is in part a reflection of unexpected, sudden and dramatic events. The country's supply of energy to provide electricity and to power its industries was greatly and suddenly affected by the 2011 Fukushima nuclear disaster. The disaster was caused by an earthquake-induced tidal wave that overwhelmed the Fukushima Daiichi nuclear-power plant, resulting in nuclear meltdown and the escape of radioactive material. This compelled the government to order the shutdown of nuclear stations across the country (which was subsequently echoed by the German government's plan to phase out nuclear energy within about a decade, as noted previously). Prior to that shutdown, those facilities had been providing one-third of the country's electricity. To make up for the shortfall in nuclear power, the country turned to coal. It commenced construction of additional coal-fired power plants, with 49 of them planned, including as many as 22 by 2025 (NRDC, 2017: 3; Tabuchi, 2020b). Partly as a consequence, Japan is the largest customer for Australia's exports of coal (Bradsher and Kwai, 2020). Even as renewable energy, which provides about 16 percent of Japan's electricity, becomes less costly for consumers than energy from coal, oil and natural gas (which together provide about 80 percent of electricity), the Japanese government has "stood by the belief that the country's utilities must keep investing in fossil fuels to maintain a diversified mix of energy sources," having learned a difficult lesson from the country's overreliance on oil imports during the oil embargoes of the 1970s (Tabuchi, 2020b), a lesson no doubt reinforced by the Fukushima disaster. Accordingly, METI declared that "[t]he most responsible policy is to forge a concrete path that allows for both energy security and a battle against climate change" (Tabuchi, 2020b).

The cases of Australia, Canada and Japan reinforce the recurring theme that national-level considerations *other than climate change* largely, and sometimes exclusively, determine perceived national interests of developed countries and thus their policies for climate governance. These countries show the persistence of carbon in national energy mixes and, closely related, its persistence in what their governments perceive to be a national interest more important than mitigation of climate change: near-term economic vitality. Something that is remarkable about the case of Japan is that it shows how a completely unexpected event – a *geologic* event, no less – can have a dramatic impact on climate governance. An earthquake reshaped the climate-related policies of one of the world's most developed and affluent countries. In this case, a completely natural disaster resulted in changes to energy policies that will have the effect of extending further into the future Japan's reliance on fossil fuels and thus its GHG pollution.

Japan is certainly not alone in being vulnerable to natural events. What happens when "natural" disasters that have been exacerbated by climate change strike *developing* countries? Do national politics play a different role there, or do we see the same pathologies that are exhibited in the developed world? The next chapter looks into these and related questions

6

Pathologies of National Politics
in the Global South

The preceding chapter's description of the national politics of climate governance focused on developed "industrialized" countries of the Global North –
those that reached or exceeded levels of economic development in the twentieth century to give them the ability to meet far more than the needs of their
own citizens. Those countries are particularly important to the story of climate
governance, and the pathologies of national politics in that story, because they
were the major sources of the GHG pollution that created the climate crisis.
Together, those countries (EU members, Russia, Australia, Canada and Japan),
along with China and the United States (Chapter 4), account for nearly two-
thirds of global carbon emissions from the burning of fossil fuels (Crippa *et al.*,
2019: 12). In addition to most of them being far more responsible than the rest
of the world for historical GHG pollution, the countries of the North are, due to
their economic wealth (even if it is not always distributed fairly or wisely
within their borders), far more capable of taking action to govern climate
change effectively. The principle of CBDR that has nominally guided the
evolution of global climate governance regime is based on these important
considerations. Consequently, the developed countries are often the focus of
attention for *mitigating* climate change.

But what of the developing countries of the Global South? Collectively they
are currently the source of one-third of the global pollution causing climate
change. If one still classifies China as a developing country (something that is
difficult to justify given its great wealth and power), then all developing
countries combined currently produce far more than half of global GHG
pollution. That pollution is on course to rise without far more effective
governance measures. This is a recipe for extending and exacerbating the
climate crisis well into the future. Thus, the future of climate governance,
and indeed of the climate crisis, will very much depend on whether more
attention is given to what is happening in the Global South.

Vitally, many countries of the South are the most vulnerable to climate change. For some of them, climate change is becoming an existential threat, as it certainly will be for millions, and potentially hundreds of millions, of their citizens. Developing countries are in precarious positions in the context of global climate governance. The majority of them are somewhere between being victims of the problem and mostly hidden causes of it: all will be affected to varying degrees, but most of them host cohorts of middle-class and wealthy people who have, in their ways, contributed to the problem. For some developing countries – the term is used loosely here because many of the officially developing countries harbor extreme wealth – their complicity in causing the problem is extreme. The most obvious examples are the Persian Gulf oil and gas exporters. For a few economically emerging countries, such as India, their contribution to climate change is very substantial, but they deserve more sympathy than blame because they suffer from extremely widespread poverty. Many developing countries – the least-developed countries (LDCs) of the world, and many small and highly vulnerable island states – are often hapless victims of a problem created almost entirely by others.

India: Development vs. Climate Change

India is an important case for understanding climate governance in the developing world. Climate change presents India with tremendous long-term challenges due to its geography, underdevelopment and large population. At 1.4 billion people, its population is matched only by China, which it is expected to surpass around 2027 (UNDESA, 2019b: 1). Indians and their descendants will bear a disproportionate share of the suffering brought on by climate change. The country's vulnerabilities are numerous: its vast coastlines will be affected by sea-level rise and tropical storms; it is extremely dependent on water from melting glaciers for agriculture; it is subject to increasingly severe droughts from lack of rain and to recurring flooding from storms; and its population will be faced with increasingly frequent and deadly heat waves, to name only some of the challenges (IPCC, 2014b: 1327–70).

Adding insult to injury, India is one those countries that bears a relatively small share of the responsibility for causing climate change, at least if one considers this in terms of population: with 17 percent of the global population, it has produced 3 percent of historical GHG pollution (Ebinger, 2016: viii). The country's CO_2 emissions are now about 7 percent of the global total (Friedlingstein, 2020), making it the fourth-largest national source of carbon pollution (Crippa et al., 2019: 12) (see Figure 2.1). Its emissions are less than one-third those of China, despite both countries having similarly sized populations. India's per capita CO_2 emissions, at 1.9 tons (in 2018), are quite low, perversely so for many millions of its citizens whose individual emissions are well below this national average – one-fourth those of China and the European Union, and one-eighth those of the United States (Crippa *et al.*, 2019: 12, 14). Very important, especially from the perspective of climate justice, within India's per capita emissions statistic are hidden millions of middle-class and wealthy Indians whose individual emissions are many times higher than those of most people in the developed world (Harris, 2016c: 127–9). Partly as a consequence, India's contribution to climate change is growing. Between 1990 and 2018 its CO_2 emissions increased by 3.4 times, and both its share of global emissions and its per capita emissions have been rising (Crippa *et al.*, 2019: 5).

From Justice to Development

In the early decades of the international climate negotiations, Indian diplomats argued that climate change was a problem for the developed world to solve. They focused on promoting principles of international economic and climate justice that would recognize India's role as a victim of climate change, and they sought to have the CBDR principle implemented (Gupta, Kohli and Ahluwalia, 2015). The Indian government argued that efforts to reduce GHG emissions should not adversely affect the country's economic development or indeed its related ability to use domestic reserves of coal (Chasek, Downie and Brown, 2014: 231). Toward that end, the CBDR principle was codified at COP3 in the Kyoto Protocol by not requiring developing countries to limit their GHG emissions and through the CDM and other benefit-transfer mechanisms (see Harris, 2016c: 81–4). India was one of the countries that benefited most from the CDM, albeit not nearly as much as China. India's demand for climate justice was evident when it hosted COP8 in 2002. Indian negotiators resisted attempts by some developed-country diplomats to persuade developing countries to take on emissions-reduction burdens.

While its demand for implementation of CBDR did not go away, as time went on India's foreign policy on climate change evolved away from purely blaming the developed world for the problem to accepting that climate change presented a threat to India, and that it could not be addressed effectively in the long term without Indian participation in efforts to limit global GHG emissions (Saryal, 2018: 4). Economic development remained the government's overriding priority, but mitigation of climate change was no longer viewed as solely the domain of developed countries. One result was a shift toward policies that would continue to prioritize development while simultaneously enabling the limitation of GHG emissions. Thus, in 2008 the government adopted the National Action Plan on Climate Change. A major aim of the plan was to promote the country's development and economic security in such a way as to produce, in the words of the Prime Minister's Council on Climate Change, "co-benefits for addressing climate change effectively" (Saryal, 2018: 10). In 2011, Prime Minister Manmohan Singh said that "the world" – presumably including India – "must move away from production and consumption patterns which are carbon-intensive and energy-intensive," and he argued that ending poverty would require access to cleaner sources of energy (quoted in Saryal, 2018: 11). He had previously pledged that India's per capita GHG emissions would never exceed those of the developed countries, and the government's emphasis on climate justice was already increasingly focused on gaining equitable access to sustainable development (Atteridge *et al.*, 2012: 70).

While India has recognized that limiting its own GHG emissions can bring economic benefits, much like China and the United States it has been unwilling to accept top-down international mandates for doing so. The government of Prime Minister Narendra Modi (who expressed a strong interest in environmental issues, including climate change) declared "India's aversion to being dictated to by outsiders" and, matching China's attitude, expressed the view that international review of its actions on climate change would be tantamount to interference in its sovereign affairs (Saryal, 2018: 11). Like other countries, India clearly has had a preference for *nationally determined* policies and a bottom-up approach to international climate governance, as codified in the Paris Agreement. In that context, India still has not pledged to reduce its total GHG emissions. To demand that it do so makes sense from a scientific perspective – cutting those emissions would help to mitigate future climate change – but doing so would evoke claims of injustice and would violate the CBDR principle (at least insofar as the principle is focused entirely on the responsibilities of states; see Chapter 8).

Instead, India has pledged in its NDC for the Paris Agreement to reduce the *intensity* of its GHG emissions 33–35 percent by 2030, as compared to 2005 (India, 2015). It proposed doing this in part by increasing the use of solar and wind power, increasing new forest carbon sinks and building domestic capacity to introduce new technology for mitigating emissions and adapting to change. The government made clear that implementing its NDC pledge would depend on receipt of major financial and technological assistance from developed countries, for example, via the Green Climate Fund. Although the government has scaled back plans to build new coal-fired power plants and is closing older facilities (Mathiesen, 2016), coal will likely continue to provide the bulk of India's electricity for many years, if not for decades. In 2017 the country's energy minister told the parliament that coal "will continue to remain our mainstay and there was no such agreement in Paris that will stop us from continuing to encourage coal-based generation of power" (Mathiesen, 2017), and this was reflected in the 2018 National Electricity Plan. Consumption of fossil fuels in India continues to rise, with 61 percent of it being coal (Crippa *et al.*, 2019: 14).

Despite the government's commitment to coal, it recognized the economic benefits of "green" technology for economic development and environmental sustainability (Saryal, 2018: 2). It said that continued use of coal would come alongside increasing use of renewable energy, and that no new coal-fired plants would be built before 2026 (NRDC *et al.*, 2017: 1). The supply of renewable forms of energy is growing rapidly, receiving more investments than those in fossil fuels. The government has aimed to obtain 40 percent of electricity from non-carbon sources by 2030 (NRDC *et al.*, 2017) and 60 per-cent of energy from them by 2040 (Dessler and Parson, 2020: 185). The cost of solar energy in India has fallen substantially, and investments in solar have exceeded those in coal (Climate Action Tracker, 2020). According to some analyses, India is on track to meet its Paris pledge (see, e.g., NRDC *et al.*, 2017), while others foresee that that is unlikely due to, among other things, political, economic and social obstacles to reforming the country's energy sector (see, e.g., Ebinger, 2016), Most likely, even as India transitions away from a heavy reliance on fossil fuels, its aggregate GHG emissions will continue to increase substantially as its economy grows in size.

Construction of India's National Interests

Just as in other countries, climate change is not the most influential force in shaping India's approach to climate governance (see Dubash, 2019). Other interests are perceived to be more important, with economic development being the overriding priority. Domestically, public demand for action on climate change has been relatively low, with most citizens much more con-cerned about development and economic growth (Andresen, 2015: 432). With about 300 million people in India still without access to even a single light-bulb, affordable access to energy is a major concern (Ebinger, 2016: viii). Demonstrating the extent to which economic considerations have influenced India's climate-related policies, it temporarily led opposition by a number of countries to efforts to phase out economically important hydrofluorocarbons (HFCs), potent GHGs used for refrigeration and related purposes. After Indian industry determined that there would be benefits in replacing HFCs, India shifted its position and, in 2016, became a leader in negotiating cuts in those pollutants under the Kigali Amendment to the Montreal Protocol on Substances that Deplete the Ozone Layer (mirroring what happened in the United States in the mid-1980s when the US position on chlorofluorocarbons shifted dramatically based on the priorities of US industry [Benedict, 1998]).

Furthermore, like Japan, India wants to be viewed as a leader in international climate governance, partly to garnish its credentials as a regional and, increasingly, global power (Atteridge *et al.*, 2012: 70). India has at times gone so far as to side with some developed countries in international climate negotiations. For example, at COP15 in 2009, alongside some other Southern countries (e.g., Brazil, China and South Africa), it joined with the United States to draft the Copenhagen Accord (see Chapter 3) (Ciplet, Roberts and Khan, 2015: 114). This shift showed that as India was becoming a "great power," its economic interests were diverging from those of other, smaller developing countries (Vogler, 2015: 18–21). It was putting its own national interests first in its climate diplomacy, mirroring closely the early stages of China's shift away from what had been a largely unbreakable developing-country bond of solidarity in international climate negotiations.

As in most countries, India's national interests with respect to climate change are "socially constructed" (Isaksen and Stokke, 2014), arising in large part from competing discourses among domestic actors about whether India should continue to focus on its role as a suffering poor country or instead embrace technological and other opportunities, including through the international climate regime, to realize environmentally sustainable development. Increasingly, there has been an institutionalization in India of a "win-win" discourse that views climate change not only as a threat to the country but also as an opportunity for its development and diplomacy. This discourse advocates "greener" economic growth and national policy action to address climate change, and the use of proactive climate diplomacy to pursue the country's interests (Isaksen and Stokke, 2014: 114). This suggests that it is possible for a major developing country, one with an enormous stake in ready access to affordable energy, to gradually start making the cognitive and policy transition away from blaming the developed countries for climate change (an entirely understandable position to take in terms of justice, among other things), toward viewing climate change as both a long-term environmental risk and an opportunity to advance national interests domestically and internationally. India would not be making this cognitive shift if there were no perceived benefits to the national interest (again, defined in terms of the interests of those with political influence) in doing so.

The evolving discourse within India regarding the country's climate change-related national interests suggests that increasing the benefits for India, and presumably for other developing countries, of climate action would increase the likelihood of effective climate governance globally. Indeed, this is precisely the formula that was built into the climate regime from almost the outset, although it is one that has been largely implemented in the breech.

The case of India reinforces the idea that governing climate change can be more closely aligned with perceived national interests when doing so does not undermine other things of importance, not least economic development or, more ideally, when it can complement that development, as, for example, when new carbon-free sources of energy (e.g., solar) can be deployed to drive economic development at a lower cost than would older, carbon-based sources of energy. India reaffirms that national politics hold sway in determining perceived interests with respect to climate change.

Brazil: Sovereignty vs. Climate Change

With a large, developing economy and considerable poverty, Brazil shares many of the attributes of India. It has allied with India, notably as a member of the "BRICS" group (Brazil, Russia, India, China and South Africa), to promote the interests of developing countries in the international climate negotiations. It has a special role in climate governance because its borders contain about one-third of Earth's remaining rainforests, including about 60 percent of the Amazon (Mufson and Freedman, 2019). The Amazon rainforest is a massive sink for carbon, absorbing one-third of all CO_2 taken up by forests globally (Kintisch, 2015), among its many other attributes with global significance, not least being the habitat for extremely rich biodiversity. While healthy and intact, the Amazon forest slows global warming; when degraded, it stops storing carbon and becomes a source of it. This gives Brazil a unique role in international efforts to govern climate change, particularly as efforts to protect the world's forests become increasingly important for managing global GHG concentrations.

Brazil also has its own very significant vulnerabilities to climate change (many of which it shares with other countries in the region [see IPCC, 2014b: 1499–566]). It is vulnerable to extreme precipitation and flooding, increasing temperatures and droughts, wildfires and loss of biodiversity, sea-level rise and storm surges, and numerous adverse effects on human health, among many other undesirable impacts of climate change. With regional warming and deforestation, it is possible, perhaps even likely, that the Amazon rainforest will be transformed into a vast grassland with little biodiversity and without the capacity to sequester carbon (Marengo et al., 2011: 260). These and other consequences of climate change will harm agricultural productivity, food security, infrastructure and livelihoods.

Brazil's national contribution to climate change is substantial but relatively small given its circumstances. It produces 3.5 percent of global GHG pollution, making it the sixth-largest national source globally, and it accounts for 1.3 percent of global CO_2 emissions (Crippa *et al.*, 2019). At 9 tons, its per capita GHG emissions are quite high, due in no small part to high levels of deforestation (NRDC and Climate Observatory, 2017: 1). Its national CO_2 emissions are relatively low because a substantial amount of its transport is powered by ethanol and it derives much of its electricity from hydropower (although it is important not to overstate the carbon-neutrality of hydropower, given evidence that dams, particularly in tropical environments, may be significant sources of GHG emissions [see, e.g., Fearnside and Pueyo, 2012]). From 1990 to 2004, Brazil's GHG emissions increased substantially, partly due to economic growth and partly due to deforestation and the conversion of forests to agriculture. Emissions then declined until 2012 as forest-protection policies took effect, only to start rising again as those policies were reversed and deforestation increased (Londono and Casado, 2019; Dessler and Parson, 2020: 185). Brazil's total GHG emissions are likely to continue increasing from what they have been in recent years due to economic growth, rising per capita energy use and further deforestation (NRDC and Climate Observatory, 2017: 1).

Brazilian Politics and Brazilian Forests

Brazil hosted the 1992 Earth Summit in Rio de Janeiro, at which the UNFCCC was signed. In the UNFCCC negotiations, Brazil took a position that endured: it argued that the developed countries had historical responsibility for climate change. However, unlike most other developing countries, Brazil was open to the idea of *voluntary* limitation on its emissions, and by 2009 it made clear that it would not require funding from developed countries before taking action itself on climate change. At the 2012 Rio+20 Conference on Sustainable Development (which it also hosted), it even pledged US$10 million to help poorer countries that were most vulnerable to climate change (Viola and Hochstetler, 2015: 245).

Brazil's international positions on climate change "arise from a complex domestic process" (Viola and Hochstetler, 2015: 237). Up until about 2010 there was a domestic coalition between, on one side, actors in favor of reducing the country's GHG emissions (particularly through forest protection) and, on the other side, actors that perceived short-term economic gains to be had from doing so (Aamodt, 2018). The administration of President Luiz Inácio Lula da Silva (known as Lula), which held office from 2003 to 2011, strengthened environmental institutions and greatly reduced illegal deforestation. Environmental issues generally had been growing in importance among the public. This increased pressure on Lula and, to a lesser extent, his successor, Dilma Rousseff, who was in office from 2011 to 2016, to take climate governance seriously.

Internationally, the Lula administration sought opportunities to benefit from the CDM's forest-protection provisions. One objective of its climate diplomacy was to enhance its role as a "key emerging power" (Viola and Hochstetler, 2015: 245). Under Lula, the Ministry of Environment's desire to undertake action on climate change was able to prevail, albeit temporarily, over the Ministry of Foreign Affairs. The latter ministry tended to ally with other developing countries in opposing requirements that they take action on climate change, and it viewed growing calls to protect tropical forests as threats to Brazil's sovereignty over the Amazon region (Viola and Hochstetler, 2015: 240). For the 2009 Copenhagen Accord, Brazil pledged to implement policies that would result in a reduction in its GHG emissions of about 36–39 percent below the 2005 level by 2020 (Embassy of the Federative Republic of Brazil, 2010). Domestically, the country adopted the National Policy on Climate Change and the National Adaptation Plan. However, from 2010, "economic and political sectors unfriendly to climate reasserted their influence over Brazilian climate action" (Viola and Hochstetler, 2015: 237). Concerns about economic growth and international competitiveness resulted in an end to the political coalition that was favorable to climate action (Viola and Hochstetler, 2015: 239).

Dilma Rousseff was politically "reliant on pork barrel politics" (Viola and Hochstetler, 2015: 241) that were focused on the state of the economy, so when she replaced Lula in 2011 her administration promoted policies that were intended to stimulate growth, such as lowering energy prices and encouraging manufacturing. These policies resulted in the increased use of fossil fuels nationwide and were reflected in the country's climate diplomacy. Affirming its developing-country status in international efforts to govern climate change, Brazil's 2015 NDC for the Paris Agreement attached a condition to its pledge: that the CBDR principle of the UNFCCC would be fully implemented (Brazil, 2015: 1), mirroring India's commitment to the principle. However, unlike many other major developing countries, Brazil pledged not just to *limit* its GHG emissions but to *reduce* them, specifically to bring them 37 percent below what they were in 2005 by 2025, and to aim for a 43 percent reduction by 2030 (Brazil, 2015: 1–2). This pledge assumed that Brazil would take advantage of its forests and land-use alterations to sequester a proportion of emissions.

Where both Lula's and Rousseff's governments were quite successful, at least compared to what happened before and since their times in office, was in reducing deforestation. By protecting its forests, Brazil would be well placed to meet its overall long-term emissions objectives even if emissions increased from other sources. Like some of the other countries described previously, Brazil used a base year of 2005 in its NDC pledge. This is especially significant because that was a year with high levels of deforestation and land-use change in Brazil, and thus high national GHG emissions. When Brazil made its NDC pledge, it had plans to strengthen forest protections at all levels so as to achieve "zero illegal deforestation" and to restore or reforest 12 million hectares of land by 2030 (Brazil, 2015: 3). According to one projection, *excluding* forests and land-use changes from calculations of the country's GHG emissions would put them 76 percent above 1990 levels by 2025 (Climate Action Tracker, 2020).

Unlike India's NDC, Brazil's was "not contingent upon international support," although it did specify that achieving greater-than-pledged reductions in emissions would require a "large-scale increase of international support and investment flows" (Brazil, 2015: 3), along with technology assistance and transfer. However, an assumption was that agreements made at the COPs to provide assistance to Brazil for forest protection would be fulfilled, showing that its motivations were not much different than India's. Also like India, Brazil said that it would try to transform its energy infrastructure toward renewable sources. It committed in its NDC pledge to obtain 45 percent of its energy from renewables by 2030, a slight rise from what they were at the time of the pledge but no more than what they were a few years prior to that (NRDC and Climate Observatory, 2017: 1–2). This lackluster dedication to increasing the use of renewables may be attributed to plans to direct more than two-thirds of energy investments toward fossil fuels, including construction of new coal-fired power plants (NRDC and Climate Observatory, 2017: 2).

This dedication to coal may have been a harbinger of the shift in Brazil's climate-related policies that came with the advent of President Michel Temer, who held office from 2016 to 2018. Temer became president after a political scandal pushed Rousseff out of office. He garnered support from congressional legislators who came from rural areas. They were keen to see more of those areas developed into farms and ranches. An erosion of forest protections and environmental regulations resulted.

"Trump of the Tropics"

President Temer was succeeded by Jair Bolsonaro in 2019. The Bolsonaro administration aimed to take Brazil in precisely the opposite direction of what was pledged by Lula. When campaigning for the presidency, Bolsonaro threatened to follow President Trump and withdraw Brazil from the Paris Agreement, arguing that it violated Brazil's sovereignty over its forests (Maisonnave, 2018). He withdrew his threat only after an international backlash (Viscidi and Graham, 2019). However, soon after he won the presidential election in late 2018, he rescinded Brazil's offer to host the COP25 conference (see Chapter 3). Just like Temer, Bolsonaro derived much of his support from "ruralist" members of the National Congress who had long advocated development of the Amazon region. Upon taking office, Bolsonaro's government reaffirmed the importance in future decades of using the Amazon rainforest for the country's economic development. Mirroring opposition to environmental regulation in the United States under the Trump administration, the Bolsonaro government cut funding to agencies responsible for protecting the Amazon rainforest, even going so far as to eliminate the power of the environment ministry to do so. It also curtailed enforcement of laws and regulations against illegal logging, ranching and mining in the Amazon region (Londono and Casado, 2019).

In the first year of the Bolsonaro administration, deforestation *doubled* from the previous year (BBC, 2020). This was especially noteworthy given that in 2018 Brazil's deforestation was among the highest in the world, 72 percent above the 2012 level (Climate Action Tracker, 2020). Major increases in deforestation, which reduced the country's carbon sinks, came alongside increasing emissions from agriculture and energy use. Parroting the arguments from leaders of some other heavily forested developing countries, Bolsonaro reasserted Brazil's complete sovereignty over its forests. He was especially adamant in declaring this position when his government faced widespread international criticism in 2019 for apparently allowing, and implicitly encouraging, the razing of forested areas so that they could be used for ranching and farming (Casado and Londono, 2019).

The Bolsonaro administration also sought to weaken climate-related policies and to expand the use of fossil fuels for energy, resulting in policies that have been classified as insufficient for meeting the objectives of the Paris Agreement (Climate Action Tracker, 2020). Under President Bolsonaro, Brazil's GHG emissions were set to rise substantially, making meeting the country's Paris pledge difficult. Bolsonaro seemed to have justified the sobriquet he earned while campaigning for the presidency: the "Trump of the Tropics" (Phillips, 2018).

President Bolsonaro's radical dislike of environmental protection is a fascinating case study of how perceptions of the national interest can vary greatly when the constellation of power in national politics changes. Indeed, the brief period under Lula, when Brazil was most proactive in climate governance domestically and internationally, was an aberration from the norm. Within Brazil there are persistent and strong pressures from powerful political actors to exploit the country's natural resources. Even when there is growing concern about the impacts of climate change on the country – when global climate action is perceived as being an important national interest – there are stronger incentives to perceive effective climate governance as an obstacle to short-term economic development and growth. Because both the rich and the poor in Brazil see benefits from taking this approach, action on climate change remains, at best, a means to an end – economic benefit – rather than an end in itself. As Eduardo Viola and Kathryn Hochstetler (2015: 246) note, for Brazil, climate politics "is mostly domestic politics. . . . [S]hifts in Brazil's positions can be best explained with a close view of environment and development stances within the country." Once again, pathologies of national politics undermine effective climate governance.

In many ways, Brazil and India are similar. Due to the size of their economies and populations, both countries emit more GHG pollution than other developing countries. Their individual national politics largely determine their approaches to climate governance. Generally speaking, each of them has perceived national interests other than climate change to be more important than climate change itself, although in both cases climate change is, over time, moving closer to the front burner of both countries' national politics and foreign policies. Each has wanted to have a prominent role in international climate negotiations to further their status, whether real or self-perceived, as regional and even global powers. Each has consistently argued for implementation of the CBDR principle internationally. Each has sought to take advantage of any benefits that the climate regime might offer them. Each has at times seen potential advantages in policies (e.g., promotion of renewable energy or protection of forests) that might assist economic development while also (albeit mostly coincidentally) mitigating GHG pollution.

Many of Brazil's and India's positions on climate governance are mirrored in those of other Southern countries. But, in some ways, there is considerable divergence. This is not surprising given the great variety of countries that occupy the Global South. Their varied attributes, disparate political systems and contrasting perceptions of national interests can result in radically different approaches to the climate crisis.

Other Southern Countries: Island States vs. Oil States

At one end of a spectrum, the Global South includes the world's least-developed countries where climate change is often a near-term danger. For some of them, it is perceived to be, and probably is, an existential threat. Global action on climate change – effective climate governance – is among those countries' top priorities. It is imperative for them that climate change be mitigated as much as possible, but even more urgent for them is being able to adapt to it. They are almost entirely reliant on convincing the Global North to help them to do so. At the other end of a spectrum, the South includes petroleum exporters that want the world to remain addicted to fossil fuels and to profit from that addiction for as long as possible (unless other countries fully compensate them for the trillions of dollars in revenue that they would lose in the event of global decarbonization). Their perceptions of their own national interests lead them to conclude that global action on climate change – effective governance of climate change, at least the mitigation of pollutants causing it – is something that they would prefer to see occur later rather than sooner. To get a picture of these contrasting perspectives on climate governance in the developing world – admittedly a restricted picture given the great diversity of countries there – it can be useful to look at both ends of this spectrum: small-island states, on one end, and an oil-rich state, on the other.

Small-Island Developing States

Small-island developing states – formally the Small Island Developing States (SIDS) group in the contexts of the UNFCCC and the COP negotiations (UN, n.d.[a]) – are officially described by the United Nations as "a coalition of some 40 low-lying islands, most of which are members of the G-77 that are particularly vulnerable to sea-level rise" (UNFCCC, n.d.). Considered less officially, the actual number of SIDS is closer to 60, most of which, such as Nairu and Vanuatu, are genuinely poor, while some of them are relatively well-off economically. These countries have done little to cause the climate crisis. Combined, they produce less than 1 percent of global GHG pollution, meaning that nearly all of them barely register among the world's emitters (UNDP, 2017b). Despite their relatively small contribution to causing climate change, the SIDS are among the countries that are most vulnerable to the impacts of climate change. This vulnerability arises from their geographies, which often leave many of them with, at the best of times, insufficient fresh water, extreme shortages of land for agriculture and reliance on imports for much of their energy and food supplies.

The SIDS are threatened by climate-induced or climate-exacerbated extreme weather events, such as cyclones, hurricanes and typhoons; storm surges and coastal erosion; and ocean warming, with devastating effects on their coral reefs and fisheries (IPCC, 2014b: 1613–54). More than one-quarter of the total land area of the SIDS is less than 5 meters above sea level, and nearly one-third of their populations live below that elevation (UNDP, 2017a: 4). For a number of SIDS, sea-level rise is likely to make substantial portions of their territories uninhabitable, in the meantime causing extensive damage to existing property and infrastructure. These and other impacts will harm these countries' economies, threaten their populations' health and undermine their food security. Many impacts of climate change have already been observed in SIDS (IPCC, 2014b: 1619–26). For example, water supplies and croplands have been destroyed by salt-water intrusion in some of them. For those SIDS facing the existential threat of sea-level rise that might swamp or submerge their territories and cause their shorelines to change or disappear, there is concern about what might happen to the status of the offshore exclusive economic zones from which many of them derive most of their income, and even worries about their long-term viability as recognized sovereign states (Sharon, 2019).

Consequently, unlike most other countries, particularly those in the developed world, many of the SIDS perceive climate change to be an immediate threat to their most vital national interests, not least their economic vitality but also, in a number of cases, the viability of – the ability to thrive on – their national territories. As the prime minister of Tuvalu, Enele Sopoaga, argued on behalf of the SIDS in 2017, "[c]limate change is a security issue and a survival issue for our countries ... " (UNDP, 2017b). Thus, the mitigation of climate change is among the SIDS' top national priorities. It is in their long-term national interests (as it is for most countries) to see the rapid curtailment of the pollution that causes climate change. However, a more urgent priority for them is effective adaptation to the impacts of climate change, particularly for those island countries that are already experiencing impacts (Robinson and Dornan, 2017: 1103). For some of them, migration to safer places has become a priority over adaptation – or, one might argue, migration itself has become a means by which to adapt to climate change (Betzold, 2015: 483).

Most SIDS are very weak diplomatically. They have pooled their otherwise meager bargaining power in the international climate negotiations by participating in the Alliance of Small Island States (not all members of which are poor). Many AOSIS members are also part of the G-77 and LDC groupings in climate negotiations, further bolstering the otherwise limited influence of SIDS. Like most developing countries, the SIDS have strongly supported the CBDR principle and advocated for recognition in the climate regime of their special vulnerabilities and need for additional financial assistance. Since at least 2007, they have argued that the nominal 2°C target for stopping global warming, which guided climate negotiations, would result in disaster, instead pushing for it to be reduced to 1.5°C (UNDP, 2017a: 4). The collective influence of the SIDS and AOSIS was reflected in the 2009 Copenhagen Accord (see Chapter 3), specifically its consideration of the 1.5°C warming target and of the SIDS' exceptional needs for adaptation finance, among other things (Corneloup and Mol, 2014).

The SIDS' arguments were clearly reflected in (if not wholeheartedly embraced by all signatories of) the Paris Agreement by its codification, at least as a nominal aspiration, of the 1.5°C global warming limit. According to one SIDS diplomat at the Paris COP, "without AOSIS, the agreement would not have set 1.5 degrees as the global goal" (UNDP, 2017a: 16). The Paris Agreement also included recognition of other key issues dear to AOSIS countries, particularly recognition of their "loss and damage" associated with climate change (Broberg, 2020), provision of additional financing, including special access to Green Climate Fund resources, and additional assistance for capacity building (UN, 2015a; UNDP, 2017a: 5, 8, 11). In 2017, Fiji became the first small-island developing state to chair a conference of the parties to the UNFCCC when it presided over COP23 (which met in Bonn, Germany), with the subsequent Talanoa Dialogue (see Chapter 3) possibly helping to raise global awareness of the special needs of SIDS.

It is clear that for most SIDS, effective action to govern climate change is in their vital national interests. Many of the SIDS governments *perceive* their national interests in those terms. However, as the earlier descriptions of both developed and developing countries demonstrate, the SIDS perspective is an exception that proves the pathological rule that prevails in most other countries: the "propensity to frame climate policy in relation to the economic costs of international attempts to mitigate greenhouse gas emissions" (Vogler, 2015: 15). Indeed, as the Russian case exemplifies, some developed countries go so far as to prefer that steps *not* be taken to govern climate change effectively because doing so would reduce their (and the world's) dependence on fossil fuels. For them, the calculation is that action to address climate change is *itself* a threat to their vital national interests, exactly the opposite of the SIDS perception.

Significantly, some countries of the Global South share this perspective. The obvious examples are countries that produce and export large quantities of fossil fuels. Like Russia, the natural consequence of their national business models is *more* climate change, not less. Not surprisingly, a number of these countries have actively tried to thwart international efforts to reduce global

GHG pollution and decarbonize the global economy. They have spread the pathogens of their national politics, and specifically their fossil-fuel addictions, to the international governance of climate change. The prototypical exemplar of such a pathogenic country is Saudi Arabia.

Saudi Arabia

As a non–Annex I party to the UNFCCC (see Chapter 3), Saudi Arabia participates with developing countries in the international climate regime. It is classified as a non–Annex I party because its heavy reliance on fossil-fuel production for income and commerce makes it "feel more vulnerable to the potential economic impacts of climate change responses" (UNFCCC, 2020). This feeling may be justified. For many decades, Saudi Arabia's economy has been almost entirely based on the production and export of fossil fuels, specifically oil and natural gas. The petroleum sector accounts for about 40 percent of the country's gross domestic product (GDP) and more than 90 percent of its export earnings (Forbes, 2018). Saudi Aramco, the national energy corporation, is by some measures the most profitable company (Reed, 2019), and the most valuable listed company (Jolly and Ambrose, 2019), in the world. It is also history's largest corporate source of GHG pollution by far (Griffin, 2017). The vast majority of the Saudi government's revenues derive from the sale of petroleum products. Thus, Saudi Arabia shares important attributes with Russia, helping to explain the perception in each country that action on climate change is not in the national interest because its economy (or at least powerful actors in the country) would suffer if the world economy were to greatly reduce or end its reliance on fossil fuels, particularly oil and natural gas. If that were to happen, the market for Saudi (and Russian) exports would dry up. The government's longstanding national business model would become obsolete.

But Saudi Arabia is not just vulnerable to the impacts of the world's responses to climate change; it also has some vulnerabilities to the impacts of climate change per se. For example, it has already experienced substantial warming and is likely to experience much more, its already limited rainfall will be even more limited, and sea-level rise will adversely impact settled areas and infrastructure along its coastlines (Met Office, 2011). However, unlike many developing countries – certainly unlike many SIDS – Saudi Arabia may be able to cope with these and other impacts of climate change, especially if its economy continues to provide the financial resources necessary to produce or import food and other necessities.

The domestic and foreign climate change policies of Saudi Arabia have been premised on maintaining the world's addiction to fossil fuels, and indeed to increase that addiction, for as long as possible. For decades, the country's position on global efforts to govern climate change has been "clearly founded on its fears over the potential negative impacts of climate change mitigation policies on its economy" (Depledge, 2008: 12). It has been a "persistent obstructer of climate action" (Dessler and Parson, 2020: 221) and it has "sought consistently to block measures that might restrict the use of fossil fuels and compromise the future of its economy" (Vogler, 2015: 15). The Saudi government has used a range of means to promote these objectives, including through diplomatic tactics, especially in the formal international climate change negotiations; by allying with like-minded governments and corporate lobbying organizations in other countries; and by encouraging skepticism whenever possible, among other methods. By definition, the international climate negotiations require that countries compromise to reach agreement. Saudi Arabia has taken advantage of this requirement with a very simple diplomatic approach: to say "no" whenever possible, and thereby either formally to block agreements at different stages of negotiations or, at minimum, to slow their progress by "souring the atmosphere" (Depledge, 2008: 9).

Saudi Arabia's ability to influence climate negotiations has been bolstered by like-minded international organizations in which it plays a leading role, especially the Gulf Cooperation Council (Luomi, 2014: 10), OPEC (Barnett, 2008) and, paradoxically, the G-77 (Depledge, 2008: 17). The latter paradox is explained by Saudi Arabia's chairing of the G-77 relatively often, its financial ties with G-77 members, mutual interest among members in the adaptation aspects of climate agreements, and the unity of members vis-à-vis the developed countries, including more than a little common historically rooted distrust of them (Depledge, 2008: 16–18). While Saudi Arabia has very often worked alongside other developing countries and their negotiating groups in the international climate negotiations, it has not done so when this involves supporting robust cuts in global GHG pollution. In such instances, it has instead often allied with the likes of Australia, Russia and the United States in opposing action on climate change. The latter alliances have been especially evident in recent years. For this reason, climatologist Michael Mann has described an "axis of evil" comprising the "fossil-fueled triumvirate of Trump, Putin, and Saudi Arabia who have colluded to sell out the future of this planet for their own short-term financial gain" (Mann, 2018). As such, Saudi Arabia is increasingly at odds with the LDCs that are most vulnerable to climate change, not least many of the SIDS.

In addition to trying to thwart action on climate change through its role in international climate negotiations, Saudi Arabia and Aramco (including its American subsidiaries) have for decades been active in lobbying the US government and members of Congress to prevent and dilute their support for such action (Fang and Lerner, 2019). During negotiations of the UNFCCC, along with the United States, Saudi Arabia worked closely with the Global Climate Coalition, the then-influential US-based lobbying organization of the fossil-fuel industry that made the promotion of climate skepticism its raison d'être (Climate Investigations Center, 2019). This collaboration between Saudi Arabia and the American (and Australian) coal and oil lobbies created a "broad coalition of fossil fuel interests" that opposed strong action to address climate change (Depledge, 2008: 16).

As a key component of that opposition, throughout the international negotiations on climate change Saudi Arabia has tried to limit the impact of science on climate policy. It has consistently emphasized the uncertainties of climate science. As certainty about climate change increased over the years, Saudi Arabia doubled down on arguments that the problem might not be caused by human activities. For example, as the IPCC was meeting in 1995 to prepare its second assessment report (IPCC, 1996), Saudi Arabia joined with Kuwait to insist that uncertainties about the anthropogenic causes of climate change be highlighted in the document. The head of the Saudi delegation at the meeting explained the underlying motivations for his government's focus on scientific uncertainties: "Saudi Arabia's oil income amounts to 96 percent of our total exports. [W]e will not agree to what amounts to a tax on oil" (Masood, 1995).

This pattern of Saudi efforts to limit the extent to which science informs and influences the climate regime is still apparent. For example, at COP24 in 2018, Saudi Arabia, along with Russia and the United States, opposed the conference "welcoming" the IPCC's special report on 1.5°C of global warming (IPCC, 2018), thereby taking exactly the opposite position of the SIDS (IISD, 2018: 28–9). Earlier on, the Saudis tried to block the report, "searching for ways to scuttle the findings of the world's top scientists that countries must substantially curtail their fossil-fuel use," relenting only when other countries singled out Saudi Arabia as the only remaining opponent (Chemnick, 2018). Similarly, in 2019, Saudi officials emphasized scientific uncertainties in the same report at climate negotiations in Bonn, even as SIDS demanded concrete emissions targets to comply with the IPCC's findings (Farand, 2019b; McGrath, 2019). According to the comments of one observer from the Union of Concerned Scientists (which suggested that the Saudi position had not changed over more than two decades), the Saudi's traditional behavior is to "try to block, water down, delay, and then, when they fail at that because they're overwritten by other countries, they fall back on uncertainty. To them, scientific certainty is anathema because it would impact their oil sales" (quoted in

Chemnick, 2018). These efforts to sow doubt about the human causes of climate change seem to have rubbed off on some Saudis. More people in Saudi Arabia (16 percent) doubt that humans are causing climate change than in almost any other country (Milman, 2019).

Saudi Arabia's national climate governance has been consistent with its broader international approach to climate change. Its NDC pledge toward the Paris Agreement, which has been classified as "highly insufficient" (Climate Action Tracker, 2020), was to reduce its annual CO_2 emissions by 130 million tons by 2030, apparently relative to what they were in 2000 (the base year was not clearly specified in the NDC) (Saudi Arabia, 2015: 1). The pledge was contingent on many things, including continued economic growth, diversification of the economy, international climate policies not causing a "disproportionate or abnormal" burden on the Saudi economy, and continued "robust contribution from oil export revenues to the national economy" (Saudi Arabia, 2015: 1). The pledge was revealing, stating that "Saudi Arabia desires to actively contribute to the UNFCCC negotiations [while] minimizing potential negative side effects for Saudi Arabia" (Saudi Arabia, 2015: 1).

Nevertheless, it appears that some Saudi officials realize that eventual global decarbonization points to the need for a diversification of the Saudi economy, and that improving energy efficiency and investing in alternative energy sources could be part of this process. The government has made some moves in that direction even as it has used all diplomatic means to impede global cuts in GHG pollution. As part of its "Vision 2030," the government planned to increase the use of renewable energy domestically, although details are difficult to find (Saudi Arabia, 2020). Such a move could be a fruitful step given the country's ample land for solar-energy installations. Yet, there are still signs that Saudi Arabia, like Russia, will persist in supporting fossil fuels. One area in which the government has expressed repeated interest, including in its NDC, is in CCS technologies. If such technologies could be used widely, which is a tall order given the many obstacles to implementing them, they would prolong the world's demand for Saudi oil exports.

This look at Saudi Arabia and SIDS reveals the very wide range of perceptions regarding climate change and national interests in the Global South. What happens in developing countries in coming decades will, to a large extent, determine the long-term efficacy of global climate governance. What they do matters enormously because the impacts of climate change – the hardships and suffering that it will bring – will be felt by many more people there than in the North. What is more, if they continue to rely substantially on fossil fuels for the development of their economies, the majority of the GHG pollution that will ultimately cause those impacts will come from these countries. That is exactly what they may do if the pathologies of national politics around the world are not overcome.

Perceptions of National Interests in Climate Governance

Climate governance has been undermined by pathologies of national politics. Those pathologies are functions of the actors, institutions and forces that shape the domestic and foreign policies and behaviors of individual countries. They are manifested in the processes through which national interests are perceived and defined. National interests related to climate change are not divorced from what is happening internationally and globally, but, ultimately, they are mostly determined by domestic politics. Yet, each country's national politics are not always effective in bringing about a clear perception of all actual threats to national interests; even when they are able to do so, they are not always efficacious in translating perception into effective policies and actions. Most countries do not yet *perceive* climate change to be enough of a threat to motivate action that is sufficient to prevent it from becoming much worse. Every country is threatened by climate change to one degree or another, now or in the future, but each country perceives the threat – defines its related national interests – in its own way. Perception often involves more than a little self-denial and even willful ignorance, perhaps especially so among governments. Degrees of self-denial come when the threat of climate change is recognized but weighed alongside other considerations, thereby resulting in perspectives that do not see climate change as being as urgent a problem as it happens to be. This continues to occur despite the experience and threat of climate change worsening decade after decade (see Chapter 2).

To illustrate the importance of perceptions, imagine that a young child wanders away from a family's holiday safari, only to encounter a hungry hyena, a creature that the child's parents had told her is not dangerous. If the child listens to her parents and does not perceive any danger, she might treat the hyena as she does the family's puppy, by trying to give it a cuddle. Alternatively, if the child relies on what she learned at school – that hyenas are dangerous predators – and thus perceives that she is in extreme danger, she would likely exert all effort to climb the nearest tree. Both actions have potentially existential consequences for the child. In both scenarios, the hyena is *de facto* a threat, but in only one of them is it perceived that way. The child's vital interests depend on how she *perceives* the hyena. Something similar prevails for countries as they face climate change, albeit less immediately (in most cases). If they tend toward climate skepticism and perceive little or no serious threat from climate change, they will, all things being equal, likely act in ways that do little or nothing to confront it. If they instead perceive climate change to be a major threat, they will, all things being equal, likely act in ways intended to minimize their related vulnerabilities to it insofar as their capabilities allow.

Calculations of the national interest are heavily biased toward established conceptions of what is important. Climate governance ends up being subjugated to desires to protect national economies and influential actors with vested interests in business as usual. In such circumstances, it is difficult for governments to shift priorities. In democratic countries, what citizens want can be particularly important, not least in periods leading up to elections. In most countries, especially democracies or where governments' hold on power may be fragile, officials do not want to bear the short-term political costs of climate-related policies that will produce benefits in the long term (Howlett 2014; cf. Harris, 2015). Most governments fear the political consequences that might result if they implement policies that require many citizens to experience increased costs or lifestyle changes, even when people are being asked to do new things that will benefit them, for example, if they are asked to ride bicycles in city centers or consume less meat, activities which can promote health and well-being. In most developing countries, both governments and citizens believe that it is unfair for them to bear the burdens of policies intended to solve a problem largely created by developed countries and their citizens, least of all if doing so requires holding back the developing countries' economic development. The consequence of these sentiments, among others, are pathological biases toward the status quo. This results in forms of climate governance that are far too restrained to curb the climate crisis. Indeed, the consequence is that the crisis becomes worse.

No government of a major country has yet perceived climate change to be its top national priority. This has not even happened in many countries that are most greatly affected by the ongoing and especially future impacts of climate change, as evidenced by Russia, where tundra cities are sagging as the permafrost melts beneath them, and Brazil, where the biologically diverse Amazon rainforest appears increasingly likely to desiccate and become a vast savanna that is relatively devoid of life. (Worryingly, both the melting of Russian permafrost and the desiccation of Brazilian forests will transform those places from enormous carbon sinks into gigantic sources of GHG emissions.) Some governments of countries that are clearly threatened and even hurting already from climate change remain in a state of political denial about whether climate change is of greater importance to their national interests than are specific economic actors or sectors that remain wedded to fossil fuels. Australia (at the time of this writing) is a case in point. Only a very few countries – some SIDS, for example – that are most immediately vulnerable to climate change, but which have no ability to prevent it and precious little capacity to adapt to it, see climate change as very clearly a greater national interest than most other issues.

This is not to suggest that climate change is unimportant to most countries; clearly it *is* important to most of them. Climate change is moving up the ranking of national interests. This is demonstrated by a wide range of policies around the world intended to do something about the problem. Yet, with few exceptions, climate change has not yet broken through the influence of alternative, often quite narrow, relatively short-term, country-specific interests. As the descriptions of national politics in this and the preceding two chapters show, there is an overall trend of insufficient action to meet the Paris Agreement's goal of limiting global warming to 1.5°–2°C. (Let us not forget that global warming has already exceeded 1°C and continues to increase. Two-thirds of this warming has occurred since 1975 [NASA, 2020].) Very few of the national pledges (NDCs), including those of the major economies that produce a large share of GHG pollution, are sufficient to realize the Paris Agreement's goals, least of all in ways that share the burdens of doing so fairly (see Table 6.1). Assuming all of the pledges to implement the Paris Agreement are implemented fully, global warming is likely to be three times what it is now by the end of this century (UNEP, 2019: 8). More ambitious pledges will be forthcoming from many governments, but they are very unlikely to be enough in the end.

While the SIDS show how climate change has the potential to push national politics and foreign policy, even in those countries, and very much so in most others, climate change is one of many factors influencing national priorities. The experience of the SIDS highlights that the countries that are most likely to perceive climate change as a major threat to their national interests are the ones least able to do anything about it. In many other countries, national politics contribute to weak climate governance and sometimes sudden and quite radical shifts in related policies.

The advent of Donald Trump as president of the United States reveals the waxing and waning of economic nationalism (and nationalism more generally) and the politicization of science (climate skepticism and denial) that existed before him and will likely continue to taint climate governance after his presidency. His administration also shows how quickly and substantially policies can change. China's climate-related policies, while characterized as "climate leadership" by some observers (especially the Chinese themselves [Xinhua, 2019]), are predominantly an outgrowth of national politics – much of it unique to China, but some of it at play in most other countries. In the

Table 6.1 *NDCs of selected major economies: motivations, adequacy and recent developments*

	Pledged NDC toward Paris Agreement goals	Selected motivations for current policies	Adequacy of NDC*	Recent developments in climate governance
United States	Reduce GHG emissions 26 percent below 2005 level by 2025	Economic growth Economic competitiveness Protection of fossil-fuel industry Resistance to regulation Mix of scientific skepticism, denial and concern	Critically insufficient	Trump administration declaration of US withdrawal from Paris Agreement Disabling of federal environmental institutions and regulations Attempts by some state and non-state actors to implement pledge Unlikely to meet pledge without additional action
China	End growth in CO_2 emissions by around 2030 Increase share of non-fossil fuels in primary energy to around 20 percent Reduce CO_2 intensity 60–65 percent below 2005 level	Economic growth Economic competitiveness Maintaining legitimacy of the government Desire to be viewed as great power and international leader	Highly insufficient	Increasing use of alternative forms of energy domestically, but coal predominant Belt-and-Road projects will contribute to CO_2 emissions Business-as-usual pledge is likely to be achieved
European Union	Reduce GHG emissions at least 40 percent below 1990 level by 2030	Economic growth Economic competitiveness Desire to be viewed as climate leader Growing concern about impacts	Insufficient	Strong support for pledge in European Commission and several member states Resistance in some member states Proposals for increased ambition, e.g., reducing GHG emissions 55 percent by 2030 On track to achieve pledge *(continued)*

Table 6.1 (*cont.*)

	Pledged NDC toward Paris Agreement goals	Selected motivations for current policies	Adequacy of NDC*	Recent developments in climate governance
Russia	Limit anthropogenic GHG emissions to 70–75 percent of 1990 level by 2030 (a long-term indicator, subject to maximum possible account of absorbing capacity of forests)	Economic growth Economic competitiveness Fossil-fuel export revenue Foreign investment Official skepticism of human causes	Critically insufficient	Climate targets and policies delayed Continued reliance on fossil fuels Very weak pledge is likely to be achieved
India	Reduce emissions intensity of GDP 33–35 percent from 2005 level by 2030	CBDR Economic growth Economic competitiveness Foreign investment	Compatible with 2°C but not 1.5°C	Renewable-energy investment exceeds that of fossil fuels Continued reliance on coal On track to achieve pledge
Brazil	Reduce GHG emissions 37 percent below 2005 level by 2030	Economic growth Economic competitiveness Rural development Sovereignty over forests Mix of scientific denial and concern	Insufficient	Recent presidential administrations have rolled back environmental protections and supported development in protected areas Large increase in deforestation and associated GHG emissions Unlikely to meet pledge without additional action

*Adequacy of the NDC to meet fairly the Paris Agreement's goal of limiting global warming, as calculated by effort-sharing methodology of Climate Action Tracker (2020).

European Union, where some members want to take more aggressive action on climate change, its potential for leadership on climate governance is diminished by a few members that fear the domestic consequences of implementing that leadership. In a few countries, such as Russia and Saudi Arabia, action to govern climate change effectively is itself viewed as a far bigger threat to national interests than are the impacts of a changing climate. If anything, the latter countries' positions on climate change have been the most unwavering over time.

Of the three groups of pathologies of climate governance, those of national politics are bulging in the middle. The pathologies of international relations channel climate governance into the hands of states, pushing their governments to conceive of climate change in narrow, nationalistic terms at the expense of robust and effective collective action to govern it as a common global threat. For some countries, national and common interests overlap, and for a few of those countries most immediately vulnerable to climate change, those interests converge precisely. But for many more countries, national and common interests have been converging only very slowly, at least insofar as interests are perceived. The pathologies of national politics mitigate against wider convergence of narrowly perceived national interests and common global interests. This disconnect is exacerbated by the pathologies of human nature (the subject of the next chapter), which also channel climate governance toward relatively narrow and short-term perceived interests of people.

In some countries, the climate crisis is real enough for people there to recognize the need for concerted action, and thus to push their governments to respond accordingly. But the voices of such people are often drowned out by calls from other actors to slow down or do nothing. In many countries, people see the need for action, but only if it does not very noticeably threaten – or is not perceived to threaten – their established ways of life. And in some countries, the wider public barely perceives the climate crisis at all, thereby putting little pressure on governments to take climate governance seriously. Looked at globally and holistically, the result of all of these various perceptions of interests is climate governance that results in far too little happening to cut GHG pollution and to help those that are most adversely affected by the climate crisis.

7

Pathologies of Human Nature

In addition to the pathologies of international relations and national politics described in the preceding four chapters, there is a third group of pathologies that greatly undermine climate governance: the pathologies of human nature. These pathologies are associated with people and especially their behavioral responses to the social, economic and political milieus in which they live. This chapter highlights some of the features and consequences of these pathologies. The chapter's first objective is to describe why human population matters for climate governance, especially insofar as it is associated with voluntary material consumption. The process of consumption involves extracting resources from the environment, using those resources directly (e.g., for unprocessed foods) and indirectly (e.g., in manufactured products) and then returning them as wastes, often in highly concentrated forms, to the environment. Consumption almost invariably involves the direct or indirect use of energy, which globally still comes disproportionately from fossil fuels and thereby contributes to GHG pollution. All things being equal, more people result in more consumption and hence more pollution. But things are not equal; some people consume more than others, by orders of magnitude. (Many of the world's poorest people still consume too little to meet their needs. Justice demands that these people be aided to consume more [see Harris, 2016c], the environmental consequences of which need to be factored into climate governance.) This means that, while the size of the human population matters greatly for climate change, what matters even more is how many people are consuming more than necessary to meet their needs. Billions of people are doing just that, and the rate at which they are doing so is increasing faster than the rate of population growth.

A second objective of this chapter is to describe some of the individual, social and economic forces that stimulate people's consumption behaviors. Thousands of years of history demonstrate that human nature is inclined toward material consumption. People generally enjoy consuming, they often desire to consume more rather than less and they live in socio-economic and political environments that encourage vastly more consumption than is necessary to meet their needs. Being able to consume that which is necessary to meet basic needs, especially those things that sustain survival, is a fundamental human right (Shue, 2014: 47–67). But nearly all modern affluent societies encourage everyone who is capable of doing so to consume far beyond what is required to meet needs and indeed to do so far beyond what is good for most people (an example being the consumption of too much food). Thus, one of the contemporary pathologies of human nature is increasing materialism and over-consumption, an influenza of affluence – affluenza – characterized by an addiction to consuming more than one needs to the point of doing harm to oneself (and almost always to the environment).

Finally, a third objective of this chapter is to highlight how the impact of human nature on climate change and its governance is being exacerbated enormously as more people around the world obtain the economic resources to consume much like people of the Global North. Material consumption and affluenza are spreading and mutating around the world by means of the processes of globalization, not just trade in products but also by way of the diffusion of ideas that encourage more people everywhere to aspire to, and to adopt when they can, highly consumptive lifestyles. A growing global middle class is consuming more energy-intensive and material-hungry products, services and activities, ranging from "fast fashion" and private automobiles to hamburgers and airline travel for tourism. In recent decades, the spread of material over-consumption has contributed to large increases in global GHG emissions. Much of this increase has been experienced in the countries of the Global South, to the point where their collective emissions (if we include China's) now greatly exceed those of the Global North. The globalization of consumption – the global stimulation of the ability and inclination of people to consume – is a growing force that has made effective climate governance extraordinarily difficult.

Pathologies of Consumption: Environmental Dynamics of Human Population

There are many explanations for the climate crisis and the corresponding failure of climate governance to prevent its outbreak. Arguably the most important single explanation can be found in human population, specifically the number of persons on the planet and especially the manner in which, and the amount that, they consume.

Population: Rapid Growth in the Number of Potential Consumers

A very brief (but gruesome) thought experiment can help to illustrate why people are so significant for climate change and its governance. Imagine that a global pandemic kills every person on Earth except for the remaining uncontacted peoples who live in more or less prehistoric conditions (such groups still remain in the Amazon rainforest, for example). In such a scenario, most anthropogenic GHG pollution would all but cease immediately. Some of it would continue due to the vestiges of civilization – such as methane emissions from landfills – but within a few years most other GHG emissions from humans, especially CO_2, would come to a stop. This would be a scenario for curbing climate-changing pollution quickly and effectively. Under such an unthinkable situation (although the 2020 coronavirus pandemic suggests that it may not be impossible), climate change would still occur; historical GHG emissions would remain in Earth's climate system, resulting in global warming and related impacts, albeit only for a handful of surviving humans, for hundreds or possibly thousands of years. Nevertheless, the most ambitious aspiration of the Paris Agreement – to avoid global warming of more than 1.5°C – would have a chance of being realized, perhaps ahead of schedule.

What this thought experiment emphasizes is that people are, by definition, the essential drivers of anthropogenic climate change. Without people, unnatural climate change ends insofar as physics and chemistry allow (a potential exception being the deployment of technologies that reverse climate change). Something that is also implicit in the thought experiment is that with more people, all things being equal, there will be more GHG emissions. Other pathologies of climate governance matter greatly for the climate crisis, but the fact remains that none of them would matter if there were few people on Earth to do the things that result in emissions of CO_2 and other GHG pollution. Yet, despite the obvious importance of population for climate change and the effective governance of it, much, perhaps even the vast majority, of the literature on climate governance has had little to say about human population and particularly about its growth (Bongaarts and O'Neill, 2018). That may be partly explained by the limited explicit role that population plays in the domestic and international politics of climate change, and indeed the limited explicit place for it in the climate change regime and the underlying official climate science (Stephenson, Newman and Mayhew, 2010). Where population does feature is primarily as an attribute of some countries. China and India, most prominently, are viewed differently (or want to be) because they have very large populations.

Some might argue that it is unfair for the developed world to say too much about the importance of population for climate governance because doing so implies that billions of poor people in the developing world deserve blame for climate change. Others might argue that a larger human population is always a good thing, possibly for religious reasons (e.g., Catholic convictions about the value of procreation) or for economic reasons (e.g., the argument that a larger population would include a greater number of innovative people to solve future problems, or at least more workers and consumers to stoke supply and demand). To look in too much detail at population also has the potential to broach pesky questions about how people live their private (sexual) lives and about consumer choice (and potentially the need to restrict it). It may be no exaggeration to identify this general failure or unwillingness to highlight the role of human procreation and human numbers as a separate pathology of climate governance.

The most important reasons that population is so important for climate change, apart from rates of material consumption (see below), are the extraordinarily *high total number* of people and, at least until recently, the *high rate of growth* in human numbers. It took a century and a half, from the start of the Industrial Revolution in the middle of the eighteenth century to the turn of the twentieth century, for human population to double and reach 1 billion people. In two-thirds of the time – 100 years – the world's population grew sixfold, reaching 6 billion people by the turn of the twenty-first century (Van Bavel, 2013). The rate of growth in population peaked in the late 1960s, but human numbers nevertheless grew by another 2 billion in the 25 years from 1994 to 2019, including by 1 billion from 2007 to 2019 (UNDESA, 2019b: 5). The world's population reached 7.7 billion in 2019, 4 billion more than it was just half a century before (UNDESA, 2019b: 1). According to the UN's medium-variant predictions, human population is expected to reach about 8.5 billion in 2030, 9.7 billion in 2050 and 10.9 billion at the end of the century (see Figure 7.1) (UNDESA, 2019b: 1).

Many of the world's 47 least-developed countries are expected to double their populations by mid-century (UNDESA, 2019b: 1). Over the next three decades, more than half the growth in population will occur in sub-Saharan Africa (UNDESA, 2019b: 1). Population there is expected to grow through the end of the century, but in other regions it is likely to peak and start to decline before then. Of the expected increase in human population up to 2050, more than half will occur in eight poor countries (e.g., Ethiopia, India, Tanzania) and a single wealthy country – the United States (UNDESA, 2019b: 1). The latter is extremely problematic if Americans and their government fail to take climate change much more seriously than they do at present. Population

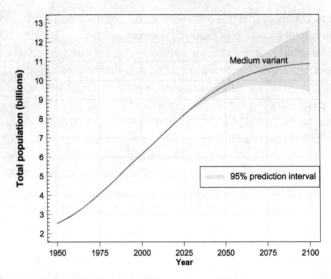

Figure 7.1 World total population.
Source: UNDESA (2019a). Reproduced with permission of Creative Commons license
CC BY 3.0 IGO, https://creativecommons.org/licenses/by/3.0/igo/

growth for the next few decades is probably unavoidable because two-thirds of
it will result from the fertility of people who are currently young (UNDESA,
2019b: 1). Although the environmental burdens of the behaviors of older
people, especially in the developed world, will weigh very heavily in the
future, the behaviors of those young people will be very important in determining the scale of GHG pollution and thus the climate change to come.

Population predictions are notoriously difficult; the actual population in the
future could vary substantially from what has been suggested here, meaning
that it could be lower but also that it could be significantly higher. Much will
depend on how population growth is governed alongside climate change.
Nevertheless, it is safe to assume that during the entire period of time that
most countries will be expected to aggressively reduce their carbon pollution
to near zero so as to achieve the objectives of the Paris Agreement (see
Chapter 3) – that is, the period up to mid-century – the world's population
will be growing. Most of that growth will be in countries where the impacts –
and the suffering – of climate change will be felt most severely and where there
have been too few resources to cope with the impacts of it, or indeed to
participate fully in the global move toward decarbonization.

Around the end of this century, global population may level off and begin
declining (see Figure 7.1) as reduced fertility, which is already common (and
often officially lamented) in many developed countries, takes hold in

developing countries. However, a stabilization or even a substantial decline in human population does not necessarily mean that the human contribution to climate change will stabilize or decline. If it does not, calls for reducing human population growth will grow louder and more urgent (see, e.g., Lovejoy, 2011).

Consumption's Consequences: Multiplying Environmental Impacts

There are substantial uncertainties regarding the future relationship between population and climate change (Bongaarts and O'Neill, 2018). It might be assumed that slowing the growth in the world's population would result in a reduction in global GHG pollution. This assumption would be correct only if people's consumption in the future falls accordingly. If rates of consumption increase enough to offset slowing population growth, the impact on climate would be correspondingly unchanged. If rates of consumption were to increase beyond what they are currently, which seems likely to be the case as more people join the global middle class (see below), GHG pollution may in fact increase in the future despite reduced rates of population growth. Past trends suggest that the latter is what is most likely to happen without substantial changes to the ways in which people consume, directly and indirectly, carbon-based energy. During the twentieth century, the human population grew by six times, but fossil-fuel consumption grew more than two and one-half times as quickly – by 16 times (Flannery, 2007: 77). What is more, even if consumption rates were to be reduced, potential reductions in GHG emissions that may result from slowing population growth will not be experienced until sometime after mid-century – that is, after the point in time when emissions must approach zero if the global warming objectives of the Paris Agreement, and probably that of the UNFCCC (i.e., avoiding dangerous climate change), are likely to be achieved.

There are other uncertainties about population. For example, the impacts of urbanization are difficult to predict. Already, more than half the world's population lives in cities, and that proportion is expected to reach 68 percent by 2050 (UNDESA, 2018: 10). Cities have the potential to be energy efficient, partly because there is less need for longer-distance transportation. Heating homes in an apartment building generally requires less energy than heating separate houses with the same number of people (unless those houses are built to, and operated at, sufficiently high energy-efficiency standards to exceed those of the apartment building). However, cities are also associated with economic growth, which is still correlated with more GHG pollution. If people living in cities consume at substantially higher levels than do people elsewhere, which is often the case now, they will, in effect, be importing (and be responsible for) GHG emissions from the places where the things that they consume are produced. This may be the case even if a city obtains most of its energy from non-fossil-fuel sources.

These uncertainties reinforce the practical reality that, for climate change, levels of consumption can be more important than levels of human population. Even if one is greatly worried about climate change, it may be possible to argue that the number of people on Earth is not yet too high. What is definitely too high, however, is the level of consumption of too many of those people. If their consumption can be brought down, and if the energy needed to supply the remaining consumption comes from non-fossil-fuel sources, there need not be an incompatibility between a large human population and effective climate governance. (As noted below, other questions of environmental sustainability will still apply.) When taking such a rosy view of population, however, we must be reminded that there is every likelihood, short of new policies implemented globally, that consumption will continue to increase, and that much of the global economy looks destined to rely heavily on fossil fuels for quite some time. After all, as mentioned in Chapter 2, four-fifths of global energy comes from the burning of fossil fuels. What makes this statistic especially worrying is that it has not changed much since well before the climate regime was crafted. All of the efforts around the world to rein in the use of fossil fuels over the past several decades have been diluted by the growing demand for energy. Coal-fired power plants, which are designed to operate for many decades, are still being constructed.

Reining in consumption, specifically the consumption activities that contribute to environmental harm (as most material consumption does), will not be easy. Consumption has exploded since the mid-twentieth century, and it is "the driving force" behind extraordinary impacts on the environment (WWF, 2018: 6). The impact on Earth arising from human consumption has been so great that scientists now refer to a new geological epoch: the Anthropocene (Carrington, 2016). Humanity's "ecological footprint," a calculation of the consumption of natural resources, far exceeds the carrying capacity of Earth. It has increased by 190 percent over the past half century (WWF, 2018: 28). In the 1960s, humanity was consuming resources and polluting at a rate equivalent to about half what the environment could sustain, with that rate jumping by the middle of the 1980s to a rate equal to *all* that Earth could sustain (Flannery, 2007: 78). Today, humanity is devouring the equivalent of 1.75 Earths, extracting vastly more resources and producing much more waste – including carbon pollution – than the environment can sustain in the long term (Global Footprint Network, 2020). Emissions of CO_2, when quantified in terms of how much land and ocean would be needed to absorb them, account for 60 percent of the humanity's ecological footprint, and those emissions are the fastest-growing component of it (Global Footprint Network, 2017).

Thus, humanity is currently consuming many natural resources faster than the environment can sustainably provide them and pouring pollution into the environment at a much greater rate than can be sustainably absorbed. And things are expected to grow worse in coming decades. Looked at from the perspective of the ecological footprint, it is very unlikely that Earth could support even the world's current population for very much longer, let alone the larger population of the future, without creating unbearable environmental conditions – at least in the absence of dramatic reductions in levels of consumption and pollution, including GHG pollution.

The idea that humanity might one day surpass the ability of Earth to provide for everyone's needs is not new. Around the turn of the nineteenth century, English economist Thomas Malthus forecast that the growing human population would eventually go beyond the carrying capacity of nature: "[t]he power of population is indefinitely greater than the power in the earth to produce subsistence for man" (Malthus, 2015: 47). A century and a half after Malthus made that argument, Paul Ehrlich proclaimed that humanity was facing a "population bomb" that would lead to widespread famine (Ehrlich, 1968). History, and the statistics on human population growth introduced above, demonstrate that Malthus's and Ehrlich's arguments were flawed in one respect: humanity has found ways to produce more than enough food to meet the nutritional needs of a growing world population. However, the Malthusian notion that there are limits to the number of people that the earth can sustain was prescient. Humanity experienced many famines in the time between Malthus and Ehrlich, and there will probably be more, showing that at local and regional levels, there is much truth in what they had to say. More to the point, as the statistics above on humanity's ecological footprint reveal, the real concern is the ability of the earth to sustain current and future levels of consumption and associated global pollution. This concern was at the heart of statistical analyses in the 1970s highlighting "limits to growth" (Meadows, et al., 1972) in resource consumption and pollution, and affirmation in the 1990s that humanity had already gone "beyond the limits" (Meadows, Meadows and Randers, 1992).

Malthus's and Ehrlich's arguments, and others like them, are valuable and important because they focus attention on the implications of population on the environment and humanity's relationship to it. They also show that warnings about the consumption that has led to the climate crisis are not new. To be sure, it seems likely that human ingenuity will make it possible to feed everyone – at least everyone that can afford to pay – for the foreseeable future. The scarcities to worry about may not even be the lack of most resources because substitutes are likely to be found for them when needed – although not everyone will be able to afford those substitutes. Instead, the fundamental scarcity will be the shortages of natural sinks for human pollution, not least CO_2 and other GHG emissions, and the environmental consequences of those shortages.

As the ecological footprint described above makes clear, at today's consumption levels, humanity is *already* exceeding the earth's capacity. Climate change is the most profound expression of this. Indeed, Ehrlich noted four decades after warning of a population bomb that "increases in greenhouse gas flows into the atmosphere, a consequence of the near doubling of the human population and the near tripling of global consumption, indicate that the results likely will be catastrophic climate disruption caused by greenhouse heating" (Ehrlich and Ehrlich, 2009: 8). As Tim Jackson (2009: 13) has argued, "the climate may turn out to be the mother of all limits." Thus, the predictions of Malthus and Ehrlich have proved to be correct in an important way: there are environmental limits to the demands of the human population. The world can produce more food than Malthus anticipated, but in a future characterized by dangerous climate change, even having enough food globally will not prevent enormous human suffering and death.

Before considering further what is driving global consumption – examining why people consume so much, and thus produce so much GHG pollution – it is important to emphasize that levels of consumption vary tremendously among countries and among people. Consequently, the levels of GHG pollution also vary tremendously. This was evident in substantial differences in per capita CO_2 emissions of the countries described in the previous chapters, ranging from 16 tons in the United States to less than 2 tons in India. Of total global CO_2 emissions, 10 percent arise from consumption by the poorest 50 percent of the world's population, whereas half of all emissions are attributable to the richest 10 percent of the world's population (see Figure 7.2) (Gore, 2015: 1). The per capita carbon footprint of the latter group is 11 times the size of that of the former, and the per capita carbon footprint of the world's richest 1 percent is 175 times the size of the poorest 10 percent (see Figure 7.3) (Gore, 2015: 1). And these figures disguise the extremely high levels of GHG pollution arising from the behaviors of the world's wealthiest individuals. Around the world, those people with assets over $1 million have average per capita carbon footprints of almost 65 tons (Otto *et al.*, 2019), a figure which itself disguises far higher emissions by the richest individuals. If the levels of consumption by the latter people are taken into account, per capita GHG pollution globally can quite easily vary by a factor of 1,000 or more (Hartmann, 2011). What is more,

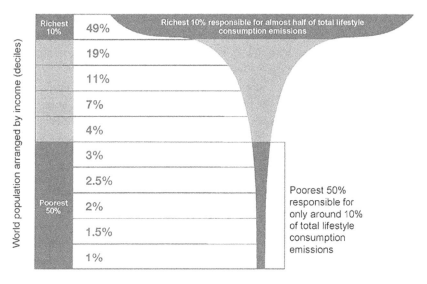

Figure 7.2 Percentage of CO_2 emissions by world population.
Source: Gore (2015: 4). Reproduced with permission of Oxfam.

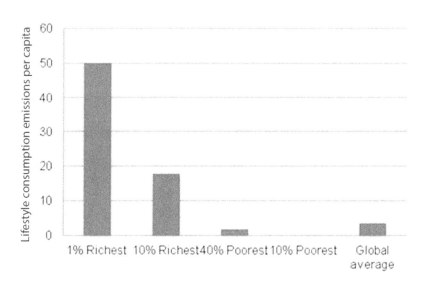

Figure 7.3 Lifestyle consumption emissions of CO_2 per capita.
Source: Gore (2015: 4). Reproduced with permission of Oxfam.

the richest people around the world often have investments in fossil-fuel companies, use their political influence to thwart more effective climate policies and otherwise leverage their wealth in ways that add to their disproportionately high responsibility for climate change (Kenner, 2019).

These statistics highlight that what matters for climate change is the great disparity in consumption by people around the world. While the world's poorest people lack the ability to consume enough to meet their needs, and thus have relatively little practical role in causing climate change (and no moral responsibility for doing so), billions of people are voluntarily consuming vastly more than they need, thereby producing most of the avoidable pollution that is causing the climate crisis (and thus have the moral responsibility that goes with their pollution). As Andrew Simms and Joe Smith (2008: 3) have noted, "by the time a typical British family sits down to its evening meal on 3 January, they will already have been responsible for a volume of greenhouse gases being pumped into the global commons of the atmosphere equivalent to that produced by a similar sized Tanzanian family in a year." If we were to make the same comparison between families in, say, South Sudan and the United States, the same level of GHG emissions would probably be reached by the Americans before they were to sit down to breakfast on the second day of January.

What becomes clear from these comparisons is that, while the very large human population does have great significance for climate change, what matters much more is how affluent people are, and more specifically whether and to what extent they use their affluence to consume in ways that result in GHG pollution. Thus, in coming decades, a bigger concern than population will be whether and to what extent people consume beyond their needs.

Pathologies of Growth: The Evolution of Overconsumption

People's consumption directly and especially indirectly contributes to climate change. Anyone who uses fossil fuels directly, for example by driving a traditional automobile or burning natural gas to heat a home, is consuming in ways that immediately contribute to climate change: the burned fuels are converted to GHG pollution, including CO_2 in these examples, which causes global warming and other manifestations of climate change. These kinds of direct consumption that eventually lead to climate change occur almost everywhere, although they are the most polluting in many developed societies and among affluent people around the world. However, for most people, certainly in developed countries and enclaves, the connection between consumption and climate change is more indirect. For example, when using electricity at home or in an office, if that electricity is generated by the burning of coal or natural gas, one is contributing indirectly to the climate change that will be caused by the CO_2 pollution coming from the power plant. Consumption can often be even more indirect, as when people consume products and foods whose production, transport and disposal result in emissions of GHG pollutants. Indirect consumption can also often contribute to the destruction of carbon sinks, for example when forests are cut to make way for cattle ranching or palm-oil plantations.

Importantly, GHG pollution arises both from the consumption of the necessities of life and from consuming luxuries. The former consumption is unavoidable – although it can often be done in ways that are more or less likely to result in GHG pollution – but the latter is, by definition, unnecessary, raising serious questions for climate governance as to why people do it and what can be done to eliminate the adverse environmental impacts of it. Much as human population per se is not necessarily a critical problem for climate change, neither is consumption per se; the problem is that billions of people are and will be consuming far beyond their needs. The failures of climate governance are substantially failures to mitigate climate-changing consumption. If climate governance is to be more successful in the future, it will have to grapple with consumption in new ways – to discourage climate-causing consumption where possible and to decarbonize the consumption that is necessary and unavoidable.

Human Nature and Pathogenic Consumption

The tremendous growth in human population has serious implications for climate change (and the natural environment more generally), but the population-related equation that matters as much or more is the number of people multiplied by what and how much they consume, and the climatic impact that results from that consumption. If the current world population – let alone the number of people later this century – is multiplied by current levels of consumption associated with GHG pollution, extremely dangerous climate change is certainly unavoidable. It should be emphasized that much of the consumption around the world, and especially that which occurs in developed countries and in pockets of affluence in developing countries (on the latter, see the next section), involves people's desires for the accoutrements of modern lifestyles. When assessing the significance of population for climate change and climate governance, we must therefore consider the manner of modern life and specifically whether people consume, and thereby pollute the atmosphere, to fulfill their actual needs or instead because they are trying to fulfill pseudo "needs" that arise from the apparent requirements of modernity. The latter seems to require that we consider the role of capitalism, neoliberal economic (and political) paradigms and globalization (see later in this chapter).

Everyone must consume food and water, along with other things essential to survival, such as material for adequate shelter and clothing. Humans evolved to consume; it is inherent to human nature (Hantula, 2003). Because there was seldom a surplus of resources during most of human evolution, there was no need for people to develop a genetic trait that might put a brake on their consumption. In primitive human communities characterized by scarcity of food and other vital resources, the people who thrived were those who consumed the most. Individuals with the ability to acquire more than enough resources, such as those with especially effective hunting skills, probably had higher social standing and were considered to be the most desirable mates, thereby favoring the propagation of genetic traits inclined toward overconsumption (Gondor, 2009). Thus, evolution has bequeathed people the proclivity to consume.

A vital question to ask is why so many people consume *much* more than necessary, to the extent that is especially common in the developed parts of the world. They do so in part because they find or believe that there is some value or benefit in doing so (Krogman, 2020). Thorstein Veblen (2009) observed more than a century ago that it is a normal human trait to be concerned about social status. The most prominent way to project that status is visibly to consume at least as much as is consumed by other people in one's community or reference group (Dubois and Ordabayeva, 2015). This "keeping up with the Joneses" (in the American parlance) happens at all levels of society as people attempt to acquire the things that enable them to have lifestyles at least as good as their neighbors or, increasingly, other people that they become familiar with via modern media. Importantly, the reason that people do this is not just that they want to do so; it is also that they are capable of doing so. The world economy today provides billions of people not only enough money to meet their needs, but also enough to consume far beyond that – to *over*consume.

The human inclination to consume is exacerbated in terms of climate and environment by modern lifestyles, which are partly characterized by the economic independence of individuals, the availability of easy mobility, an intensification in the use of time and a discouragement of relaxation, a prolifer-ation in novelty (of both products and experiences), diets that comprise historically large proportions of meat and imported foods, and the propagation of conveniences and comforts in daily life, such as home air conditioning (Ropke, 2010: 123–4) (although there is a case to be made that air conditioning is becoming a necessity in many localities due to global warming). In such an environment, people increasingly live as if they are divorced from nature, with the impacts of their consumption – from the extraction of natural resources for making products to the deposition of wastes, including GHG pollution, into it – being hidden from the view of billions of people much of the time. Brian Elliott contends that this "consumption paradigm has colonized virtually every domain of social existence" (Elliott, 2016: 100).

Because people's appetites for consumption tend toward insatiability if the right conditions exist, the limiting factor is not so much lack of desire to consume but lack of money to do so. When there are great disparities in visible wealth and the capacity to consume, people with sufficient money will often do what they can to reduce the disparities between themselves and those with more visible wealth through consumption. It is not that people always want to have more things in absolute terms. How much they have seems to matter less than how much they have relative to other people around them, and often compared to what their parents had and what they themselves had when they were younger. This tendency means that consumption increases in societies where some people have more wealth and possessions than others; inequality begets overconsumption. In such circumstances, people compete in a perpetual cycle of consumption, characterized most obviously by the prototypical American way of life and similar lifestyles. Even people with many possessions – the world's wealthiest people – consume more than they might do because they want to establish their social status relative to other wealthy people around them, most of whom consume even more for the same reason.

One response to such observations might be to argue that wealthy people seem to be happier than less affluent people. While this may be true some of the time, it is not simply a matter of affluence. It is a matter of *relative* affluence (Highfield, 2007). Consumption is a means to some measure of expressed happiness for affluent people primarily because they are consuming more than other people, and many of those other people want to consume more because they see what more affluent people have. This is a recipe for chronic overconsumption.

People also consume because they obtain pleasure from doing so. However, they often become bored quite rapidly with what they have consumed. A customary way to alleviate boredom with the things that one already possesses is to consume yet more things, often novel ones. Even the most affluent people seem to become quite bored with their extreme luxuries, hence the market for the ever-more extravagant watches, jewelry, home furnishings and so forth. Additionally, people quickly become habituated to affluence, and consumption becomes a form of sybaritic behavior even for people who would not be considered wealthy (Durning, 1992). Products that were once thought by almost everyone to be luxuries quickly become perceived as necessities. Current examples include televisions, microwave ovens, mobile telephones and the myriad software applications ("apps") for them, and near-constant access to the Internet. (Few people below a certain age can easily tolerate going without an Internet connection for very long, but the Internet is now one of the fastest-growing sources of GHG emissions, producing as much carbon pollution as the entire airline industry [Griffiths, 2020].) In many places, cars are considered to be essential even when they are not (e.g., to visit a nearby shop for necessities or frequently to travel long distances independently for recreation). In short, affluence brings the ability to consume things at an accelerating pace, but it never seems to be enough to satisfy many people's desires – despite the fact that hundreds of millions of people around the world have more luxuries than monarchs did in the not-too-distant past (cf. Brand and Wissen, 2021).

Thus, global consumption has become a kind of collective addiction arising from modernity and affluence: a pandemic of affluenza. This pathology can be characterized generally by the persistent urge to consume more than one needs or, more specifically, as "a painful, contagious, socially transmitted condition of overload, debt, anxiety, and waste resulting from dogged pursuit of more" (De Graaf, Wann and Naylor, 2014: 1). A key feature of affluenza is *over-consumption* of products, services and experiences. This is routinely taken to extremes, especially when viewed in historical terms and when compared with people's actual needs. It is a "new consumerism" distinguished by "an upscaling of lifestyle norms; the pervasiveness of conspicuous, status goods and of competition for acquiring them; and the growing disconnect between consumer desires and incomes" (Schor, 1999).

The Economy of Pathogenic Growth

The new consumerism did not explode innately from human nature. It has been cultivated and nurtured by forces external to each person. In particular, the inclination of people to overconsume has been stimulated and exacerbated by modern capitalism and the neoliberal preoccupation with free-market expansion that has dominated the world economy, and indeed much of global governance, for about the past five decades (cf. Elliott, 2016; Brand and Wissen, 2021). Consumption is strongly encouraged almost everywhere. More consumption is the raison d'être of the global capitalist economy. To be sure, contemporary capitalism has been a vehicle for lifting many millions of people out of poverty, with China providing the most profound example of this phenomenon. Capitalism has also facilitated the acquisition of modern conveniences and luxuries by billions of people and, in the process, made some of them extraordinarily wealthy. But the assumption of capitalist economics as practiced for decades has been that there are no limits to growth; capitalism has cultivated "the consumption mantra: there will always be more" (Elliott, 2016: 61). This assumption of growth disregards the environmental limits described above. In most countries, a disproportionate share of the national economy consists of personal consumption. That consumption is still correlated with the direct and indirect use of climate-changing fossil fuels. The magnification by capitalism of the natural human penchant for consumption has thus fueled the climate crisis (see Klein, 2014).

The paradigm of growth is the prism through which the success of the global economy is viewed. Correspondingly, economic growth, ideally occurring as fast as possible, is the measure of health for national economies. Indeed, as the descriptions of several countries' national climate politics in the preceding chapters demonstrate, economic growth is routinely considered to be a vital national interest – in most cases, it is perceived to be the *most vital* national interest day to day. (Even for countries that one might expect to be more concerned about national security, economic growth is seen as the means to pay for military preparedness.) Many governments join with corporations to encourage people, even those with more than enough already, to believe that having more is better and will make them better off – that it will make them happier and promote their interests. During economic slowdowns, when the natural inclination of many people is to consume less and thereby save money for the future, governments often encourage people to shop, buy services, travel and so forth as means to stimulate economic growth (even if this might leave many people worse off).

Interestingly, in few countries is national success measured by whether individual well-being is growing, at least not to anywhere near the extent to which national economic growth is taken as the measure (see Chapter 8). Even in developed economies with ageing and declining populations, where it should be possible for citizens to be better off without the national economy growing at all (and even if it is declining, assuming it does so at rate that is somewhat less than population decline), growth remains the measure of success (Gotmark, Cafaro and O'Sullivan, 2018). This seems to support the contention of Clive Hamilton (2015: 49) that political leaders have internalized and fetishized economic growth to the point where "[t]he state itself, which once represented the interests of the people ... has been reshaped since the 1970s to serve the interests of the Economy [*sic*]."

Consumption is encouraged by marketing of every imaginable kind. Marketing is certainly not new, but as Hamilton (2015: 70) observes, in today's "consumption society, marketers are now engaged in an endless process of creating and transforming, as well as responding to, consumer desires." The process is endless because consumer capitalism is premised on "a constant feeling of dissatisfaction to sustain spending," meaning that "[e]conomic growth no longer creates happiness: unhappiness sustains economic growth" (Hamilton, 2015: 71). As Peter Newell (2012: 267) has argued, "[o]ne of the most indelible features of the global capitalist economy over the last 40 years has been the exponential increase in mass consumption that has been achieved through advertising and marketing strategies and the internationalization of production and transport networks, fueled until now by cheap and abundant energy supplies." Gabriella Kutting (2016: 208) puts it succinctly: "the rise of consumerism is embedded into the economic system" of modern capitalism.

What is more, marketing has been made much more powerful by modern communications and computer technologies. Most profoundly, the power of the Internet is now being harnessed to boost consumption of products and services. Marketers are able to tap even more deeply into the primordial aspects of human nature to stimulate consumption, using online computer apps to tailor these stimuli to each individual's impulses and desires. Various forms of online social media platforms use algorithms to learn which products or experiences individuals find most attractive. Those platforms then use the resulting data to target people through advertising or by using online personalities (influencers) to promote the things that people are most captivated by, while simultaneously enabling instant purchases and (in the case of physical products) rapid delivery. These methods are designed to take advantage of human nature, particularly people's tendencies to seek status and novelty. These online platforms have thereby accelerated mass overconsumption. They are some of the most environmentally harmful manifestations of the modern global economy.

James Gustave Speth (2008: 7–8) is scathing in his description of the ingredients of today's global economy and its impact on the environment. He points to "[a]n unquestioning society-wide commitment to economic growth at almost any cost; enormous investment in technologies designed with little regard for the environment; [and] powerful corporate interests whose overriding objective is to grow by generating profit, including profit from avoiding the environmental costs they create." He argues that global capitalism comprises "markets that systematically fail to recognize environmental costs unless corrected by government; government that is subservient to corporate interests and the growth imperative; rampant consumerism spurred by a worshipping of novelty and by sophisticated advertising; [and] economic activity so large in scale that its impacts alter the fundamental biophysical operations of the planet." By way of emphasizing the consequences for Earth's climate, Joachim Radkau (2008: 250) has observed that the current global economy is "utterly unlike anything that has ever existed before in history: in a *single* year, this economy burns and vents into the atmosphere fossil fuels that took a million years to create." As Peter Dauvergne (2008: 5) has put it, "[m]itigating the environmental impact of this global political economy of rising consumption is one of the biggest governance challenges of the twenty-first century, if not the biggest."

Yet, mitigating the impact is the opposite of what is happening. Instead, consumption is rising globally. The "fetish" for maximizing the growth in consumption has been exported from the Global North to most of the South. Nowadays, to "develop" is to grow, and the fastest way to grow is still to consume as much as possible.

The Metastasis of Overconsumption: Emergence of the Neoconsumers

The global economic system is geared toward promoting consumption. Economic actors and forces persuade people to overconsume as a way of playing their part in the expansion of economic output. Consequently, an end to population growth would not necessarily mean that there would be an end to the growing consumption that results in GHG pollution. If the rate of people's consumption plateaus or declines in one part of the world, it may very well continue to rise in another. That is precisely what has been happening in recent decades. As some developed countries have experienced slow or stagnating economic growth, many developing countries have grown rapidly, some of them by double-digit percentages over several decades. This growth has been driven partly by exports to the developed world and increasingly by domestic consumption. Western-style, high-consumption lifestyles have become both possible and popular in larger parts of the Global South, aided in their spread by the processes of globalization, especially the enormous increase in the scale and pace of international trade, extreme efficiencies in economies of scale and new superfast means of communication. The pathologies of consumption and growth have metastasized, saturating the developed world and now engulfing the developing world.

Neoconsumers Join the Global Middle Class

For decades the developed countries, with far fewer people than countries of the developing world, were in combination by far the largest sources of global GHG pollution. This phenomenon shows that population per se is not the greatest cause of climate change. The developed countries were the largest historical polluters because their citizens had, as they still do, far higher consumption levels. But this is changing. Levels of consumption in the developing world are increasing, meaning that the larger population there is now of far greater significance for climate change than it was until quite recently. Indeed, the countries of the Global South combined (including China) now produce substantially more GHG pollution than do the countries of the Global North, and most of the projected increase in global GHG emissions will come from them. This has been made possible by the rise of many millions of "new" consumers – neoconsumers – in a number of Southern countries. These neoconsumers have been defined in different ways. Norman Myers and Jennifer Kent (2003: 4963) defined them (in 2003) as individuals in the developing world living in a four-person household with spending capacity (in terms of purchasing power parity at that time) of at least $10,000 per year. Myers and Kent found that it was at about this spending capacity that people began to consume home appliances, air conditioners, televisions, computers, cars, grain-fed meat, large quantities of water and other "perceived perquisites of an affluent lifestyle" (Myers and Kent, 2003: 4963). The rise of the neoconsumers began in the 1980s, most prominently by the economic opening of China, and it accelerated in the 1990s. During those two decades the number of neoconsumers multiplied several times, substantially exceeding 1 billion people by the turn of the century, nearly one-third of them in China alone (Myers and Kent, 2003: 4964). Over the past two decades, the number of neoconsumers has multiplied again.

As of about 2018, about 4 billion people around the world – more than half the world's population – had enough discretionary income to classify them as being middle class, enabling them to consume washing machines, refrigerators, motorcycles and other "consumer durables," and to spend on entertainment and vacations (Kharas and Hamel, 2018). According to Homi Kharas and Kristopher Hamel (2018), "this marks the start of a new era of a middle-class majority." In many ways this can be interpreted as good news – more people are free of poverty and its afflictions. But this is probably not good news for the effective governance of climate change because more than two-thirds of global GHG emissions arise due to the consumption behaviors of households (Dubois *et al.*, 2019), and two-thirds of consumption by households around the world can be attributed to the middle class (Kharas and Hamel, 2018). (To be sure, each super-rich person consumes much more, but altogether they are relatively few in number, and the world's poor are simply unable to consume as much as they need to, let alone as much as they might like to.)

What is more, the number of people in the global middle class continues to increase, possibly rising to 5.3 billion people by 2030, on top of another 300 million rich people (Kharas and Hamel, 2018). The majority of this growth will be in Asia, where 88 percent of the next 1 billion people to enter the middle class are expected to live (Kharas, 2017: 20). By 2030, two-thirds of all members of the middle class will live in Asia, including 380 million people in China and 350 million in India (Kharas, 2017: 13) (figures that would be far higher if the calculations of Myers and Kent were adopted). Put another way, by 2030 the number of middle-class consumers in China alone will likely be at least tens of millions of people greater than the entire population of the United States. The middle class in India may equal or exceed the total number of Americans, to say nothing of the rise of the neoconsumers in Brazil, Malaysia, South Africa and other developing countries. Neoconsumption – the growing consumption of the neoconsumers – is well on its way to colonizing the world. (A wild card is the global coronavirus pandemic, which could greatly affect projections, at least in the short term.)

Neoconsumption of Western Lifestyles

What is the added environmental impact of the neoconsumers? Much as the world's population has increased, the number of overconsumers has increased. And much as the world's population matters for climate change because of consumption (i.e., population multiplied by consumption), the contribution of the world's neoconsumers matters even more because their exploding consumption contributes greatly to rising GHG emissions. Just when a number of countries in the developed world are waking up to the importance of the climate crisis and starting the shift away from fossil fuels, the neo-consumers are taking lessons from the Western world's past and present when deciding how they want to live. Indeed, one argument that is often made is that people of developing countries have the right to live as people in the West have done. The CBDR principle, and specifically its admission that developed countries (and people there) are the most responsible for climate change, is persuasive to both the governments *and* the citizens of the Global South. It is natural for the latter to want to consume, and to believe that they have the right to consume, just as people of the West have done for so many decades.

However, lifestyles of people in the West (and other longstanding developed areas, such as Japan) are not compatible with mitigating the climate crisis. As economies around the world have developed, and as more people have acquired incomes that enable them to consume what they want, demand for resources from the environment (e.g., food, water and minerals), manufactured products, experiences and services have increased greatly, resulting in growing negative consequences for climate change. To put this into perspective, imagine what things would be like if all of the world's population were to adopt a typical American's lifestyle. In such an environmentally horrific scenario, total consumption would grow eleven times (Diamond, 2008) and annual energy demand would increase by a factor of at least ten (Le Page and Ananthaswamy, 2012), meaning that carbon emissions would be roughly eight times what they are at present. It follows that if only one-eighth of the world's population were to live like Americans, climate change would continue unabated.

The experience of China epitomizes the rise of the neoconsumers and the degree to which they have multiplied the human impact on the environment. China warrants special consideration because many countries aspire to copy its economic model – a model that made it the largest national source of GHG pollution. Over the past four decades, millions of people in China have become affluent enough to overconsume and to afford luxuries that have been enjoyed in the developed world for much longer. The newly affluent Chinese have been described as the new "vanguards of global consumerism" (Gerth, 2010: 36). There were very few neoconsumers in China in 1980, but by 2020 there were projected to be 400 million "mainstream" consumers "able to afford family cars and small luxury items" and an additional group of 61 million elite "affluent" consumers (Atsom *et al.*, 2012: 15), with other projections putting the number of "middle class" Chinese at from 550 million (Iskyan, 2016) to 630 million by 2022 (Barton, 2013). The actual figure depends on precisely how one defines the Chinese consumer class, but we can safely assume that the number of neoconsumers in China has grown rapidly from almost nothing to *hundreds of millions of people*, and the growth continues. The only country that comes close to matching this number is the one where the middle-class lifestyle of consumerism became very deeply rooted in the mid-twentieth century: the United States. Thus, it is no coincidence that China is the largest polluter of the atmosphere and likely to remain so.

Despite the efforts of the Chinese government to increase the use of renewable energy, the rise of the country's neoconsumers creates a growing demand for energy to heat and power Chinese homes and to produce consumer products, in the process outpacing those efforts, to say nothing of the growing impact of tens of millions of Chinese who travel abroad every year for holidays. At the time of this writing, the world is experiencing a major economic slowdown due to the global coronavirus pandemic (which apparently started in China, very possibly due to heightened demand from neoconsumers for meat from wildlife [Woodward, 2020]). This will push both the government's and the public's support for moving away from fossil fuels down the list of priorities. While GHG pollution dropped sharply in China during the pandemic, pent-up demand during preventive "lockdowns" there, alongside the government's economic stimulus measures, could more than make up for that decline (Myllyvirta, 2020). More consumption will be encouraged to help lift the economy out of the pandemic-induced slowdown. After all, following the global financial crisis of 2008, the world looked to the Chinese consumer to make up for demand that was lost in the West. To a great extent, the Chinese did just that, and they may do it again, with the help of neoconsumers in the clusters of affluence across the developing world.

Through their consumption choices, neoconsumers have been emulating the lifestyles of Westerners in many ways. They are following fashion trends, consuming more processed foods, living in more energy-hungry homes and enjoying all manner of leisure activities. Changes in their lifestyles in recent decades are especially evident in two trends that are contributing very substantially to the growth in GHG pollution coming from the Global South: increasing consumption of meat, particularly that from livestock fed by grain, and the growing popularity of highly polluting forms of transport, specifically private cars and air travel. These trends are highly significant because the animal-farming sector is the third-largest contributor to global warming, road vehicles are the first and airline emissions have been rising steadily (Unger *et al.*, 2010). These trends showcase the extent to which *nonessential* consumption with direct implications for climate change has migrated beyond the developed countries of the Global North. Few people need to eat meat (some people lack alternative food choices, of course), most of the rise in car ownership is a matter of lifestyle and airline travel is very rarely essential. In other words, people's desire to consume these things, and the lifestyles associated with them, is largely unnecessary. Greenhouse gas pollution often goes up for relatively frivolous reasons.

Between 1961 and 2014, global per capita meat consumption doubled, increasing at a faster rate than population growth (Devlin, 2018). By 2050 meat consumption is projected to expand another 75 percent (Alexandratos and Bruinsma, 2012). While meat consumption in developed countries is stable or on the decline, in middle-income countries it is rising, often rapidly, especially in China and East Asia. China alone accounts for more than a quarter of the world's meat consumption, with per capita consumption there increasing fivefold from the early 1980s to the late 2010s, and it is likely to increase substantially more over the coming decade (Pan and Sherrard, 2017). Global meat consumption is already highly damaging to the environment. It requires vast tracts of land, whether for grazing or for the production of grain feedstocks, and enormous quantities of water. The GHG pollution that results includes methane emissions from ruminants and emissions of CO_2 from meat-related land clearing, production, transport and so forth. Nearly 80 percent of the GHG emissions coming from global agriculture are a consequence of livestock production, accounting for 14.5 percent of all GHG emissions globally (UNDP, 2019: 189). According to a study of people in the United Kingdom, where meat consumption is modest by global standards (below that of Brazil and the United States, but about 20 percent above that of China [Ritchie, 2019b]), those individuals who consume meat are responsible for double the GHG pollution of those who do not (Scarborough *et al.*, 2014).

Without a major reduction in global meat consumption, it will not be possible to achieve the objectives of the Paris Agreement (Springmann *et al.*, 2018). If it were to continue doing business as it does today, the livestock industry would, by 2030, produce 49 percent of the allowable global emissions budget for limiting global warming to 1.5°C (Harwatt *et al.*, 2020). Although there are methods for mitigating the GHG pollution coming from livestock, even if they were to be implemented the rapid rise in demand for meat by the neoconsumers would likely more than offset their effects. This is especially tragic because the consumption of meat in the quantities that are already commonplace in most of the developed world and increasingly among the neoconsumers is a recipe for a number of life-threatening diseases (Godfray *et al.*, 2018). Alongside the climate crisis is an expanding global health crisis directly associated with changes in lifestyles characterized by overconsumption.

Another way that the neoconsumers are adding to global GHG pollution is through their growing interest in joining Western consumers (especially Americans and Germans) in owning automobiles. By some accounts, automobiles together are the largest net source of pollution contributing to climate change (Unger *et al.*, 2010). Rising incomes in developing countries have resulted in a growing reliance on private cars for transport. The number of private cars owned by the neoconsumers increased dramatically in the decade up to 2000, rising by 445 percent in China and 259 percent in India (Myers and Kent, 2003: 4965). Between the turn of the century and 2030, total global vehicle ownership is expected to increase by about two and one-half times, reaching 2 billion units, with well over half of that rise occurring outside the developed countries, and the number of vehicles in China alone is expected to reach 390 million (Dargay, Gately and Sommer, 2007: 1). China, which has more than 300 million registered vehicles (Zheng, 2017), has overtaken the United States as the country where the most cars are produced and purchased (Ecola *et al.*, 2014). The vast majority of cars today are still powered by petrol/gasoline or diesel. In 2019 the total number of privately owned cars of this type in China reached 207 million (Xinhua, 2020).

One might argue that a global shift to mostly electric-powered cars is beginning to occur, although, to continue using China as a case in point, fewer than 4 million of the private cars there in 2019 were powered by "new energy" sources (Xinhua, 2020). If a big shift to electric cars does happen, whether their impact on climate change can be mitigated will depend on whether and how quickly countries decarbonize (and expand) the electricity grids that will be needed to charge all of those cars. And it will depend on how much GHG pollution comes from making them.

The aviation sector is one of the fastest-growing sources of carbon pollution. In 2019, it produced about 2.6 percent of energy-related CO_2 emissions globally (IEA, 2020a). According to one projection, by 2050 carbon emissions from aviation are likely to double if high-efficiency improvements are implemented by airlines and triple if they are not (Kommenda, 2019). Another projection foresees global GHG emissions from international aviation growing by 300–700 percent between 2020 and 2050 (European Commission, n.d.). Regardless of the precise change in emissions, it seems likely that they will rise substantially in the long term (once the effects of the coronavirus pandemic on travel are overcome). While there are many opportunities to decarbonize the car sector, even optimists are unlikely to suggest that aviation has a similar potential to shift away from fossil fuels to a substantial degree anytime soon, notwithstanding experiments with electric aircraft engines and biofuels (the latter having their own potentially very adverse implications for the environment).

Consequently, the neoconsumers' growing demand for air travel is worrying. According to an official at the International Air Transport Association, "[t]he upsurge in middle-class households in major nations like China and India in particular is 'pulling people into air travel'" (Rosen, Valino and Nowakowski, 2017). Globally, air travel grew by 300 percent between 1990 and 2019 (Kommenda, 2019). The number of air travelers is expected to increase from 3.8 billion in 2016 – nearly 1 billion of which were in China – to 7.2 billion in 2035, with China replacing the United States as the largest airline market and India likely to become the third (Rosen, Valino and Nowakowski, 2017). By 2016, 135 million people were traveling internationally from China alone, more than half of them for "leisure" (Rosen, Valino and Nowakowski, 2017).

Air travel has the ability to substantially increase the climate-related impacts of the neoconsumer class in particular. The CO_2 emissions per passenger from even relatively short flights exceed the total annual emissions of individuals in many of the world's poor countries, and many neoconsumers will take more than a single flight each year. For individuals, flying is arguably "the worst possible single action you can take for climate change" (Kugel, 2020). Significantly, the climate agreements (see Chapter 3) largely excluded regulation of emissions from airlines. However, a separate agreement was reached in 2016 to stabilize CO_2 emissions from airlines at the 2020 level, albeit not through actual cuts but instead through the use of carbon-offsetting mechanisms (e.g., carbon sinks) (ICAO, n.d.). That agreement may be short-lived. When airline travel fell sharply in 2020 due to the global coronavirus pandemic, the airline industry immediately began calling for the emissions-stabilization plan to be adjusted. Presumably the airlines did not want the upper limit of allowed emissions to be established in a year with greatly reduced demand for air travel (Farand, 2020).

Without truly radical changes to what and how people consume, the growth of the global middle class, which is happening primarily in the Global South, cannot be environmentally sustainable, nor can it be compatible with the objectives of the Paris Agreement to keep global warming below 1.5° to 2°C (cf. Kharas, 2017: 18). Among the positive aspects of a growing middle class – the most important one being the associated reduction in poverty and the hardships that go with it – is that people in the middle class have smaller families, meaning that population growth is mitigated. But the fact remains that people in the middle classes and above consume far more than do the world's poor. Most of that consumption contributes to GHG pollution. Given that the lifetime GHG emissions of some people is so much higher than others – more than 1,000 times higher in many cases – "it is not the growth in the number of people, but rather the growth in the number of consumers and the GHG implications of their consumption patterns that are the issue" (Satterthwaite, 2009: 564). With hundreds of millions of neoconsumers of the Global South joining consumers of the North in lifestyles that rely heavily on the burning of fossil fuels, the challenges for climate governance look set to increase.

Human Nature and Climate Change

Climate change is the outgrowth of the natural human inclinations to procreate, to consume and to assume that consuming more is better. The power of human nature in these and related respects has been so strong as to instigate the

Anthropocene epoch – the human mutation of Earth. The natural inclination of people to consume is stimulated and empowered by global economic institutions and paradigms, especially contemporary capitalism. People consume more than they would without the encouragement that comes from social, economic and political forces. None of that is very new; anthropologists have found artifacts from past civilizations, even from prehistoric settlements, demonstrating the durability of the human urge to have things that are not essential for survival. Yet, while it is part of human nature to consume, it is not natural for humans to live in a global capitalist economy that, with the aid of inexpensive resources and powerful modern technologies, is able to stoke and fulfill the almost endless wants – even addictions – of everyone who is capable of affording them. Human nature is in a losing battle with an economic milieu that is relentlessly pushing individuals and societies to consume as much as possible.

What is especially new is that consumerism is spreading around the world at a rapid pace as more people become affluent enough to consume well beyond their needs. As more people consume far more than is necessary to meet their needs, the potential for climate catastrophe becomes very real, perhaps even unavoidable. Even if, as projected, human population stops growing in the future, the harm done to Earth's climate system could very well continue to increase if nothing is done to stop the per capita growth in consumption. Thus, the biggest demographic challenge for climate governance is not automatically the number of people or even necessarily the rate of population growth. Rather, it is the growth in, and the global proliferation of, consumption. The pathologies of human nature – traits inherited through evolution and their stimulation by economic and social forces – have conspired to make people believe that the best way for them to promote their perceived interests is to consume. This of course means to consume that which every person clearly needs (e.g., enough healthy food), but also to consume what society and corporations signal is necessary to live a modern lifestyle. Much as most national governments wrongly perceive that it is not in their interests to negotiate strong agreements with other states to govern climate change more effectively, and to implement aggressive national policies toward that end, most people routinely perceive that restricting their consumption of things that they do not need is not in their interest.

Climate governance faces many challenges. The pathologies of international relations (Chapter 3) and national politics (Chapters 4–6) are exacerbated enormously by pathologies of human nature, including (among others) the inclination to overconsume, which converts a potentially sustainable human population into a threat to Earth's climate system and everything that depends on it, including humanity; the susceptibility of people to the officially endorsed and corporately encouraged paradigm of economic growth, which shapes perceptions of people and societies and thereby greatly multiplies the impacts of human consumption, notably from GHG pollution; and the metastasis of Western lifestyles to the countries of the Global South, manifested in hundreds of millions of neoconsumers joining the global middle class (and upper class). These pathologies combine to make it difficult or undesirable for most governments to formulate and especially implement effective domestic policies to mitigate GHG pollution and move swiftly toward decarbonization. In democracies, a public convinced that its well-being is tied to growing consumption will be less likely to accept, let alone welcome, lifestyle changes that translate into consuming less. Every person who wants to consume more is a potential vote against politicians and political parties that ask people to constrain their personal freedom to consume. In non-democratic societies, there will be similar pressure from citizens (albeit not at the ballot box) because nearly all governments want to encourage economic growth, which is still derived from people consuming as much as possible. The pathologies of human nature likewise reduce the willingness of governments to embrace international action on climate change, at least insofar as doing so requires them to go beyond their nationally determined preferences.

At the time of this writing, the world is experiencing a coronavirus pandemic. The global economy is severely affected, and the buying power of the global middle class has fallen, at least for the short term. This has resulted in a fall in consumption, revealing at least a brief silver lining in the pandemic: it will reduce GHG pollution and may buy some time to implement more effective governance of climate change (McGrath, 2020). But it is highly questionable whether this time will be used to govern climate change more effectively. It is entirely possible, even likely, that the pandemic will sideline efforts by governments and many industries to move toward decarbonization. Industries that are major contributors to GHG emissions, such as airlines, are lobbying governments for subsidies to keep them afloat during the pandemic. Some national governments are giving cash handouts to citizens to encourage consumption. And it is entirely possible that the global economy will come roaring back, at least in terms of its ability to harm the environment, once the pandemic fades. After a period of relatively austere living during the pandemic, the natural human urge to (over)consume is likely to resurface if there are no interventions to stifle it. The forces of global capitalism and the determination of governments to promote growth will almost certainly kindle and stoke that urge. Because the global economy is still heavily reliant on fossil fuels, such an outcome would mean that GHG pollution, and CO_2

emissions in particular, may very well continue to rise after a coronavirus-induced dip (Peters, 2020).

Many lessons can be learned from considering the relationship between human population and consumption. One thing ought to be clear: global population is not going to fall in time to avert extremely dangerous climate change. Quite the opposite is more likely: it will continue to rise precisely at the time when aggressive action will be needed to reduce global GHG pollution drastically. This means that other variables will have to change markedly and quickly. Among them must be (over)consumption. This is clear from the fact that as global population has increased rapidly over the past century, consumption and associated environmental pollution have increased even more rapidly. Without reducing the environmental impact – and specifically the climatic impact – of consumption, even a falling population would not avert climate disaster. The fundamental ethos of the global economy – perpetual growth – is possible in the long term only if consumption can be decoupled from GHG emissions (and other forms of environmentally unsustainable pollution).

This puts the rise of the neoconsumers into sharp focus. To be sure, it would be wrong to lay very much of the blame for the current climate crisis on them. After all, the problem mostly started with consumers in the Global North and is largely sustained by their continued overconsumption. Yet, the rise of the neoconsumer in the Global South is a phenomenon that cannot be ignored if there is any hope of realizing the objectives of the Paris Agreement. Put simply, overconsumption of the neoconsumers needs to be mitigated alongside that of consumers in the Global North. This will not be easy to do because most people have been persuaded that overconsumption is in their interest even when it is not (as discussed in the next chapter).

Without a new way of thinking, a new approach to life and that which makes it good, the pathologies of human nature will continue to conspire with the pathologies of national politics and international relations to waylay effective climate governance. What prescriptions might there be to ameliorate this conspiracy, and indeed to mitigate substantially all of the pathologies of climate governance? How likely are such prescriptions to be applied? The remaining chapters are largely devoted to exploring and answering these and related questions.

PART III

Prescriptions

8

Reconsidering International, National and Human Governance

The primary objective of this book is to highlight a number of critical governance-related pathologies that have exacerbated climate change and impeded the negotiation, formulation and implementation of policies for effectively mitigating and responding to the climate crisis. Those pathologies are far from the only important problems with climate governance, but it is vital that they be ameliorated as a matter of priority. If the pathologies of international relations (described in Chapter 3), especially those that derive from the nature of the international system and its constituent units (i.e., states), are not ameliorated, effective international cooperation to address climate change much more effectively will be elusive. If the pathologies of national politics (described in Chapters 4–6), especially narrow and short-term conceptions by states of their interests, are not modified to better comprehend the collective interest in mitigating the climate crisis for the benefit of people around the world, other attempts to govern the problem will be insufficient. If pathologies of human nature (described in Chapter 7), particularly overconsumption, continue to manifest themselves in the Global North and spread metastatically to the Global South, GHG pollution will be extraordinarily difficult, and probably impossible, to bring down to the degree, and with the speed, that is needed to avoid dangerous climate change.

Clearly, diagnoses are needed to find potential therapies for these pathologies, and it is to this secondary objective of the book that this and the remaining chapters are devoted. This chapter conducts some diagnoses of the pathologies and explores some potential therapies for climate governance. It looks at some of the issues that can and should inform prescriptions, which are described in the next chapter, while recognizing that there are unlikely to be any miracle cures for climate governance.

Before considering potential therapies for climate governance, a few points warrant some emphasis. The first is that the climate crisis is already here; it is too late to stop climate change or to avoid very serious impacts (see Chapter 2). Neither the therapies considered in this chapter nor the prescriptions proposed in the next one can change this reality. Effective governance is a matter of managing climate change and one day resolving the associated crisis. Overcoming the pathologies of climate governance would mean, in effect, very quickly reducing, and ending as soon as possible, GHG pollution of the atmosphere, as well as coping as effectively as possible with the unavoidable impacts of climate change. Doing that will require applying not just the therapies and prescriptions described in this book. It will also require doing all, or nearly all, of the things being proposed by others and already being implemented, and at a faster pace. Effective climate governance will require action by all actors – national and subnational governments, national and international organizations of all sorts, local and global businesses, and capable individuals right around the world.

It will also require that effort not be wasted on doing things that are unrealistic. For example, as described in Chapter 3, the international system of states is not well suited to address climate change, but trying to do away with this system is not the remedy because (among other potential reasons) focusing resources on trying to do so would require diverting them from more practical efforts. Such an approach would, at best, take far more time than is available to avert climate catastrophe. If someone believes that the selfishness of states, and indeed that of people, is the root of all evil in this circumstance – there is a very strong case to be made for such belief – it does not follow that the remedy is to rid the world of selfishness or to plead for more altruism by states and individuals (although there is probably no harm, and potentially much good, in trying to do so). A substantial degree of selfishness is unavoid-able – it is "natural" for states to be quite selfish, and the same can be said of individuals (as implied in Chapter 7). Rather than trying to eliminate selfish-ness, a more realistic approach is to harness enough of it to make effective climate governance more likely in the near future.

Another point to emphasize is that the pathologies of climate governance – of international relations, national politics and human nature – are very much interrelated and interdependent. For example, international cooperation on climate change depends very much on the particular circumstances of the national politics of major states (at minimum). If China and the United States are too focused on their own perceived national interests, even the combined efforts of many other countries to facilitate more effective climate governance at the international level would be unlikely to be very successful (see Harris, 2013). Addressing the pathologies of national politics in particular countries requires substantial work internationally, and vice versa. Another example of the interrelated nature of the pathologies is the capitalist growth model, which has been embraced, whether explicitly or implicitly, by most actors and institutions almost everywhere, from individuals up to international regimes. Thus, to address the overconsumption that plays a very big part in the climate crisis will require addressing growth at all levels. If corporations and citizens want more and easier consumption, national governments are hard pressed to force them to do otherwise, which in turn influences the actions of those governments at the national and international levels. These sorts of interrelationships across and among the pathologies, and all of the actors, institutions and forces involved, are in the background when diagnosing the pathologies of climate governance and identifying associated prescriptions.

International Governance of Climate Change

The international relations of climate change have not focused on the collective long-term interests of all (or nearly all) states, and certainly not the collective interests of all people (not to mention other species), to have climate change governed effectively. Instead, the international relations of climate change have focused on the short-term interests of individual states, particularly those that are most important for climate governance, as perceived by the political institutions and most influential actors within those individual states. Chapter 3 described the process of international climate governance and associated pathologies of international relations. Ways must be found to eliminate or, more realistically, to attenuate these pathologies.

A problem with international governance of climate change is that the international system has the effect of undermining the ostensible raisons d'être of the states that are the constituent parts of that system: to, at minimum, secure the survival and well-being of their citizens in both the present and the future. Put another way, in the context of the international governance of climate change, states are not doing what they supposedly exist to do. Thus, more effort is needed in international climate governance to have states do that which they ought to: protect and promote the human security and rights that are gravely threatened by climate change. One way to do that is to recognize that the CBDR principle need not, and ought not, solely apply to states. It can and should also be applied to people. When that is done, it becomes evident that climate justice among states can be bolstered by justice among people living in them, with the world's affluent people, regardless of where they live, bearing more responsibility while the poor, also regardless of where they live, bearing much less. Viewing CBDR in this way provides justifications and avenues for putting the interests of people at the top of the priorities of international climate governance.

Human Security as National Interest

International relations are largely characterized by competing national interests. Insofar as they can, states behave in ways that they believe will promote their national interests. However, oftentimes those interests are ill-defined. Indeed, as Chapters 4–6 showed, national interests are very frequently determined not so much by objective assessments of circumstances as by national politics. A country's expressed interests, as evidenced by behavior, are frequently the interests of influential actors in society, which often boils down to powerful domestic corporations. The interests that states nominally claim to represent – those of their citizens – are often not very well protected and promoted, at least not if citizens' interests are looked at dispassionately and beyond the short-term future. This is especially the case with respect to climate change, which leaves some governments and many people uncertain about where their interests actually lie. As Chapter 7 suggested, many people believe that overconsumption is in their interest, encouraged in this belief by marketing, government pronouncements and other clarions of economic growth. Yet, the science suggests that climate change poses grave challenges for human well-being. If states exist to protect and promote the interests of people who live within them, it follows that they ought to act accordingly in the context of the climate crisis. That requires prioritizing the protection and, ideally, the promotion of human interests insofar as they are threatened by climate change. Doing so would require viewing climate change as a bigger threat than it is often perceived to be by many governments and other actors. It would require increasing the influence of people and their interests during the calculation of the national interest.

Climate change is a direct and indirect threat to human security now and in the future (Adger et al., 2014). It will undermine livelihoods, restrict the availability of safe and affordable food, result in shortages of water, increase threats to human life and health, exacerbate poverty, contribute to large migrations of people (internally and internationally) and increase the threat of violent conflict (i.e., civil and international wars). Already, thousands of people around the world are dying every year as a consequence of the effects of climate change, to say nothing of the millions of people dying annually from the pollution that comes from burning fossil fuels (Ghebreyesus, 2019). According to one estimate, the number of additional deaths *annually* due to the effects of climate change is in the hundreds of thousands (Global

Humanitarian Forum, 2009), and according to another estimate these numbers will likely reach 250,000 per year between 2030 and 2050 as a consequence of malaria, heat stress, diarrhea and malnutrition arising from climate change (UNDP, 2019: 180). By 2030, 100 million people could be forced into extreme poverty by climate change (World Bank, 2016). Climate change threatens human rights as well, including the most basic right of all – life (without which no other rights can be exercised). Climate change also poses threats to the rights of those who survive. For example, as noted in Chapter 6, some SIDS are facing existential threats from sea-level rise. This means that the rights of their citizens to national self-determination may be denied one day, not to mention the potential for losing rights to the place-based cultures of their homelands.

Importantly, few countries (if any) can escape the threats posed by climate change to human security and rights. This is especially true of many or most LDCs. They are often at the forefront of the impacts of climate change. Most of the millions of people displaced by climate change will be displaced internally within developing countries. The majority of people who will die because of food shortages (or price hikes due to food scarcities) or from lack of potable water will be in developing countries. The impacts of sea-level rise, worsening storms and spreading pathogens (e.g., dengue- and malaria-carrying mosquitoes) will be felt most harshly in developing countries. This is one reason that so many of those countries have called for urgent action on climate change even as many developed countries have dithered. However, the latter countries are far from immune. Their citizens will not escape climate hazards in the future; far from it (Mora et al., 2018). Citizens of the Global North have already suffered and died because of bushfires (e.g., Australia), forest fires (e.g., Canada), heat waves (e.g., France), hurricanes (e.g., the United States), typhoons (e.g., Japan), floods (e.g., the United Kingdom) and so forth, and such experiences will become more common, more destructive and more deadly in coming decades. The death toll in developed countries will not be as high as that in developing countries, but death toll there will be.

Developed countries will also suffer indirectly from the harsh impacts of climate change in the Global South. For example, many of the people in developing countries that are displaced directly or indirectly by the impacts of climate change will be on the move. As environmental scarcities and economic challenges arising from climate change increase in the South, people there will try to move to areas where there are more resources and opportunities. As climate change exacerbates or stimulates violent conflict, those affected will look for refuge. Climate change will likely contribute to millions of people each year becoming climate migrants within their own countries and climate refugees in others (Podesta, 2019), with some predictions putting the number of people moving due to climate change and other environmental factors as high as 1 billion by 2050 (International Organization for Migration, 2014). Many of these people will find their way to the countries of the Global North. The decade-long Syrian civil war, which may have been made more likely by drought that was induced or exacerbated by global warming (Kelley *et al.*, 2015), provides a stark warning of the potential for climate change to contribute to large movements of desperate people (even if climate change did not actually contribute to the outbreak of the war [as argued by Selby *et al.*, 2017]). Millions of Syrians fled not just to neighboring countries but also to the West, resulting in profound economic, social and political consequences for host countries, notably in Europe.

Similarly, given predictions that climate change will increase the spread of bacteria and viruses as vectors (e.g., fleas, mosquitoes and ticks) expand their ranges and people are forced to move into former wilderness areas, the global coronavirus pandemic of 2020 is an extreme early warning of how severe the impacts might be for people all around the world if those predictions prove to be accurate. The climate crisis is a crisis for human security everywhere and thus it is (or ought to be) a crisis for national security everywhere.

Significantly, the implications of climate change for human security and rights have been recognized at the international level. Within the United Nations, "explicit governance connections have been made between human security and climate change" (Mason, 2015: 2), including by the UN Human Security Unit (UN, n.d.[c]), the UN Development Program (UNDP, 2015) and the UN High Commissioner for Refugees (UNHCR, 2017), as well as the World Health Organization (WHO, 2018). Human security has also been a subject for assessment by the IPCC (Adger *et al.*, 2014). Similarly, the relationship between climate change and human rights has been recognized within the United Nations, notably by the Office of the High Commissioner for Human Rights (OHCHR, 2015) and the Human Rights Council (UN, 2017). This official international recognition of the threats that climate change poses to human security and rights demonstrates that it is not idealistic to believe that countries should make the de facto protection of people a top priority in international climate governance.

To be sure, this notion has been accepted at the level of the UN organization more than at the level of many of its members states. As Michael Mason (2015: 7) argues (and, in so doing, effectively highlights a pathology of international climate governance), "the 'mainstreaming' of human security in UN activities is a politically delicate project, deferential to the *sovereignty* sensitivity of those Member States anxious that the concept could be used to justify interventionist actions" (italics added). Thus, the international recognition of human security and rights is so far only a starting point, a foundation for building greater recognition by national governments, and for making the protection of people from climate change a much larger part of the calculus of the national interests of more countries. It is a pathway with the potential to significantly alleviate some of the pathologies of international relations.

Global Ethics and Climate Change

The "politically delicate project" of raising the profile of human security and rights in international climate governance can be advanced by considering the climate crisis from the perspective of global ethics and justice, a point of view that is sometimes identified as being "cosmopolitan" (see Harris, 2016c). Taking such a perspective looks well beyond the state, revealing that many other actors matter practically and ethically for climate change (Dietzel and Harris, 2019). Considering climate change in terms of ethics and justice generally is very well established in the context of the climate regime (see, e.g., Breakey, Popovskis and Maguire, 2015; Maltais and McKinnon, 2015). This is evidenced by the CBDR principle, which is an inherently ethical approach premised on conceptions of justice applied internationally, and which has been explicitly incorporated into the climate regime (see Harris, 2016c: 81–9). (As noted in Chapter 3, this does not mean that the CBDR principle has been implemented adequately.) Having agreed to the CBDR principle, states accept, at least conceptually, that it is unfair to expect developing countries to take on the same responsibility for the climate crisis as the developed countries. The latter acknowledge that justice demands special consideration for poor countries' circumstances because they are more vulnerable to climate change.

At the core of the CBDR principle is the realization that some countries have done more to cause climate change than others; those that have done so tend to be, not coincidentally, from the Global North, meaning that they also have the greatest capabilities. In contrast, most developing countries are just the opposite: they were lesser sources of the pollution in the past that precipitated the climate crisis, and much of their GHG pollution has been a consequence of meeting their needs. Furthermore, most developing countries are much less capable of acting on the climate crisis; they lack the wealth to do so. Put simply, the CBDR principle codifies the notion that it is wrong to expect the poor, weak and vulnerable (countries) to take responsibility or to pay for a problem caused largely by the affluent, strong and capable (countries).

International ethics and justice are concerned with the rights and responsibilities (among other things) of states in their relations to one another as states. From a purely *international* perspective, questions of ethics and justice for individuals relatively rarely extend beyond state borders (at least not in an obligatory way). States can of course choose to value individuals beyond their borders and even to sign treaties codifying such sentiments, as has been done with respect to genocide and the "responsibility to protect" (see Doyle, 2011). In contrast, *global* ethics and justice are explicitly concerned with the rights and responsibilities of individuals. Their rights, as well as their responsibilities, are universal in moral terms. Importantly, the global (or cosmopolitan) perspective considers humans to be of equal moral worth, and equally deserving of being considered and treated justly, regardless of which countries they happen to be citizens of or live within. From this perspective, the state – its rights, responsibilities and the like – is not the sole grounding for determining what is ethical. States are not morally superior to people.

States certainly do matter greatly in both practical and ethical terms, but they do not matter solely. People matter too. From the perspective of global ethics, deciding what is right and wrong should, at least in principle, ignore state borders. Likewise, for global justice, the determination of what is just ignores borders, at least conceptually. What comes from this global approach is that the rights and responsibilities of states, while very important, can be moved to the back of the stage, so to speak, and the rights and responsibilities of individuals can be moved to the front, ideally illuminated under klieg lights so as to draw full attention to them. This more global perspective enables us to see the CBDR principle in much broader terms. It becomes apparent that CBDR need not be restricted to state actors in international climate governance; it can also be applied to human actors (among others, if desired). If we think in terms of global ethics and justice – that is, not only of ethics and justice among states, as the CBDR principle does formally – the roles of people, their contributions to climate change, how it affects their security and rights, and what responsibilities they may have related to it become much clearer.

Many problems facing states are more or less confined to their borders. For such problems, one might argue that related ethics and justice need not extend beyond borders. But climate change is not one of those problems; it does not respect borders at all. Burning fossil fuels in one country harms people (and the environment) in many others. Consistent with the prevailing view of CBDR over the past few decades, it is still quite common to refer to climate change as a problem caused by the developed countries. To a great extent that is true: historical GHG pollution from consumption and other behaviors of people in developed countries did contribute the most to the problem for centuries. The climate change regime largely reflects this picture. But that picture no longer gives an accurate view of climate change. For some decades, a growing and now very large proportion of GHG pollution has come from developing countries. More to the point, the *people* who cause climate change through their actions, particularly the affluent people and the neoconsumers who do so through their own voluntary overconsumption, no longer live almost exclusively in the Global North. Nowadays they live in both developed *and* developing countries – in New York *and* Shanghai, in Berlin *and* Mexico City. Something similar can be said about those who suffer the effects of climate change. The majority of them are and will be in the Global South, but it is also the case that many people in the North are experiencing climate-related impacts, too, and the number of them so affected will increase with time, perhaps very dramatically.

For centuries, especially over the past few generations, through their GHG emissions people in the Global North have been undermining human security and rights in the Global South. The expanding climate crisis means that they are increasingly doing the same to people in other countries of the North. What is relatively new is that many people in the South are harming human security and rights in other countries of the South and the North. A neoconsumer enjoying his new car on a Beijing ring-road is just as harmful to human security in the future as is a member of the middle (or upper) class speeding along a Los Angeles freeway. The harm from Beijing is just as wrong – just as unethical and unjust, arguably – as the harm from Los Angeles. Conceiving of CBDR related to climate change from a global perspective lays bare this reality. It underscores that people *everywhere*, especially the overconsumers, are undermining human security *everywhere*. International climate governance would likely be much more effective if it were to recognize and embrace this perspective. This could be done by extending the CBDR principle to people in the context of the international climate regime.

Such an approach would recognize that people are responsible for climate change regardless of the countries in which they live, and specifically that their responsibility, like that of states, is differentiated. A rich consumer in, say, Canada would be recognized by the climate regime as being part of the problem, indeed a far bigger part than a poor person in, say, Brazil. At the same time, a rich person in Brazil would be recognized as having more responsibility than a poor person in Canada. (Importantly, this would not diminish the climate-related responsibility of Canada in any way, nor increase the responsibility of the Brazilian state. The CBDR of states would remain fully applicable.) To be sure, affluent people and overconsumers in Brazil and other developing countries have always contributed to GHG pollution, along-side most people in developed countries. But in the past those affluent people in developing countries did not have very much practical significance for the climate crisis. However, the growth of the neoconsumers that was described in the previous chapter means that this is no longer the case. Yet, this is still something that the current approach to international climate governance, including the underlying CBDR principle, largely disregards, at least officially. This will have to change if the pathologies of international climate governance are to be overcome.

Human Interests in International Climate Governance

Climate governance at the international level can be made more effective if it takes the security, rights and other interests of people more seriously. A number of reasons to justify doing this could be proposed, not least the widespread assumption that states exist to protect the interests of people living within them. Insofar as the interests of people within a particular state are tied to those of people in other states, as they indeed are in the context of climate change, states not only have an obligation to protect the climate-related interests of their citizens but also to consider doing so with respect to the interests of other states' citizens. Thus, there are very practical reasons for international climate governance to do much more to consider and act upon the security, interests and rights of people in addition to those of states. Furthermore, there are normative reasons, notably those premised on ethics and justice, for putting human interests alongside national interests in inter-national climate governance, including the notion that common but differenti-ated responsibilities apply to people as well as states. It is accepted, as codified in the CBDR principle, that an affluent country becomes disproportionately responsible for climate change because it spews GHG pollution into the atmosphere (largely through its economic activity). Global conceptions of ethics and justice suggest that the same disproportionate responsibility would adhere to an affluent individual who spews GHG pollution into the atmosphere (largely through excessive voluntary consumption). If recognizing and acting upon human security and rights are justified in these (and other) ways, methodologies need to be developed to bring them into the processes of international climate governance, and specifically into climate diplomacy and the ongoing negotiations to further develop the climate change regime.

Where might that process of bringing human interests much more promin-ently into climate diplomacy place its foundations? It would have to start by acknowledging that human interests matter. Few if any diplomats would openly deny that human interests do matter. Indeed, when trying to justify, for example, the failures of their own countries to take sufficient action on climate change, diplomats may invoke the need to protect the interests of their state's citizens (even when it is apparent that other actors, such as corporations, are often the intended objects of protection). Certainly, many diplomats from poor and vulnerable countries have legitimately and consistently invoked, over decades, the dire circumstances of their citizens when calling for action on climate change by developed countries. Raising the profile of human interests, specifically in the climate change negotiations and agreements, is thus largely a matter of putting into practice much of what national governments already say that they want to happen. Doing this would require methods for shining a light upon, and raising the profile of, the interests, rights and indeed responsibilities and duties of people alongside the interests and so forth of states. One way to approach this is to consider some proposals that, in effect, direct attention to human interests, responsibilities and the like in international climate governance, and then to consider ways that people have gained a foothold in real-world climate diplomacy.

Among the proposals that highlight the role of people are "contraction and convergence" (C&C), "greenhouse development rights" (GDR), the "Princeton proposal" and practical cosmopolitanism (cf. Harris, 2013: 136–40). The C&C proposal is premised on a sound assumption that GHG emissions need to contract to a point that avoids dangerous climate change, but in so doing each country's emissions cannot go so low as to prevent people from meeting their needs (Meyer, 2004). To reach this point, countries with high emissions would reduce them substantially, and countries where emissions are too low to meet needs would increase them. In this respect, the C&C proposal is not far off the CBDR principle. What is special about C&C is that it sets acceptable levels of emissions using equal per capita allowances. Every individual would have an entitlement to produce a safe level of GHG emissions, with those emitting too little having a surplus that might be sold or traded, and those who emit too much having to cut emissions or find surpluses to purchase. The value here is in the focus on the role of persons and their needs.

Similarly, the GDR proposal recognizes that there is a limited amount of emissions that the atmosphere can sustain, and similarly it recognizes that the world's poor people cannot be expected to cut their emissions (Baer *et al.*, 2009). In short, they have rights to development. Determining how much people should be allowed to emit within the sustainable global limit would be calculated, according to this proposal, based on individual responsibilities and capabilities. Significantly, the GDR proposal makes this calculation irrespective of an individual's citizenship. While both the C&C and GDR proposals are premised on what people do, they are essentially translated into entitlements and obligations of states. Nevertheless, they are helpful in highlighting the role of both human security and rights.

The Princeton proposal apportions CO_2 emissions among the word's 1 billion highest emitters (Chakravarty *et al.*, 2009). The foundation of this proposal is, in effect, the CBDR of individuals, with the 1 billion most affluent people bearing responsibility for their disproportionately high levels of GHG pollution. Like the C&C and GDR approaches, there is recognition that individuals will have to cap their emissions at a set level to avoid dangerous climate change, and that those people (at least among the world's most affluent) who exceed the cap would need to reduce emissions, while others would not face such restrictions. What is significant here is that every highly emitting individual is treated the same regardless of state borders. The proposal is based on the reality that the 1 billion high emitters live all around the world, the majority of them in the Global North, to be sure, but also many in the Global South. While this proposal is also translated into responsibilities of states, the underlying focus on individuals means that "no country gets a pass because even in the poorest countries some individuals have CO_2 emissions above the universal emission cap" (Chakravarty *et al.*, 2009: 11888).

This discernment of individuals as separate from their states is a reminder of the potential utility of global (cosmopolitan) perspectives, and some proposals are based more or less explicitly on this viewpoint. For example, one proposal for determining entitlements to, and duties to provide, assistance for adaptation is based on practical cosmopolitanism (Harris and Symons, 2010). From this perspective, entitlements and duties, and associated international institutions, ought to be focused on promoting human welfare rather than compensating states. Those whose human security is lacking due to climate change should be entitled to assistance, and that assistance is owed by those who undermine that welfare. In short, affluent polluters ought to assist the suffering poor. The argument is that international institutions for climate governance ought to reflect emphatically and deliberately these sensitivities to human needs and capabilities.

What comes from these proposals is that international climate governance ought to be more attuned to human interests, capabilities and so forth alongside the interests, capabilities and the like of states. Instead of focusing on the responsibilities and rights of states, international climate governance also ought to devote very serious attention to human responsibilities and rights. (Some might argue that the rights and interests of non-humans deserve more or most of the attention, but even if such an approach is desirable – and there is a strong case to be made that it is – the timeline for averting climate disaster is too short to realize it.) This would contrast with the prevailing approach to climate governance. While it is the case that NGOs and individuals do now have some sway in climate negotiations – for example, they speak loudly from large COP side events, NGOs are consulted by diplomats and individuals are sometimes given prominent opportunities to lobby diplomats (e.g., Greta Thunberg's speech at COP25) – international climate governance is still a state-focused undertaking. The perceived interests of states, which often include the narrow interests of domestic actors wedded to the status quo, mostly prevail (see Chapters 4–6). This has resulted in the worsening climate crisis.

Instead, human interests and obligations – real interests and obligations of real people around the world – ought to be placed at the heart of international climate governance. Doing this would reflect contemporary realities, including growing affluence around the world. It would also help states to do what they supposedly exist to do: ensure the security of people and promote their well-being, ideally in perpetuity.

National Governance of Climate Change

The considerations of international climate governance in the preceding section point toward potential diagnoses for national governance of climate change. This is to be expected, given that the most significant actors in international relations are, by definition, states – although one must acknowledge that some states are certainly more significant than others, with many weak ones being less practically significant, at least when they act alone, than some nonstate actors, notably large corporations. More specifically, the international diagnoses point to the importance of looking explicitly at the distinctions between the responsibilities and rights of states relative to the responsibilities and rights of individuals. If the CBDR principle is assumed to include people, it can help to diagnose national climate governance and thereby identify potential prescriptions for related pathologies. What comes from such a diagnosis is that national governments ought to recognize state responsibilities *and* individual responsibilities, and with respect to the latter they should act on the responsibilities of their own citizens.

Who's Responsible for Climate Change? States and Individuals

Climate change has created circumstances in which there are common interests among, and potential solidarity between, classes of people in the Global North and South. The rich in the South have more in common with the rich in the North than they do with the poor in their own countries. This is not a very new phenomenon, but it is more significant today given the growing number of affluent people around the world and their potential to impact Earth's climate through their behaviors and their participation in the global economic system, including their support for consumption-driven economic growth and their conveyance of behavioral signals to less affluent people about how to (over) consume. Similarly, the poor of the North often have more in common with the poor of the South because their poverty is exacerbated by climate change (Fitzpatrick, 2014). Increasingly, in their communities the Northern poor are disproportionately experiencing climatic impacts caused by the voluntary behaviors of affluent people around the world. This is not to suggest that the scale of suffering among the poor of the North will approach that of the South, but instead to suggest that this growing common interest highlights the diminishing practical significance of national borders and underscores the need to focus more on individuals and less on states. There is also the implication that there may be opportunities for political gain: political parties, politicians, NGOs and so forth may be able to leverage the power of those most affected by climate change to raise the profile of people and shift the emphasis in climate governance toward their needs (in the case of the poor) and their responsibilities (in the case of the affluent).

Realizing such opportunities requires more widespread understanding of the relative responsibilities of states and individuals for climate change. A problem is that attributing responsibility to states clouds our vision of the sources of that responsibility, and indeed of who might be capable of acting on it. To find therapies for climate governance at all levels, perhaps particularly at the national level (which can greatly affect the international and human levels), there is a need to recognize, accept and act upon the reality that states *and* individuals are responsible for climate change, some of them disproportionately so. Even as this is done, it does not diminish the accepted wisdom that developed countries hold the most historical responsibility for GHG pollution and should therefore bear a disproportionate share of the burden of addressing climate change (EcoEquity and Stockholm Environment Institute, 2018). That said, many people living in the North, both in the past and at present, most obviously the poor, share relatively little (or none) of that responsibility. Just as many people in the South today consume and pollute the atmosphere because that is all but unavoidable if they are to get by in life, many people in currently developed countries did so historically for similar reasons, and too many people continue to be in that position.

To be sure, countries of the South do not bear the greatest historical responsibility for climate change. Estimates of responsibility vary greatly depending on how the calculations are performed, but it seems that they are responsible for roughly one-third of the problem so far, with that proportion predicted to rise substantially through this century (see, e.g., Wei *et al.*, 2012; Elzen *et al.*, 2013). What is beyond dispute is that affluent people in developing countries, including many millions of the neoconsumers, are now contributing to the emissions of GHG pollution that will exacerbate the climate crisis. This contribution adds up, helping to explain why the Global South is now a larger source of GHG pollution than is the North. These realities need to be taken into full account if climate governance is to be more effective going forward. To be sure, growing emissions from countries of the South are only to be expected given their very large populations, their need to overcome poverty and their reliance on fossil fuels to do so. A defense of those countries is that, while their aggregate emissions are high, their average per capita emissions – total national emissions divided by population – are still relatively low.

Yet, such a focus on national per capita emissions takes us only so far. To start with, per capita emissions in the Global South are rising. In some countries there, notably China, per capita emissions are higher than the global average and even higher than emissions in a number of developed countries (Ritchie and Roser, 2019). What is more, even in developing countries with relatively low national per capita emissions, there are affluent people, sometimes millions of them in single countries, whose individual emissions are extraordinarily high by global standards, often obscenely so. Too much concentration on national per capita emissions can distract attention from the per capita emissions of these people. It also has the effect of using averages of all citizens' emissions to lower the apparent responsibility of particular countries. It enables overconsumers and wealthy people to hide behind the relatively low average per capita emissions of their countries, and especially the very low emissions of their poor compatriots, thereby avoiding individual scrutiny and responsibility. This is not fair to the many people within the same countries who consume less and thus have far less responsibility for the pollution that causes climate change.

One counterargument points to the fact that many countries in the Global South with substantial GHG emissions export products to countries in the North. The most significant example is China, where one-third of emissions result from the production of exports (Dessler and Parson, 2020: 182). Such countries ought not be held responsible for GHG pollution coming from the manufacture of exports, or so the argument might go. This is a fair argument up to a point, especially because there needs to be more focus on the quarter of all CO_2 emissions that are embodied in traded products (Moran, Hasanbeigi and Springer, 2018), and specifically more attention given to *consumption* emissions – GHG pollution coming from what countries and people consume, not just what they produce (see, e.g., Steininger *et al.*, 2014). But this argument has its flaws. After all, many people in the South benefit financially from exports. This is true of many of the new millionaires and billionaires in China, for example, but it also applies to the many neoconsumers who are able to consume due to increased wages arising from exports. If they are benefiting beyond the point of meeting their needs, then that benefit and the GHG pollution arising from it ought to be attributed, at least in part, to them, and not solely to consumers abroad. Related to this is the fact that the centuries of economic growth in the Northern countries, from which much of their disproportionate responsibility for climate change derives, has enabled people there to purchase exports from the South. In other words, at least the affluent of the South who benefit from exports are doing so as a consequence of centuries of GHG pollution in the North. If the CBDR principle is applied here, some of that disproportionate historical responsibility attributed to the North ought to be shared by affluent people of the South.

The rise of the neoconsumers and more affluent people in the South highlights the importance of *capabilities*. The significance of capabilities is so important that the CBDR principle is formally portrayed in the UNFCCC as "common but differentiated responsibilities *and respective capabilities*" (UN, 1992: art. 3[1], italics added). Due to growing wealth in the developing world, largely a consequence of economic globalization, millions of people there are more capable of taking action on climate change than are millions of people in developed countries. Thus, if one takes a holistic approach to CBDR, including by considering capabilities, it becomes apparent that many people in the South have more differentiated responsibility and more respective capabilities than the predominant focus on the CBDR of states suggests. The common historical attribution of disproportionate responsibility to developed countries retains merit, but it gives an incomplete picture if it is not accompanied by an understanding of the role played by people as well – that is, by people regardless of whether they live in the Global North or South. (One irony is that many affluent people spend the majority of their time living, and consuming, in the opposite sphere of economic development, such as rich Chinese executives living in Vancouver and retired Canadians living in Caribbean SIDS.)

This reality of responsibility – that it is held by states *and* by individuals – has significance for climate governance in a number of ways. For example, it means that not only affluent states but also affluent individuals, regardless of whether they live in the North or the South, are responsible for reducing their GHG emissions and helping at least the poor – potentially including the poor in developed countries – to cope with climate change. Many acknowledge that affluent people in the North should be doing this as part of their obligations as citizens of countries with responsibility for GHG emissions past and present. What is less commonly acknowledged is that affluent people in the South, even those in countries with very little historical responsibility for climate change, ought to be doing exactly the same thing. Affluent people, including the world's middle classes and neoconsumers, and of course the world's wealthy, *all around the world* should be recognized for what they are: voluntary sources of unnecessary GHG pollution. They have responsibility for the problem and thus should take on more of the burden of mitigating its causes and impacts. National governments should help people to do this, and require them to do it if necessary, based on those people's disproportionate responsibilities and respective capabilities.

Discerning the Responsibilities of Individuals

The common but differentiated responsibility of states is codified in the climate change agreements, but few if any of the states with disproportionate responsibility have decided that their national interests require them to accept and act upon it fully (and more than a few ignore it). As Chapters 3–6 described, for the most part what has come from national politics around the world is the shared belief among governments that responsibilities for climate change, and associated national policy action, should be nationally determined. This belief is reflected in the bottom-up approach to international climate governance, most prominently the Paris Agreement's NDCs. It is also reflected in national policies that seldom live up to the objectives of that agreement. This is partly due to the failure to perceive that human interests are national interests, and partly a consequence of not recognizing or accepting that, for it to mesh with the world as it actually is today, the CBDR principle needs to be about people as well as states.

One reason for the pathologies of climate governance at the national level, and subsequently in international climate negotiations, is that citizens view their responsibilities for climate change as being much like those of states: they are *individually determined*. Apart from some commendable policies, regulations and taxes in some countries that affect consumption behaviors (but even in those cases the policies are probably far too weak to influence behaviors of wealthy individuals), most people are free to consume and otherwise behave as they wish insofar as their capabilities (which are normally a function of their affluence) allow. This approach might have some merit were it not for the fact that those people are routinely encouraged by corporations and often by governments to overconsume and otherwise to behave in ways that result in GHG pollution, instead of being encouraged to live sustainably (see the next section).

Similar to the way that international climate governance needs to be as much about people's interests (their security, rights, etc.) as about national interests (and rights, etc.), national climate governance needs to be much more about peoples' responsibilities. Put another way, the CBDR principle needs to apply mutually to, and be shared by, states and individuals. One way to visualize this shared responsibility is to imagine two maps of the world (cf. Harris, 2010a; Harris 2013: 154–63). Imagine first a map that shows states' responsibilities for climate change. On this map, the countries that are most responsible for causing the climate crisis are colored in shades of red, with more responsible countries shown in darker shades of red and those with lesser responsibility shown in lighter shades of red. On this map, the United States would certainly be shaded in dark red, with other countries, such as Australia, Germany, Japan and the United Kingdom, being shown in varying shades of red. This imaginary map would give a fairly accurate picture of where states' responsibilities are considered to lie in the official context of the CBDR principle.

Now imagine a very different sort of map, one without any national boundaries, placed on top of the map just described. On this borderless map there is a blue spot for every individual who has unnecessarily overconsumed since the turn of this century. This map would, as expected, show large concentrations of blue spots across most of the red-colored Global North, especially in urban areas where hundreds of millions of middle-class and upper-class consumers live – Los Angeles, Toronto, Madrid, Tokyo, Sydney and the like – and it would show clusters of blue spots in many smaller communities across the developed world. So far, the blue spots more or less coincide with the red shading of the first map because many millions of overconsumers live in developed countries. However, if we look at the second map's depiction of the Global South, we would immediately notice large concentrations of blue spots, again in urban areas – Shanghai, Kuala Lumpur, Mumbai, Doha, Rio de Janeiro and the like. Thus, this second map would fairly accurately depict where *individuals* with responsibilities for climate change are actually located: *in both the North and the South.*

There are many variables that could fairly be used to ascertain whether a state or a person is more or less responsible for climate change, so creating such maps would be fraught with complications. Nevertheless, imagining them is useful because comparison of what they depict immediately reveals that responsibility for climate change is certainly not restricted to the borders of Northern countries; it is very much located in Southern countries, too. If we were to imagine similar maps showing those countries and individuals that are least responsible for climate change, we would learn even more. We would see, as expected, that more of the people with the least responsibility are located in the developing countries that are considered to have the least historical responsibility for the climate crisis. But we would also see that many people with relatively little responsibility live in developed countries.

It is important to emphasize that expanding the CBDR principle to individuals would not necessarily involve applying any new legal or moral obligations to states (that is, the legally sovereign state entities), even developing states that should be joining the developed states in finding new ways to mitigate the overconsumption of affluent individuals living within their borders. Rather, newly recognized obligations would apply to those overconsuming individuals. By implication, this approach would have the effect of diminishing the obligations of other citizens, most obviously those who underconsume or consume primarily to meet their needs. Affluent overconsumers in the South who currently hide behind the very low differentiated responsibility of their own states would no longer be able to do so, whereas poor people in the North would correspondingly have fewer obligations because it would become evident that they ought not be required to share the relatively high differentiated responsibility of their national states (at least not while affluent people in other countries evade responsibility due to a short-sighted focus on state responsibility).

If one takes the position that formal responsibility for climate change ought to be attributed solely to states, not individuals – that whatever individuals do should be attributed to the state in which they live – then the second imaginary map suggests that the shading of the first map might have to be adjusted. At the very least, if we are looking to the future, more developing countries will become responsible for climate change because more of their citizens are becoming affluent enough to add to the problem, and thus those countries would have greater obligation to take action. They would need to be held responsible for what many of their relatively well-off citizens are doing – to be responsible for regulating those people's climate-polluting behaviors – much as it is expected that developed countries ought to regulate polluting behaviors of their citizenry.

Thus, broadening of the conception of CBDR (and respective capabilities) to encompass individuals would bring much more attention to the role played by the world's affluent people who are the largest consumers and contributors to GHG pollution. Doing this would in turn bring attention to potential new national policies for holding the most responsible individuals (represented by the blue spots in the imaginary map described above) to account, rather than expecting everyone, the poor included, to share the national and global burden of reducing GHG emissions. An obvious question for national climate governance is whether governments will be willing and able to attribute more responsibility directly to those citizens who consume and pollute the most, and indeed to their enablers in industry. Doing so would mean that affluent polluters – including individual ones – would be given more scrutiny in *every* country, in effect putting the most responsible citizens in the Global North and South under the same spotlight. The hundreds of millions of neoconsumers would have to be scrutinized alongside consumers in developed countries. New national policies would have to be designed to reduce overconsumption, whether through carrots, such as government support to install solar panels, or through sticks, such as fees (perhaps based on a percentage of a person's income or wealth) on fossil fuels. Governments might even impose outright bans on polluting luxury products and behaviors, and they would certainly have to end current policies that subsidize forms of consumption that contribute to climate change, likely shifting funds to policies that encourage environmentally benign lifestyles and provide support for the poor who are least responsible for, and most affected by, climate change (see below).

National Politics: Harmonizing Interests and Fostering Climate Citizenship

Effective therapies for the pathologies of national politics will have to result in much more concrete action on climate change – reducing GHG pollution radically, preparing for the inevitable impacts and helping the poor to cope with them. This action will have to do far more to prioritize people's interests and responsibilities, rather than focusing mostly on the narrowly perceived interests of states or, as happens often in the real world, the even narrower interests of well-connected national actors that disproportionately influence policymaking in what is probably a majority of countries. At the heart of national responses to climate change is finding ways to recalculate the national interest so that it truly values and is based on human interests. At least in the context of climate change, national interests and human interests ought to be one and the same. (Of course, national governments would claim that they are already promoting their citizens' interests. Perhaps the best proof otherwise is the climate crisis itself and specifically that many citizens suffer as a consequence, not to mention the health impacts of lax environmental regulations.) Implicit in this notion is that national politics need to be much more cognizant of people's responsibilities because the behavior of some people harms the interests of other people, often including those others' most fundamental interest of all: survival.

How might national politics harmonize the interests of the state and its citizens? Some of the prescriptions proposed in the next chapter point to opportunities, but one place to start is the economy of each country. It should be shifted away from the promotion of national economic growth, which is a primary driver of climate change, to promoting growth in people's well-being, bearing in mind their responsibilities and capabilities. Governments will have to accept that the modern growth imperative is ecologically unsustainable, and that there are better ways to promote national and human interests. This is particularly the case because so many people around the world now not only aspire to live highly consumptive lifestyles but also have the capabilities to do so. The infatuation with economic growth has not only engendered the climate crisis. It has also distracted most governments and most people from alternative pathways that can do more to promote their interests and well-being in the long term while also mitigating climate change. The national interest, especially if defined more in terms of human interests, may even be best promoted through *degrowth* in material production and consumption alongside *more* growth in ecological sustainability and human welfare.

Shifting away from material growth and associated GHG pollution will require that national governments use both positive and negative incentives to engender behaviors that simultaneously promote people's long-term interests and the long-term interests of Earth's climate system. (If negative incentives, such as regulations to push people to behave in certain ways, seem to be too draconian, it is worth bearing in mind that if climate governance is not made more effective quite soon, the resulting scarcities and insecurities will likely become so severe as to require very strict policy action. Freedom-loving people should hope to avoid such a scenario.) Doing this will involve, among other things, finding new measures for economic success that focus on human well-being, new infrastructure to make it easier and more enjoyable for people to live sustainably, new lifelong educational initiatives that encourage climate-friendly behavior by showing how it protects and promotes people's interests, reversal of subsidies so that polluting activities and fuels cost more and sustainable alternatives cost less, the outlawing of activities that unnecessarily contribute substantially to the climate crisis, and taxation policies and welfare programs that promote social and ecological justice (see more on these things below).

Central to national policies should be the project of contributing to near-total decarbonization of national economics and thereby the global economy – ending the use of fossil fuels almost completely. Nonessential uses of fossil fuels that persist will have to become much more costly and highly regulated. For example, long-distance airline travel will have to return (at most) to something more like what it was half a century ago – an activity that was expensive and which most people did very rarely – and today's frequent-flier programs, which encourage unnecessary travel by air, will have to be replaced with progressive levies that do the opposite (Kugel, 2020). Part of the process of decarbonization should involve creating national (and eventually global) economies premised on "steady-state" (Daly, 1991), "circular" (Stahel, 2019) or similar principles that draw resources from nature sparingly and produce very little waste and pollution. Wastes that are produced will have to be recycled efficiently back into production processes and ways will have to be found to ensure that unavoidable pollution is sustainably absorbed by the environment. National food systems will have to be transformed, specifically in ways that nurture the environment, eliminate unnecessary food waste and make maximum use of landscapes as sustainable carbon sinks. Meat consumption will have to be radically reduced, becoming at most a complement to plant-based diets. Unavoidable waste from food systems might be used to feed a relatively few humanely reared livestock animals. (There is a very strong case to be made for eliminating meat consumption altogether for ethical and other reasons, at least where alternative foods are available.)

Technological innovation will be highly desirable and probably essential, not least in finding ways to sustain the healthy aspects of modern life without producing GHG pollution or otherwise harming the environment. But technology will have to be more about finding solutions to problems, particularly those related to climate change, than about creating demand for new products (as is the case with much technology development nowadays). While technologies to remove CO_2 from the atmosphere may be beneficial if they are environmentally sustainable, national policies should not assume that such technologies will be forthcoming within the short time span that is remaining to avoid very dangerous climate change.

National climate policy should aim to bring people directly into the process of limiting unnecessary consumption that results in GHG pollution. One of the ways to do this could be national carbon fees, with revenues being used as rebates that favor the poor so that they do not suffer from increased energy costs, and ideally benefit from them. Governments could also implement personal emissions-trading arrangements that in effect allocate responsibilities and rights related to climate-impacting consumption, with overconsumers paying into the arrangements so that people who are unable to consume enough to meet their needs receive assistance in doing so. Such fees and emissions-trading schemes should be based on national implementation of global caps on individual emissions. Those caps should be determined based on GHG emissions and total atmospheric concentrations that stay within safe planetary boundaries, divided by the global population, with appropriate consideration for the needs of both current and future generations.

These and other policies that focus on the responsibilities and rights of individuals have the potential to be politically popular, especially if combined with effective educational policies. For example, if more people can be made to understand that it is in their interest to consume fewer things (see below), and individualized taxation and trading policies are visible in the ways that they redistribute wealth (ideally directly to individuals), such initiatives may garner substantial popular backing, possibly enough to make the policies irreversible once they have been implemented (which may explain some of the corporate opposition to such initiatives). If such schemes were joined together globally so that affluent people everywhere effectively paid into them, popularity would rise among the hundreds of millions, possibly billions, of people who would benefit. This would include poor people, and those who consume relatively little, in the Global North who would receive payments from a system into which affluent people of the South have contributed. The consequence could be more support for climate action in developed countries and a much healthier sharing of global wealth alongside reductions in GHG emissions.

For these schemes to work, it will be necessary to foster climate citizenship (Moore, 2012) – the conscious connection between living in ways that do not exacerbate the climate crisis, including by reducing unnecessary consumption, on one hand, and being a good national (and global) citizen, on the other. Building such a sense of climate citizenship begins with children's education and encourages sustainable living throughout one's lifetime. Arguably, many young people today already have a substantial sense of climate citizenship, with Greta Thunberg and her many young followers around the world being conspicuous examples. But the short time span available to reverse the failures of climate governance means that nearly everyone, young and old, will have to embrace, consciously or not, climate citizenship (regardless of whether it is called that or something else) and live accordingly, starting no later than the next decade or two. In addition to education at all levels (from preschools to universities), policies to promote climate citizenship can learn from past and present attempts to foster civic-mindedness, nationalism and even religiosity. If there is any doubt about the ability to persuade people to do things, one need only think of extreme examples, ranging from the willingness of people to fight and die for their countries (even when those countries are relatively new constructs) or, to take the most extreme example, to become suicide bombers in the unhinged belief that doing so is morally right. Some have argued for a kind of pro-climate nationalism, an approach that is premised on the endurance of the state while fully acknowledging the threats posed by climate change (Lieven, 2020).

To be sure, it will be a challenge to convince most people, particularly those who have become accustomed to thinking that overconsumption is the route to well-being, that they ought to consume and pollute less, but it is vital to try. It may be easier than one might expect given that consuming less is probably in the best interests of the majority of people in the Global North, of many of the neoconsumers and of the wealthy overconsumers in the South. For many people, doing with less is the fastest route to health and happiness. A vital role of national governments is to use all of their resources to help people to realize this as quickly as possible. This means reversing many of the current approaches to politics and policy related to climate change.

Human Governance of Climate Change

In contrast to today's pervasive epidemic of overconsumption in much of the world, consuming in ways that are environmentally sustainable and relatively benign toward Earth's climate system can do much more to promote human interests, well-being and happiness, individually and collectively (Lamb and Steinberger, 2017). What is more, despite the messages coming from media and many governments, garnering and spending wealth, beyond a level that is sufficient to meet people's needs, are unlikely to promote much greater happiness. In fact, people in countries with the highest levels of consumption and wealth often report lower levels of happiness than do people in many low-income countries. As societies go from rich to richer, happiness can stagnate and health can decline. As suggested in Chapter 7, and as will be explored more below, this is because many people who are caught up in modern lifestyles overconsume things that they do not need instead of consuming things and experiences that will make them physically fit, mentally healthy and happy. Indeed, excessive consumption can itself be the cause of unhappiness and poor health. To live and consume in ways that actually promote human interests and well-being often means doing the opposite of what marketers and governments advocate, or at least means ignoring much of what they implore people to do (cf. Harris, 2013: 171–96).

Promoting people's interests and achieving well-being are consistent with mitigating the climate crisis. An essential task of effective climate governance is to achieve a virtuous relationship between doing what is good for people and doing what is good for the climate system. The question is how best to persuade people who already live lives of overconsumption that there is a better way of life available to them, and to convince those who aspire to overconsume, including the up-and-coming neoconsumers of the world, that they would be better off leapfrogging the traditional Western path to affluence and going directly to alternative lifestyles that will do more to promote their long-term interests and well-being. Making a convincing case for this runs counter to many of the most powerful actors and forces that have created the climate crisis. However, the task is made less difficult by the fact that doing what is in the interest of more effective climate governance does not require altruistic behavior of people. What is required are behaviors, and especially modes of material consumption, that promote people's long-term interests.

Addressing climate change more effectively means doing less of what is good for corporations and more of what is good for people (perhaps in the process ending some countries' practice of treating corporations as if they have the same rights as persons). The process of overconsumption is not only causing and exacerbating the climate crisis; it is also doing harm to people's interests. This section considers whether climate governance might be made more effective if people were to understand this.

Latter-Day Paradox: Wealth vs. Well-Being

It seems commonplace to assume that having more wealth and more things – more "stuff" – will make everyone better off, more secure, healthier and happier. While this is true for people in certain circumstances, especially the very poor who lack necessities, let alone small comforts, it is not true for many millions of the people living in the Global North and in the pockets of high economic development in the South. Studies of relative life satisfaction and happiness in different countries and cultures reveal that people's overall quality of life fails to increase substantially after they acquire more than enough wealth to meet their basic needs (Gilding, 2012: 191). Beyond the poor parts of the world, well-being often remains constant, and sometimes even declines, as people's aggregate wealth increases. Growth in GDP over the long term does not generally translate into growth in happiness over time, an observation first emphasized by Greg Easterlin (Easterlin, 2016: 13–45). This failure of happiness to rise along with GDP has been eponymously labeled the "Easterlin paradox" because it seems counterintuitive to those who expect there to be a direct relationship between growing GDP and growing satisfaction with life. The paradox seems to be generally true whether one looks at entire countries or at individuals over time, and it applies to different kinds of countries (Easterlin *et al.*, 2010).

The most profound example of the Easterlin paradox is the United States, where many millions of people live in large, comfortable homes with televisions, microwave ovens, dishwashers and machines to both wash and dry clothes; have computers with high-speed connections to the Internet and smartphones with immediate access to social media, online games and videos;

and drive big cars (often small trucks or SUVs) with air conditioning and entertainment systems, among other material accoutrements of American life. Yet, Americans are no happier than they were decades previously, and a growing number of them display attributes associated with unhappiness, such as divorce, depression and even suicide (see, e.g., Ingraham, 2019).

For poor countries, rising GDP, if it is distributed fairly, can help people to escape poverty and thereby increase their felt and actual well-being. However, the American experience with stagnating and, for many people, declining feelings of well-being has been mirrored in China. Indeed, despite rapid economic growth and an economy that has multiplied in size several times over four decades, people in China have expressed a slight downward trend in feelings of life satisfaction (Easterlin et al., 2012). These developments seem to be almost incredible given the millions of people who have moved from poverty into middle-class lifestyles in China. None of them would want to return to the poverty of their grandparents, but it seems that a life of "consumerism with Chinese characteristics" – to play on the government's oft-invoked notion of "socialism with Chinese characteristics" (Ho, 2018), a euphemism for state-directed economic development that has devastated the country's environment and made China the largest source of global GHG pollution – has not brought the widespread satisfaction that was anticipated.

To be sure, the most affluent Chinese are more satisfied than the average person in China, but those left behind point to an unsavory aspect of growth- and wealth-induced happiness: it seems to be dependent on growing inequality. The happier people are often surrounded by people who are substantially less affluent, and the unhappiness of the latter individuals is, in turn, often attributable to seeing how the wealthy live. Inequality makes more-affluent people happy but makes the less-affluent unhappy. This explanation makes sense because China's decades of economic growth have been accompanied by growing disparities in wealth; the country's Gini index, a measure of economic inequality, reveals it to be among the world's more economically unequal societies (roughly similar to the United States) (Lin, 2016). What has happened in China also seems to confirm what much of the literature on happiness and well-being has found: rising incomes engender even faster-rising aspirations, undermining the satisfaction that might otherwise come from them (Easterlin et al., 2012).

To be sure, growth in the economic lot of the poor is associated with their improved well-being, as one would expect, and affluent people understandably often express higher levels of satisfaction than do the poor. That said, psychological, social and physical aspects of well-being are often highest in countries with relatively low per capita GDP, with some of the happiest people living in relatively poor countries and some of the unhappiest people living in very wealthy countries (Jackson, 2009). This seems to be associated in large part with higher levels of overconsumption in the latter.

Overconsumption, materialism and affluenza can be psychopathologies. Pursuing excessive wealth and possessions can undermine one's health. Psychologists have found that more wealth does not have much positive impact on people's sense of well-being after their basic needs have been fulfilled, and people who are extremely wealthy experience higher than average rates depression (Gregoire, 2017). People who seek material possessions and wealth have fewer positive feelings than do people without such aspirations (Gregoire, 2017). The most materialistic people tend to feel less satisfied with life, while the least materialistic people tend to feel more satisfied with it (DeAngelis, 2004). Having more wealth and possessions than one needs can increase stress and be a diversion from other things that bring happiness. Happiness and self-esteem are lower among people who desire possessions and wealth, while their relationships with other people often suffer and their anxiety can be higher. In Tim Jackson's (2009: 1) characterization, "[h]aving more stuff doesn't always make us happy. Material aspirations don't necessarily deliver well-being. And a society dedicated to materialist values sometimes undermines the conditions on which well-being depends."

Similar to wealth-seeking, overconsumption does not garner the happiness that might be expected, is not likely to prevent unhappiness and may in fact contribute to it. While consuming more than one needs can bring some gratification in the short term, it can harm long-term mental and financial health. A problem with overconsumption is that it can become a substitute for the things that bring happiness and well-being. Consumption also has the obvious downside of requiring money. People work harder, often in more than one job, to earn enough to consume, and the desire to be rewarded for all that hard work often motivates yet more consumption. The consequence is a cycle of consumption and work that results in stress, relief from which is sought through still further consumption, thereby continuing a self-destructive – and climate-destroying – cycle.

That wealth-seeking and overconsumption often fail to bring much happiness is consistent with the perpetual-growth model of modern capitalism. Indeed, consumer capitalism is premised on "a constant feeling of dissatisfaction to sustain spending. ... [U]nhappiness sustains economic growth" (Hamilton, 2015: 71). Alan Durning (1992: 48) suggested decades ago that the consumer society had already "impoverished us by raising our income," and he pointed out that it "fails to deliver on its promise of fulfillment through material comforts because human wants are insatiable, human needs are socially defined, and the real sources of personal happiness are elsewhere." That "elsewhere" is very often found by spending more time enjoying the simplest of pleasures, such as meeting with family and friends, walking among nature, learning new things or becoming engrossed in art (see below). But time becomes scarce as people work and consume to fulfil the urges induced by today's capitalist societies.

Some of these observations are subject to dispute, not least by advocates of liberal economics who believe, along with many corporations and government officials around the world, that more wealth and more possessions are the sources of happiness and well-being. But even many of these skeptics might accept, on reflection, that wealth and overconsumption can reach points of diminishing returns to individual interests, including well-being and happiness. The question is then whether the extra return that comes from the pursuit of more wealth and more belongings is worth it – whether its pursuit distracts from other things that might bring more benefits to people *and* would contribute far less to global GHG pollution and the many harms that arise as a consequence. Even if one is skeptical of the Easterlin paradox (see Easterlin, 2017), there is still the possibility that there can be more to (a good) life than the pursuit of economic growth, greater wealth and more unnecessary possessions. Living as though the climate crisis matters presents everyone with an opportunity to find that "more," and in so doing to promote their genuine interests.

Measuring Prosperity: Toward Environmentally Sustainable Well-Being

If overconsumption and related pathologies are, at best, uncertain pathways to well-being, what are the alternatives? Is it possible to secure people's well-being without at the same time destroying Earth's climate system? Doing just that is indeed possible. People can improve their well-being and happiness, and promote their genuine interests, while greatly reducing their contributions to GHG pollution and the global injustices that are associated with it. Doing this is possible by moving away from economic growth and toward sufficiency and sustainability (Gough, 2017). But it will require that more people realize the availability of alternative lifestyles that enhance well-being without exacerbating climate change. Governments should reconsider what national economies are for, question contemporary measures of economic success, notably GDP, and proactively take steps that will sustainably promote people's well-being.

If people were to act in ways that promote their genuine long-term interests, we would be well on our way to effective governance of climate change. Doing so will require some rethinking of the power that economic growth has in individual and national development. One reason that growth has become so problematic is the manner in which it is measured. Instead of measuring the human well-being that might arise from growth, or be lost from lack of it, it is measured by too many economists and political leaders in terms of GDP. While there are some merits in GDP, the way that it is interpreted has become perverse given the climate crisis. It fails to account for the profound human suffering from climate change, especially among the world's poor (because their poverty means that their suffering does not add up to very much in economic terms). Even more perversely, GDP often registers environmental harm in counterintuitive ways. Cleaning up pollution costs money, so more pollution and spending on associated cleanup would register as positive GDP growth. Consequently, if growth is what people and countries aspire to, alternative measures of it will be essential. Those alternatives should measure and value human well-being and ecological health, and their interpretation should reward policies and behaviors that promote people's interests within the carrying capacity of the earth.

Questioning the utility of GDP and arguing that alternatives to it are needed is not new. A number of alternatives have been proposed by scholars, NGOs, international organizations and governments. For example, the United Nations Development Program has been producing the Human Development Index (HDI) for several decades. The HDI is intended to measure national development that enhances human well-being, in the process considering environmental sustainability and equity (UNDP, 2011). The most recent UNDP report on the HDI includes refinements that measure and highlight inequalities in societies, recognizing that they can undermine the well-being of people, especially the least well-off (UNDP, 2019). The report specifically spotlights the inequalities and associated human suffering that arise as a consequences of climate change (UNDP, 2019: 181). For example, because climate change increases income inequality, it is both a consequence and cause of the circumstances that induce people to overconsume. Building on the HDI, since 2012 UNEP has been calculating an index of "inclusive wealth" that accounts for the environmental sustainability of countries' economies and the well-being of their citizens (UNEP, 2018).

Similarly, drawing on factors well beyond total economic throughput, the Genuine Progress Indicator (GPI) was devised to measure countries' well-being. It encompasses social and environmental elements, the latter including countries' carbon footprints (Fox and Erickson, 2020). In contrast to the tendency of GDP to interpret pollution (or, more specifically, spending on its cleanup) as adding to economic growth, use of the GPI interprets the cost of cleaning up pollution, and the adverse ecological and social impacts of it, as undermining development. The GPI has had some practical application; it has been used to inform decision making in the governments of some US states, initially Maryland and Vermont (Ceroni, 2014).

Another alternative to GDP, one that is explicitly designed to measure environmentally "sustainable well-being," is the Happy Planet Index (HPI). The HPI measures four elements – well-being, life expectancy, inequality and ecological footprint – "to show how efficiently residents of different countries are using environmental resources to lead long, happy lives" (New Economics Foundation, 2016: 1). The HPI reveals that many of the world's developed countries, including the United States, are doing poorly in promoting sustainable well-being, while some developing countries, notably Costa Rica, are doing well. The GPI and HPI show that aggregate national human well-being and sustainability can be measured and have the potential to inform policy if governments are willing to look beyond GDP growth.

Another possible alternative to GDP, although not officially intended as such, is reference to the Sustainable Development Goals (SDGs). The SDGs were established by the UN General Assembly in 2015 as successors to the Millennium Development Goals (UN, 2015b). The 17 SDGs, which the United Nations optimistically expects the world to achieve by 2030, are officially described as "the blueprint to achieve a better and more sustainable future for all. They address the global challenges we face, including those related to poverty, inequality, climate change, environmental degradation, peace and justice" (UN, n.d.[b]). Among the SDGs are things that need to grow in the future, such as good health, well-being, strong institutions and, vitally, climate action. The SDGs are clearly aspirational; many of them, such as "no poverty," will not be achieved. What is more, it can be argued that they do not give nearly enough weight to climate action – it is clustered among 16 other goals – especially when one considers how climate change will make achieving the other goals much more difficult. Nevertheless, the SDGs have value because they give governments, international organizations and other actors something to aim toward other than a short-sighted preoccupation with traditional economic growth. If the SDGs receive sufficient attention and resources, they may help to root climate action alongside the promotion of human well-being as interconnected governance objectives.

With few exceptions, these and other alternatives to GDP have been used alongside it rather than serving as outright replacements, akin to what one analyst has described as "Quality Adjusted GDP" (Pooran, 2018). However, a handful of countries have decided to move away from GDP as a measure of the success of their economies. The government of Bhutan has taken this unusually far, replacing GDP with the Gross National Happiness (GNH) index. The components of GNH include some traditional factors, such as income, but it focuses heavily on alternative elements, including physical health, psychological well-being, work-life balance, financial security, community vitality and, importantly, ecological diversity and resilience (Centre for Bhutan Studies, 2016). Significantly, the government of Bhutan actually uses GNH to inform policy. While Bhutan is a very rare example of moving away from GDP, it points to the potential for enlightened governments to change course toward more explicit measurement of human interests and environmentally sustainable well-being.

Toward Sufficiency, Simplicity and Sustainability

If governments are to accept alternatives to GDP growth, and especially if they are to use those alternatives when formulating policies, it will be important for them to have public support. That support will be possible if people come to understand that overconsumption, and the behaviors and states of mind that are associated with it, are often harmful to their interests and long-term well-being, and that there are alternatives to overconsumption that are more likely to promote human interests and well-being while drastically reducing global GHG pollution. In particular, individual efforts to reject "the emotional drug of materialism" (Gilding, 2012: 2014) and to move toward lives with less excess and complexity can result in more happiness and health in the long term. Such lives leave more time and resources to devote to friends, families and communities. They require less time spent at work to earn money to support excessive consumption, potentially giving people more freedom to choose less stressful and time-consuming jobs.

Encouraging people to live in ways that are much less harmful to Earth's climate system would not require asking them to act contrary to their interests. Instead, people should be encouraged to act in their own *genuine* interests. Rather than trying to better their lives (while polluting the planet) through overconsumption, people would be better off moving toward lives of *sufficient* consumption. For people whose material needs are already met, moving toward sufficiency would be much less about unnecessary material consumption and much more about consumption of that which is good, such as healthy food, experiences with friends, new knowledge and other things that bring greater well-being and, coincidentally, less GHG pollution. What is needed, then, is contraction and convergence toward sufficiency, whereby those who overconsume transition to consumption that is sufficient to keep themselves well, and those who currently consume too little are given greater opportunities and capabilities to consume enough to ensure their well-being. The result of such a shift would be much greater happiness and well-being globally: over-consumers would be freed from many burdens, thereby making available resources that could enable those who under-consume to have better lives, all while reducing GHG pollution.

Many possible avenues for people to achieve such an outcome have been proposed. For example, as an alternative to consumerism, people could voluntarily try to live simpler lives. There is more to voluntary simplicity, which mirrors the philosophies of Epicurus (Segal, 1999: 180–9) and Henry David Thoreau (Stoller, 1956), than might be apparent conceptually. People who voluntarily choose to avoid unnecessary material consumption have higher levels of subjective well-being (Jackson, 2009: 151). Voluntary simplicity gives people more satisfaction than consumerism because it helps them to focus on the things in life that matter most for well-being, such as relationships and community, and helps them to avoid needless clutter and frenetic busyness in their lives (Elgin, 2010). Another alternative to consumerism is mindful consumption, which aims to replace "acquisitive, repetitive and aspirational consumption" with "a sense of caring about the implications and consequences of one's consumption" (Sheth, Sethia and Srinivas, 2011: 21, 27). Mindful consumption is about explicitly consuming to maximize one's well-being alongside that of one's community and the environment.

It is vital to emphasize that these and similar kinds of lifestyles are most definitely not about sacrifice. To the contrary, they are about people finding ways to flourish and to be happier while making their lives more environmentally sustainable. To aim for sufficiency in one's life, to live more simply, is the best kind of self-interested behavior. By consuming less, overconsumers can become more prosperous, not less (Soper, 2020). Perhaps the reduced consumption that was imposed on people around the world during the coronavirus pandemic may have helped many of them to realize that their interests and happiness need not be yoked to constant consumerism and the work needed to fund it. As Meehan Crist (2020) remarked at the time, "[m]aybe, as you hunker down with cabinets full of essentials, your sense of what consumer goods you need will shrink. . . . Lifestyles that include, for example, frequent long-distance travel already seem ethically questionable in light of the climate crisis and, in an age irrevocably scarred by pandemic, these lifestyles may come to be seen as grossly irresponsible. Maybe among the relatively wealthy, jumping on a plane for a weekend away . . . will come to seem unthinkable."

Governing human nature toward sufficiency and simplicity will require that governments take a greater role in helping people to be cured of consumerism and associated pathologies, such as affluenza. Governments should move away from worshiping economic expansion at all cost and instead declare overconsumption to be something that is both harmful and wrong. This could be done in part by requiring that advertising disclose the environmental and other harmful impacts that come from producing, using and throwing away products. Many governments around the world already outlaw or greatly restrict the advertising of cigarettes and other things because they are harmful to health. Similar restrictions could be placed on the marketing of products that harm health through the pathologies associated with too much consumption and the climate change that results from it. At the very least, every product ought to have a label disclosing the GHG pollution arising from its production, consumption and disposal so that consumers can make informed choices.

This highlights the vital role for education, as noted earlier. From preschools to universities, education should be permeated with lessons on how citizens can best realize healthy and good lives. This will require replacing current lessons that in effect instruct people to consume more in order supposedly to achieve more happiness with lessons on how to consume mindfully and sustainably so as to promote their long-term interests. Historical experience shows that education (whether formal or informal) has the capacity to shift people's thinking and behavior. After all, the very notion of nationality is something that people learn, as is the related sentiment of patriotism. Similarly, religious faith – some of which advocates the kind of simple living described above – is something that is taught. Nationalism and religion stimulate and mold people's primordial inclinations, just as liberal capitalism does through media advertising. Nowadays, people are being coaxed to think and do all sorts of crazy things (such as performing deadly stunts, joining blatantly racist organizations and even committing suicide) as they use social media on their mobile phones. They can also be induced to do things that are not crazy. All of this goes to show that it should be possible to persuade the majority of people to stop harming themselves and the environment, and instead to promote their own well-being and that of the climate system.

Governments and other actors have many other tools at their disposal to encourage people to behave in ways that better promote human interests and those of the environment. For example, infrastructure that makes climate-friendly living easier would diminish opposition to government regulations intended to discourage behaviors that lead to GHG pollution. Governments can also use pricing signals to help people to consume responsibly. An obvious place to start is the elimination of subsidies that encourage pollution. Globally, over $5 trillion is spent annually subsidizing fossil fuels – 6.5 percent of global economic output (Coady et al., 2019: 5) – an incredible indictment of the current state of climate governance. An equal amount could instead be spent subsidizing non-carbon energy and access to it, especially for the world's poor countries, communities and individuals. Alternatively, part of that $5 trillion could be used to subsidize renewable energy, while another part could be transferred to the poor around the world so that they would not suffer from any costs that might rise as the world decarbonizes.

Similarly, carbon fees will need to be phased in without delay, with the associated economic impact on poor and working-class individuals and households avoided, and even made rewarding by, for example, transferring the revenue directly to people's financial accounts. Such transfers to citizens are essential to avoid backlash, as happened when the French government attempted to impose, and then later reversed, an "eco-tax" on diesel fuel in 2018 (Willsher, 2018). Carbon fees have been enacted in a number of countries (e.g., Canada, Chile, Ireland and Sweden), but mostly they have been too low to greatly reduce emissions. In the United States, a "fee-and-dividend" approach to reducing CO_2 emissions has gained some support, including among politicians on both sides of the political spectrum. A bill to implement such a scheme was introduced in the House of Representatives in 2019 (US Congress, 2019). Such initiatives will have to be adopted and implemented widely in the near future.

People's general overconsumption – consuming more than needed – matters enormously because that is what can undermine well-being and send demand signals to industries to run their factories and plants, thereby producing GHG pollution. In addition, as the previous chapter observed, the proliferation of private automobiles and the growth in air travel are insidious forces in the climate crisis that need to be brought under control. Some forms of overconsumption clearly harm the interests of people in the long term while contributing to the climate crisis. An important example is meat consumption, which, as noted previously, is growing globally and thereby adding substantially to GHG pollution. Levels of meat consumption, especially in the Global North, will have to fall to reduce GHG emissions and to improve health. Indeed, by reducing (or ending) the consumption of meat, people who already eat substantial amounts of it would greatly reduce their contributions to GHG pollution, especially if they were to focus on not eating ruminants, and in so doing they would increase their long-term health, especially if they were to minimize eating red and processed meats (Godfray *et al.*, 2018; Harvard Medical School, 2020).

To demonstrate the full potential of cutting meat from diets, one analysis determined that adoption of vegetarian diets throughout the United Kingdom would reduce the countries' GHG emissions by 22 percent, while vegan diets would cut it by 26 percent (Berners-Lee *et al.*, 2012). If, in addition to holding back on meat consumption, everyone in the United Kingdom (to continue with this example) that does not need a car were to choose not to buy one, and everyone were to recognize that flying on holidays (and for most other purposes) is unnecessary and refrain from doing it, and otherwise they were to strive to consume more of what they need and little of what they do not need, the fall in emissions – just from changes in individuals' behaviors – would be very substantial indeed.

There is justifiable skepticism regarding whether people will be willing to make such changes. Many of the people who understand and accept the science of climate change, and even many of those who worry about the climate crisis, continue to behave in ways that make the problem worse. They are implicitly or explicitly waiting for governments and corporations to do all of the legwork to reduce pollution. To quote Lisa Pryor (2020), we "need to ask ourselves hard questions as individuals and communities. The question I have been asking myself is, what does it matter that I accept the science of climate change if I continue to live my life as if climate change were a hoax? Who cares how many people accept the data if we are still consuming, traveling, investing, eating, dressing, voting and planning for the future as if global warming were imaginary?"

However, while skepticism is certainly warranted, there ought to be no doubt that people are definitely *capable* of consuming and living differently. After all, they have demonstrated time and again that they can restrain their inclination to consume if called on to do so, whether that be by taking doctors' advice to avoid unhealthy foods, following religious traditions to fast during certain periods or refrain from sexual activity, or to take a recent and extreme example, staying at home and going without many of the nonessential trappings of modern life during the global coronavirus pandemic. Often people hold back on consuming things because they believe that doing so will promote their interests and the interests of their loved ones and their communities, or because they believe that by doing so they will find greater happiness. The very same can and should be said of refraining from doing unnecessary things that cause and exacerbate the climate crisis.

Synopsis of Diagnostic and Therapeutic Considerations

The diagnostic and therapeutic considerations related to international, national and human governance outlined in this chapter imply certain prescriptions for the pathologies of climate governance that were described in Chapters 3–7. Those prescriptions, or rather some of them that might be administered, are the subject of the next chapter. Many considerations will have to be brought to bear if the right prescriptions for the pathologies of climate governance are to be identified and put into practice. Alleviating the pathologies of international relations will require, among other things, shifting states' perceptions of their national interests much more in the direction of protecting and promoting human security. International climate governance will benefit greatly from explicit recognition by states (and other actors) that human interests should be prioritized and that they are, in the context of climate change at least, borderless. National climate governance will be more effective once it is recognized that both states and individuals have responsibility for climate change, and that common but differentiated responsibility applies (bearing in mind respective capabilities) to individuals regardless of where they live. National policies related to climate change should seek to harmonize the interests of people in different countries and to foster climate citizenship. More effective governance of the human dimensions of climate change requires understanding that too much consumption can undermine well-being, and that ensuring well-being without exacerbating the climate crisis requires

Table 8.1 *Climate governance: dominant pathologies and diagnostic considerations*

Dominant groups of pathologies	Selected diagnostic and therapeutic considerations
Pathologies of international relations (Chapter 3)	Human security is central to the national interests of states Global ethics and justice point to the borderless nature of human interests International climate governance should prioritize human interests
Pathologies of national politics (Chapters 4–6)	Both states and individuals are responsible for climate change Common but differentiated responsibilities (and respective capabilities) apply to individuals regardless of their nationality National climate politics should be aimed at harmonizing interests and fostering climate citizenship
Pathologies of human nature (Chapter 7)	The relationship between consumption and human well-being is not direct; too much of the former undermines the latter Securing human well-being requires moving away from growth and toward sufficiency Individual efforts to realize simplicity and sustainability can enhance well-being and give rise to lives that are more fulfilling

moving away from economic growth toward sufficiency. Individual lives that are more fulfilling can be fostered, as can collective well-being, if both governments and people do their best to realize environmental sustainability.

It is important to emphasize that any serious reconsideration of climate governance needs to be done holistically. In the real world, there is seldom an actual separation among international, national and human governance of climate change. Each affects the others, often in complex ways. The therapies and specific prescriptions for the pathologies of climate governance ought to be devised with this in mind. Table 8.1 highlights some of the diagnostic considerations that should be involved. The next chapter draws on these considerations to identify a number of potential prescriptions for making climate governance more effective.

9

Prescriptions for Governing Climate Change

This chapter identifies a number of prescriptions for climate governance that could, alongside other actions being taken worldwide, mitigate the climate crisis (cf. Harris, 2013: 197–223). Success in this regard would entail dramatic and quite rapid declines in GHG pollution globally and successful adaptation to the impacts arising from past pollution. These outcomes would engender greater protection of human interests and substantial reductions in the many injustices arising from climate change, all while enhancing environmental sustainability in the long term. The prescriptions outlined here are intended to address corresponding governance pathologies described in Chapters 3–7. They illustrate the kinds of steps that will be required to make climate governance much more effective. Before they could be applied in practice, much more explication would be required. They will have practical significance for the climate crisis only if they are taken seriously.

By definition, the prescriptions may be difficult to realize; if they were easy to implement, that would have been done already. It can be assumed that most and perhaps all of the prescriptions will face opposition of one kind or another. At the very least, vested interests, particularly those that benefit from the world's continued appetite for fossil fuels and material overconsumption, will do what they can to push back against these prescriptions and similar approaches. Just as significantly, if not more so, customary ways of living and doing things are almost always difficult to change. Governments and people normally do not like change, especially if they perceive the status quo to be to their advantage, or if the idea of change evokes worries that things might become worse than they are at present. What is more, even when the experts agree that change is needed, they may disagree on the best courses of action. All of this, on top of the considerations outlined in previous chapters, increases the difficulty of addressing the pathologies of climate governance promptly and effectively.

However, none of these obstacles gives reason not to attempt more effective governance of climate change. Not to try is to accept the inevitability of the climate crisis and to believe that there is little that can be done to avert the catastrophes that await those individuals and communities that are most vulnerable to the impacts of climate change. An assumption here is that it is not acceptable to continue down the path that has led the world into the climate crisis. From the realm of international relations to the ministries of national governments and on to people's homes around the world, as many capable actors as possible need to do what they can to help mitigate the pollution that is causing climate change, to at least cope with the climatic impacts to come, and ideally to prosper amidst it all (the latter objectives considered briefly in the next chapter).

From Pathologies to Prescriptions

Parts I and II described the worsening climate crisis and detailed some of the major governance-related pathologies behind it. Understanding the crisis and its causes is important, and indeed that understanding is the primary objective of this book. But many readers will want more; they will want to know what can be done to address the climate crisis. Part III (including this chapter) is aimed at satisfying that desire for solutions, at least a little bit. However, while this is the point in the book where increasingly specific solutions to the pathologies of climate governance are proposed, it is also the point where there may be the most disappointment. It is assumed here that there are indeed solutions to be had, and it is believed that the following prescriptions should be among them. But it is also assumed that none of these prescriptions can have the intended effect if they are not implemented robustly. If the response is something like "governments will never do that" when a prescription indicates that governments should do something new, or "people will never do that" when a prescription calls on people to alter their behaviors, then we are right back where we started. In other words, there needs to be some faith that governments and other capable actors, individuals included, will have the good sense to do what is required.

If actors will not do what is necessary to alleviate the pathologies of climate governance – given the history of climate governance so far, the cynic is certainly forgiven for questioning whether they will do so – then it is still possible to understand what is happening and to bear witness to it. Put another way, even if little practical good results, it is not wasted effort to identify the serious pathologies of climate governance and, in turn, to identify prescriptions for alleviating them. That is because undertaking this task at least prompts us to think more clearly about the climate *problematique*. It is, after all, human nature to want to understand our predicaments. The process of diagnosing climate governance and identifying prescriptions for it also sends an important message to present and future generations. For the present, it reminds the actors able to make the necessary changes that they cannot claim ignorance of the problem, including its causes and consequences. Neither can they claim ignorance of the many alternatives to the status quo and to business as usual. To be sure, excuses can and will be made for slow action or lack of it, but denial is no longer a credible option. Future generations can look back at the prescriptions for climate governance, alongside the many other proposals from experts, activists and politicians for climate action, and understand that we, in the present, were fully aware of the climate crisis and how best to navigate our way out of it. It is cold comfort to contemplate that one's role may ultimately be more about bearing witness to the climate crisis than to alleviating it. But consciously bearing witness is in an important act of humanity (and better than doing nothing).

Before laying out a selection of prescriptions for climate governance, it is useful to acknowledge some realistic limitations. As suggested in Chapter 1, the relationship between prescriptions and associated outcomes is akin to what happens when physicians prescribe therapies for sick patients. Some patients are extraordinarily ill, with multiple chronic ailments arising from lifetimes of unhealthy behavior, often complicated by genetic predispositions. It is often easier to identify what is wrong with a particular patient than it is to select the most effective therapies. So, too, with climate governance. Furthermore, alleviating sick people's pathologies can happen only if patients accept their physicians' diagnoses and are committed to implementing the prescribed therapies. It is likely that even the best medicines will cure only some of the sickest patients' ailments. Climate governance is similar to such patients – multiple pathologies, some exacerbated by predispositions (e.g., assumptions related to the national interest and growth) – so it requires at least as much acceptance and commitment. In other words, the diagnoses and prescriptions are meaningless if the patients do not act accordingly, and, even then, we cannot expect miracles. Much as some patients ignore their physicians' advice, or at least do not follow it precisely enough, the history of climate governance suggests that at least some governments and many other actors will be reticent (at best) about acting on advice intended to alleviate the pathologies of that governance. Much as many patients do, they will insist on continuing with their individually and communally destructive behavior.

The prescriptions proposed here are largely based on the diagnostic and therapeutic considerations described in the previous chapter (and summarized in Table 8.1). While the prescriptions are organized in the same way as the pathologies – international, national and human – it must be acknowledged again that this separation is largely artificial; it is a means of focusing analysis and thus prescription, not an exact replica of the infinitely complex actualities of climate change and climate governance. In the real world, the causes of the climate crises are crosscutting and interrelated, and so too are the associated pathologies of climate governance (see Figure 1.1). Consequently, the prescriptions will invariably apply to all groups of pathologies to varying degrees.

It is believed that these prescriptions are important and ought to be applied, but they are hardly exhaustive. There is no shortage of ideas for how to make climate governance more effective. Some of them were mentioned in the preceding chapters. Already, many of those ideas are being implemented around the world by national and municipal governments, by corporations and NGOs, by families and individuals. The prescriptions proposed here cannot be applied independently of existing and planned efforts by governments and other actors. They are intended to supplement all of that activity and most definitely not to substitute for it. Furthermore, no prescription is powerful enough on its own to alleviate adequately the collective pathologies of climate governance. What is needed for every pathology is the application of a cocktail of therapies. The same perhaps ought to be said about all proposals for addressing climate change and related governance more effectively: they are rightly viewed as being complementary parts of a much larger global undertaking.

Ultimately, climate change cannot be avoided; it is happening already, and further global warming is baked into the climate system, as is ocean acidification (among other horrors), due to past and ongoing GHG pollution. Therefore, if climate governance is about preventing significant climate change, it has failed utterly. Humanity has already created the most complicated and extraordinary mess in all of its history. Much that has been said in the preceding chapters has been aimed at explaining that mess. Yet, despite all that has happened, it may not be too late to mitigate significantly future climate change – to make it less dangerous than it might be and to reduce the hardship, including the dying, that will result from it. That is what implementing the following (and related) prescriptions, and the policies that logically follow from them (see Chapter 10), can do.

Prescriptions for International Relations

Alleviating the pathologies of international relations described in Chapter 3 will require a number of prescriptions. This section proposes five of them as a way to illustrate what could be done to overcome the pathologies and thereby bring about more effective climate governance at the international level. As noted in the previous chapter, the aims of these prescriptions, among other things, are to bring human security and national interests closer together, to recognize the borderless nature of human interests and to prioritize those interests in international climate governance. Again, it is essential to emphasize that these prescriptions are just some of the steps that will be needed. They should be applied alongside the many other steps toward more effective international climate governance that have been proposed by others. The same applies to prescriptions for national politics and human nature identified below.

1. In the international climate negotiations, including annual COPs, and in resulting agreements (conventions, protocols, etc.), treat human security as if it is the most important interest of states individually and, thus, collectively.

The lack of effective climate governance at the international level is largely attributable to the nature of the international system in which it occurs. Insofar as possible, prescriptions for climate governance ought to face the flaws in that system head on. One appropriate approach might be to search for ways to eliminate or replace the international system, which (as noted in Chapter 3) has been in existence for centuries, with something much more capable of mustering collective action on climate change. Even if such an approach would be the best one in the long term (and there is reason to believe that it might be), it is – to put it bluntly – not going to happen, certainly not in the time that is available to bring about much more effective global governance of climate change and thereby mitigate extremely dangerous impacts. The extant international system in which climate governance occurs seems to be more or less inviolable for the foreseeable future. This means that we can expect states to continue to act in their quite narrow self-interests. (The 2020 global coronavirus pandemic reinforces this notion. The pandemic cried out for a coordinated international response. Instead, many countries reverted to nationalist and at times xenophobic behavior, even to the point where some governments ordered embargoes on exports of foodstuffs and others blocked the sharing of vital supplies, such as protective medical equipment, needed to save lives in other countries.)

If at all possible, this tendency of states to act selfishly, at least in the context of effective collective action to address climate change, has to be converted into an asset. One way to do that is to push states (and their diplomats) to behave as they would claim that they do already – to promote the vital interests of their citizens. By accepting that protecting and promoting human security is the most important interest of the state, it follows that, at least in the context of climate change, doing so is also a collective interest of the international community. By promoting the common interest to address climate change more effectively, states promote human security and thus their national interests. Deliberations should return to this reality as often as possible, and future climate agreements ought to reflect it prominently in their stated objectives and in the processes through which they are realized.

2. In the international climate negotiations, including annual COPs, and in resulting agreements (conventions, protocols, etc.), recognize that human and thus national interests related to climate change are borderless, and act accordingly.

If states, as well as the diplomats involved in international negotiations, are to conclude that it is in their common interest to address climate change more effectively, it is necessary for them to recognize that vital human interests (and indeed less-vital ones) are, in this context, borderless. As noted in previous chapters, human interests are borderless because neither the causes nor the consequences of climate change are restricted to particular national territories. Human security and other interests, and thus national security and other interests, are threatened by what happens all around the world. Neither states nor individuals can isolate themselves from global climate change. This is most obviously the case for the world's poor countries and people, but, as noted previously, even affluent countries and affluent people are not immune. (One need only be reminded of recent events, such as deadly and destructive wildfires in Australia, the United States and other developed countries that occurred during 2019–2020.)

To make this prescription is hardly to say anything that nearly all of the diplomats involved in climate negotiations do not know already. They recognize, at least intellectually, that climate change is a global problem requiring collective responses. That is why they gather together in COPs, for example. But too often they act as if some countries can safely free ride on the action – or lack of it – of others to address climate change, or that they need not cooperate fully because their own countries and citizens can escape the consequences of climate change. To be sure, if national interests continue to be defined in narrow terms, often focusing on the short-term interests of influential actors within powerful countries, there is some truth for some countries to this logic. However, if national interests are defined in terms of human interests, even if interpreted narrowly to fellow citizens, then collective and national interests overlap because human interests are borderless in the context of climate change. Climate negotiations and the agreements that result should reflect this. Doing so will best promote genuine national *and* human interests.

3. In the international climate negotiations, including annual COPs, and in resulting agreements (conventions, protocols, etc.), prioritize long-term human security and rights.

It follows from the first two prescriptions that certain outcomes are required from climate governance at the international level. It is not enough to proclaim the vital importance of promoting human security and other interests, including human rights. It is also necessary to reach agreements that, when implemented, actually promote human security, rights and other interests. One criticism of this approach might be that it does not prioritize environmental protection, which should be the objective of climate governance. That would be a misinterpretation. One assumption is that to prioritize the long-term interests of people will require the elimination of resource depletion, habitat destruction and environmental pollution, which are not sustainable in the long-term. That is, instead of trying to protect the environment for its own sake, the aim is to protect people by protecting the environment upon which they rely. The latter motivation is different – it is consciously biased in favor of people instead of the environment per se – but the result is likely to be more or less the same.

This approach has the value of capitalizing on the presumed selfishness of governments to prioritize their citizens over the environment. To protect citizens effectively during the climate crisis requires international cooperation to reduce GHG pollution rapidly and to put in place policies that address the needs of those affected around the world. The latter is required because climate-induced hardships in the Global South will increasingly threaten the Global North in many ways. (For example, as noted in the previous chapter, those who are severely impacted by climate change will move in great numbers, many of them crossing borders, including from developing countries to developed ones.) Implementing this prescription means that it is no longer appropriate to muddle along in climate negotiations, agreeing to individualized lowest common denominators (i.e., the Paris Agreement's NDCs) that are often predicated on protecting domestic economic interests. Instead, it means agreements and associated policies that decarbonize the global economy as quickly as possible, along the way caring for those affected by the transition and the impacts of climate change that cannot be avoided.

4. In the international climate negotiations, including annual COPs, and in resulting agreements (conventions, protocols, etc.), expand the CBDR principle to encompass capable individuals regardless of where they live.

Currently, international climate agreements attribute the responsibility for climate change to states in accordance with the longstanding CBDR principle, and accordingly the associated burdens of addressing climate change are also attributed to states. In attempting to promote their perceived national interests (and not yet following the prescriptions above), this has discouraged the states that are more responsible for climate change from doing as much as they should to govern the problem effectively. This has in turn discouraged the less responsible states from doing as much as they could to govern climate change effectively. One way to escape this trap is to expand the CBDR principle to encompass capable individuals, of course including those who live in the countries of the Global North (who are already indirectly encompassed by the principle simply because they live there), but also including those who live in the countries of the South (who are not currently encompassed by the principle, even if they are very wealthy, by virtue of where they live). Genuinely to encompass individuals within CBDR when it is considered and applied in international climate negotiations would require that resulting agreements explicitly take into account what individuals should and must do as part of global efforts to address climate change.

This approach has the potential to be very influential politically because it would mean that affluent people in developing countries would be required, alongside most people in developed countries, to change their behaviors to reduce GHG pollution and contribute to schemes designed to aid those countries and people most affected by climate change and that are in need of help. The result of the latter might be, in effect, transfers of wealth from the rich people of the South to the poor people of the North as a trade-off for more (long-overdue) transfers of wealth from the most affluent Northern countries to the poorest Southern ones. In other words, by folding individuals into the CBDR principle, new opportunities for global cooperation arise and look much more politically acceptable, even desirable, to more people and thus more governments (and their diplomats).

5. In the international climate negotiations, including annual COPs, give people, particularly those most threatened by climate change, direct access to, and genuine influence in, diplomatic deliberations and decision making.

The prescriptions above require that states and the officials that negotiate new international climate agreements and the further implementation of existing agreements prioritize human security and other interests. Doing that will require seeing national interests a bit differently – viewing them as actually being congruent with human interests – and also devoting disproportionate negotiating time toward that endeavor. The objective of international climate governance according to such prescriptions becomes protecting and promoting people's interests. The associated agreements therefore need to encourage the formulation of policies that are necessary for doing that, and they need to promote the implementation of those policies. But it is not enough to simply deputize state diplomats to negotiate on behalf of people. Decades of climate governance suggest very strongly that they will need help in fully understanding and effectively promoting people's interests. Consequently, it is necessary to allow people to be much more meaningfully involved in future climate negotiations. They ought to have full access to the negotiations, including what were closed-door deliberations, whether in person or via modern communications technologies (e.g., videoconferencing). Extra effort should be put into bringing more women (particularly from poor countries) into the process because they tend to be more concerned about climate change and bear more of the burdens of it than do most men (Richler, 2019).

Not everyone can participate in negotiations, but individuals who represent different groups of people around the world could be democratically chosen to do so. While the mechanisms for doing this would need to be developed, a starting point could be to give a representative sample of the NGOs that meet in COP side events, which are now standardly conducted nearby the annual conferences, greater access to the actual negotiations (while accounting for the fact that not all NGOs represent people's interests and that some, such as those that in fact represent many industries, actively oppose them). Very importantly, the people newly given access to negotiations must have genuine influence; they must be both heard and allowed to have a role in shaping negotiating outcomes.

Prescriptions for National Politics

This section proposes five prescriptions for alleviating the pathologies of national politics that were described in Chapters 4–6. These prescriptions are intended to illustrate the types of policies and actions that can overcome those pathologies and make national climate governance more effective. As described in Chapter 8, therapies for the pathologies of national politics ought to focus on, among other things, shared responsibility of states and individuals, recognition that the CBDR principle applies to individuals (as well as to state governments) regardless of nationality, and the promotion of climate citizenship.

1. Accept the sharing of responsibility for climate change between the state and its citizens.

Responsibility for climate change has been attributed to states despite the reality that it is other actors that are the proximate causes of the problem. While the state of, say, the United Kingdom certainly shares substantial responsibility for climate change due to government policies since the advent of the Industrial Revolution, it is also the case that most people who live in the United Kingdom have responsibility. Similarly, while the state of, say, Costa Rica, shares little responsibility for climate change compared to developed states, the affluent people who live there certainly have disproportionate responsibility. A primary driver of climate change is in fact the behavior of individuals, disproportionately the affluent ones, and specifically their choices about which things, and how much of them, to consume, which forms of transportation to use and which politicians and corporations to support through their voting and spending.

It is now past time for state governments (and other actors) to accept that responsibility for causing climate change ought to be shared among multiple actors, and particularly between the state and its citizens. Accepting the sharing of responsibility in this way has many advantages, as noted in previous chapters, not least exposing the large contribution to climate change made by people who live in states that have contributed relatively little to it. Doing this lifts some responsibility from the shoulders of national leaders who may feel overly burdened by what happened in the past. It redistributes responsibility to non-state actors whose behaviors substantially determine the future course of the climate crisis. This implies new kinds of agreements that states could reach at the international level and new policies that they could formulate and implement domestically. Such agreements and policies would require all affluent people around the world to share the burden of addressing climate change more effectively.

2. Apply the CBDR principle to individuals regardless of their citizenship, with due regard to respective capabilities.

Once it is accepted that affluent and capable individuals share responsibility for climate change alongside states, it is necessary to apply that conception in the form of real-world action. Government policies for doing this should aim to enable, encourage and, if necessary, require individuals to act in accordance with their relative responsibilities related to climate change. For example, policies and regulations might be developed that limit the allowable GHG emissions of individuals, thereby preventing anyone from exceeding sustainable limits. These schemes could come in the form of mandates or they might entail market mechanisms (e.g., personal emissions trading), assuming they have provisions to ensure that all citizens are able to easily meet their needs (e.g., personal emissions trading should not allow the wealthy to buy up essential emissions allowances of the poor). Such policies should be implemented in all countries, meaning that there would be a large majority of the population in, say, Canada, that would face limits on their personal emissions, but also meaning that there would be a substantial minority of the population in, say, Colombia, that would face similar limits.

These limits would in no way derive from the respective responsibilities for climate change of the state per se; those state obligations would remain unchanged. Individual responsibilities would be ascertained by considering both individuals' climate-harming behaviors and their circumstances – their capabilities and options for behaving differently. In some circumstances, individuals may have no choice but to live in ways that produce more GHG pollution than is produced by people living in different environments. For example, even affluent people living at high latitudes may have no choice but to use fossil-fuel energy for heating until alternatives become available. Correspondingly, policies regarding individual responsibility should not in any way prevent those individuals with few capabilities, most obviously the poor, from meeting their needs.

3. Harmonize the interests of states and individuals by replacing traditional economic growth with growth in citizens' long-term well-being.

As a national priority, state governments should find better ways to harmonize national economic interests with growth in the actual well-being of citizens over the long term. Gross domestic product should be downgraded (or abandoned) as a measure of success (or failure) of governance. Alternative measures should attempt to capture more than economic activity; they ought to enable assessment of changes in citizens' actual well-being and in environmental sustainability, specifically to address the climate crisis. Furthermore, economic growth should be abandoned as an assumed positive objective of governments. It should be recognized and accepted that economic and material growth does not necessarily translate into growth in human well-being, and indeed that such growth can translate into diminishment thereof, particularly in already highly developed economies. This is especially the case given the consequences for Earth's climate system. However, growth per se need not be abandoned if what is sought is growth in well-being and environmental sustainability. Policies that promote growth in the economic well-being of the poor are desirable, especially so when they are implemented sustainably. Equally desirable are policies that promote growth in health, happiness and satisfaction with life, along with growth in measures of environmental vitality, such as reductions in GHG emissions and preservation of biodiversity.

At the same time, economic *degrowth* and declines in material throughput should be policy objectives in many countries. For example, in economically developed societies with declining populations, there is no need for further expansion of the economy, unless perhaps it is to increase resources for sharing with other societies that are not yet developed enough to meet people's needs. In developed countries, most obviously those where people already consume much more than they need, further growth in consumption should be viewed as perverse given the climate crisis and its roots in overconsumption, not to mention the impacts that climate change has and will have in the future on many of the world's least well-off people.

4. Formulate and implement policies that foster climate citizenship and make it easy for people to be good climate citizens.

As noted in the previous chapter, climate citizenship involves reducing unnecessary consumption and otherwise living in ways that do not exacerbate the climate crisis, insofar as possible. Good climate citizens do this while also being good national and global citizens. Governments have the responsibility to formulate and implement policies that make it possible for citizens to do this. Policies should also make it relatively *easy* for people to be good climate citizens. It is also necessary, given the gravity of the climate crisis and the failure of governments to take more action sooner to reduce global GHG pollution, to formulate and implement policies that discourage people from being bad climate citizens. In addition to education policies and programs that make citizens more literate in the importance of acting as good climate citizens (see the next section), policies are needed to enable and encourage people to act on that awareness and to push people who lack the awareness to do so as well.

The most obvious approaches would include increasing the cost of climate-harming activities and products in the short term and perhaps medium term, followed by regulating (and potentially outlawing) such activities henceforth. Associated programs would be needed to compensate the poor and probably the middle class for the added costs of doing so. Good climate citizenship might be rewarded with financial payments, possibly funded by ending fossil-fuel subsidies or by distributing the proceeds of personal emissions trading schemes. Importantly, policies that empower people to live as good climate citizens are essential. Examples of such policies include convenient and inexpensive (or free-to-rider) public transport systems, public services that enable emissions-free leisure and recreational activities, and food and product-quality regulations to ensure that foods and other things on the market have the lowest possible embodied GHG emissions. A fundamental objective of all such policies must be the environmentally sustainable promotion of citizens' genuine long-term interests.

5. Treat fossil fuels as threats to the long-term national interest and the interests of citizens.

Implicit in these prescriptions – but this notion will have to become explicit in policy – is that fossil fuels are, due to the climate crisis, threats to the long-term interests of people and thus to national interests. In addition to being the largest sources of GHG pollution, fossil fuels create other threats. According to one assessment, use of fossil fuels leads to 4 million premature deaths around the world each year (Taylor, 2020). As noted previously, the threats to people from climate change apply in both the Global North and the South. There is every reason to believe that making the transition away from dangerous fossil fuels will bring benefits for both citizens and states, including cleaner air almost immediately (the global coronavirus pandemic demonstrated how air quality improves dramatically when fossil-fuel burning declines [McGrath, 2020]), reduced healthcare costs and the elimination of the perceived need for some countries to prepare for (and to fight) wars to protect access to oil, not to mention the long-term benefits of mitigated climate change.

As good citizens concerned about the future of their compatriots and their homelands, even citizens of countries whose economies are now heavily reliant on fossil fuels have interests in seeing that global decarbonization occurs sooner rather than later. Some of them might even benefit greatly in the medium term (e.g., Australia might be better off using solar energy to power its economy and produce alternative fuels for export rather than to rely on export earnings from coal, and Saudi Arabia would do well to become a regional exporter of solar energy instead of an exporter of petroleum). Policies that arise from this prescription would aim to eliminate fossil fuels from each country's national energy mix as soon as possible. This will require adjusting government spending and regulation to discourage the use of fossil fuels and to encourage the development and use of alternatives to them, alongside very aggressive, long-term demand management. As with the other prescriptions, long-term thinking suggests that national and human interests are best protected and promoted by implementing this one.

Prescriptions for Human Nature

This section outlines five prescriptions for addressing the pathologies of human nature that were described in Chapter 7. The objective of making these proposals is to suggest the types of approaches that will be necessary to alleviate those pathologies and thereby improve the effectiveness of climate governance. Chapter 8 pointed to several considerations (among others) that need to be emphasized if the pathologies of human nature are to be alleviated. First, the assumption that more consumption can bring happiness needs to be overcome. Second, promoting people's well-being will require moving away from the objective of perpetual growth toward the objective of sufficiency. Third, efforts to realize simplicity and sustainability can increase people's well-being as the world moves toward decarbonization, elimination of unnecessary GHG pollution and adaptation to climate change.

1. End the fixation on material consumption and wealth as supposed sources of well-being, and treat overconsumption as a disease.

There is some truth to the widely held assumption that material consumption and wealth can, up to a point, benefit well-being. Having said that, it must be acknowledged that this effect is not universal, that the relationship between highly consumptive lifestyles and well-being can be the opposite of what is assumed – unnecessary consumption can, in fact, diminish many people's well-being – and that overconsumption comes at great cost in the form of climate change and all of the negative impacts thereof. The people who ought to be consuming more and achieving greater wealth are the world's poor. But for those whose needs are already met, wanting more, working harder and longer for more, and consuming much more than necessary can quickly become self-destructive to one's mental health and financial security, with adverse side effects for families, communities and the environment. In short, overconsumption is a human disease that contributes to GHG emissions and exacerbates the climate crisis. If overconsumption and excessive wealth did not have adverse effects – if they consistently contributed positively to human interests – they might be understandable and justifiable in narrow human terms. However, when they undermine human well-being *and* environmental well-being, they make much less sense. Given the climate crisis, one might say that they are perverse.

To be sure, many people, perhaps most, do not *perceive* consumption and wealth in this way. The assumption, reinforced by observing the behavior of others, listening to government pronouncements, watching television, imbibing social media and being subject to ubiquitous advertising, is that to consume things is good for people. For many millions of affluent people around the world, life very largely revolves around putting such a perception into practice: getting an education to get a well-paying job to acquire progressively more things over time, often falling into debt along the way because the things that one desires are beyond one's reach in the short term. As noted in Chapters 7 and 8, these sentiments are pathological. The key prescription therefore involves recognizing this and then looking for, and experiencing, alternative lifestyles that bring well-being to more people while lowering global GHG pollution.

2. Replace material growth with sufficiency to maximize the sustainable well-being of society.

Maximizing the environmentally sustainable well-being of the most people – that is, doing so while alleviating the climate crisis – is not possible if too many people continue to assume that the world will be better off with perpetual material growth. Alongside changes in the ways that governments view growth, people will have to make changes as well. Instead of looking for happiness in more things, it is important for the world's relatively affluent people to ask whether it is time to conclude that enough is enough, to consider whether having more than enough to meet everyone's needs and make life enjoyable might be not only be a major contributor to the climate crisis but also self-destructive and thus quite foolish. It is also important for everyone who already has enough, based on an objective and dispassionate assessment, to ask how they might live differently, to ask whether there is an alternative way of living that can ensure happiness without contributing to the destruction of Earth's climate system.

As suggested in Chapter 8, such a way of living does indeed exist. It is a lifestyle that is premised, in one version or another, on the notion of sufficiency. Sufficiency is about acquiring the things and the wealth that are needed to meet one's needs and those of one's family, to have all of the necessities of life (which will vary from one place to another depending on geography, social welfare programs and so forth), even to have a feeling of security in life (which for most people would mean savings in a bank), but then to stop – to accept that one has enough, and then to enjoy what one has, rather than always striving for more. For many affluent people around the world, the coronavirus pandemic of 2020 was an opportunity to realize that it is possible to live happily with fewer material things (although millions of people, including many who were already living beyond their means, suffered economic insecurities that the pandemic engendered). Recognizing that it is possible to replace always wanting more – to replace growth in everything – with sufficiency would set the stage for lives that no longer exacerbate the climate crisis and instead create a foundation for effective individual and collective self-governance of climate change.

3. Strive as individuals, families and communities to live happier and healthier lives through simplicity and sustainability.

People who overconsume and live associated lifestyles do so not to become overburdened with possessions and debt. They do it because they are trying to do what they have been told by media, corporations and even governments is good for them, their families and their communities. There are few messages imploring people to accept, let alone embrace, sufficiency, especially not in places where having more is viewed as a principal measure of success in life. However, if people's genuine well-being is to be promoted, there is an alternative narrative that needs to get a foothold in societies and to be acted upon: that greater happiness and health can be found in simpler lives that result in much less GHG pollution and indeed less suffering of the people who are and will be most impacted by climate change.

For many people, particularly the affluent of the world, voluntarily striving for simplicity presents opportunities to contribute to alleviating the climate crisis while enhancing their well-being. Simple living means garnering satisfaction, even joy, from slowing down, consuming less, avoiding debt and building a nest egg for hard times or, just as important, peace of mind. It means finding satisfaction in making things last longer instead of in buying and soon replacing fast fashion and the latest smartphones or even (in much of the Global North, especially) the latest-model cars. It means devoting more time to simple pleasures – literature, conversation, birdsong and the like – and less to the aspects of modern lifestyles that can be so infuriating – sitting in traffic, working long hours in demoralizing jobs and doing all of the things necessary to keep up with the Joneses. Living simply often means doing more for others than for oneself and being much happier as a consequence. Living sustainably means avoiding those things and behaviors that pollute the environment and contribute unnecessarily to the climate crisis, especially when those things and behaviors do oneself little or no good, and quite possibly do oneself more than a little harm.

4. Educate for the maximization of human well-being through informed, self-interested behavior and climate citizenship.

Fundamental to these prescriptions for human nature is awareness and appreciation of what comprises the human interest and where happiness and well-being can be found. They require knowledge and understanding of the relationship between living in ways that lead to self-harm and contribute to the climate crisis and, conversely, the positive relationships between promoting one's genuine interests and contributing to resolution of that crisis. Education is needed to establish these varieties of knowledge and appreciation, and to help them develop and flourish so that people have the comprehension and willingness to exercise good climate citizenship. It is through education that more people can come to realize where their real interests actually lie. People need to know that to promote their actual interests is not to live as too many people have done in the past and continue to do in the present. It is instead to live much more as if the future matters. But being a good climate citizen is not to be altruistic (although altruism and civic-mindedness should be promoted in educational programs, too). It is instead to be self-interested in a way that simultaneously protects and promotes one's actual interests while doing the same for others, all while minimizing the human impact on the environment, including the climate system.

As noted above, governments have a very big role to play in this undertaking, particularly through education policies and programs. It is vital to educate children now and in the future. (One must acknowledge that many children already appreciate the importance of being good climate citizens more than most adults do.) It is also crucial that adults – those who are less frequently in formal education and may never be again – learn about the value and importance of climate citizenship. This is going to require some willingness on their part to be curious and concerned about the world, to heed widely available information about the climate crisis and to proactively learn how to respond to it as individuals and in families and communities. But this may take us only so far. Consequently, much of the burden may be on children to educate their parents, local government officials to educate their neighbors and community organizations to educate their members. An important message of education for climate citizenship should be that the way that many people have been living is not actually about them being self-interested but instead about them doing self-harm. To be self-interested is to be a good climate citizen, and vice-versa.

5. Individually and collectively, act politically to foster more effective climate governance.

To be a good climate citizen means to behave in ways that are good for the climate and for one's fellow citizens (which, depending on one's sense of citizenship, can extend well beyond the borders of one's country). Certainly, it involves avoiding overconsumption and other unnecessary behaviors that add GHG pollution to the environment. But it also involves other kinds of behavior, both as individuals and as groups, that aim to alter the trajectory of society so that the climate crisis is mitigated and those who need help in coping with it get that help. Thus, being a good climate citizen also means being political. Naturally, this should come in the form of the activities we would normally associate with citizen politics: voting for candidates, and reelecting politicians, who understand climate change and want to implement more effective policies for governing it (and not voting for those who want to do the opposite) and supporting (perhaps by canvassing or donating money to) political parties that advocate and have reputations for supporting more effective climate governance. It might involve running for political office oneself, whether locally or nationally, to advocate for initiatives that address the climate crisis and otherwise encourage environmental sustainability.

Being a good climate citizen might also involve joining and supporting NGOs that lobby publics to support, and governments to implement, more effective policies for climate governance. It could include writing letters to newspapers, creating Internet blogs or using online social media to persuade fellow citizens, corporations and policymakers to take climate change more seriously. It might involve going on strike, whether from work or school, to declare (as Greta Thunberg and many other young people have done) that one can no longer tolerate the world's achingly slow response to climate change. It might involve becoming an activist, perhaps to the point of civil disobedience, so as to send a message to those in power that the status quo is no longer acceptable. It would ideally involve being and acting in solidarity with, and aiding if possible, those people who are most adversely affected by climate change around the world – that is, it would involve being a good *global* climate citizen.

Synopsis of Prescriptions for Climate Governance

The prescriptions for climate governance outlined above indicate some of the major directions for policies at all levels of pathology – international, national

Table 9.1 *Prescriptions for climate governance: a synopsis*

Pathologies of climate governance	Selected prescriptions for climate governance
International relations (Chapter 3)	1. Treat human security as if it is the most important interest of states individually and collectively 2. Recognize that human and thus national interests related to climate change are borderless, and act accordingly 3. Prioritize long-term human security and rights 4. Expand the CBDR principle to encompass capable individuals everywhere 5. Give people, including the poor, direct access to, and genuine influence in, diplomatic deliberations and decision-making
National politics (Chapters 4–6)	1. Share responsibility for climate change between the state and its citizens 2. Apply the CBDR principle to individuals regardless of their citizenship, with due regard to respective capabilities 3. Replace traditional economic growth with growth in citizens' long-term well-being 4. Formulate and implement policies that foster climate citizenship 5. Treat fossil fuels as threats to the long-term national interest and the interests of citizens
Human nature (Chapter 7)	1. End the fixation on material consumption and wealth as sources of well-being, and treat overconsumption as a disease 2. Replace material growth with sufficiency to maximize the sustainable well-being of society 3. Strive to live happier and healthier lives through simplicity and sustainability 4. Educate for the maximization of human well-being through informed behavior and climate citizenship 5. Individually and collectively, act politically to foster more effective climate governance

and individual (see Table 9.1). The more of them that are taken seriously and acted upon, alongside actions proposed by others and those that are already being implemented in fits and starts around the world, the more likely the world is to avert the worst of the climate crisis in the future. For the prescriptions to result in much more effective climate governance, there will have to be substantial congruence in their application. For example, it does little good if many of the diplomats at future climate COPs agree that their first priority is to protect and promote long-term human security if their home governments believe that their first priority is instead to promote the short-term interests of influential corporations that thrive when GHG pollution is allowed to continue. It does little good for people to have access to, and influence in, climate negotiations if they themselves are not adequately cognizant of their true interests with respect to climate change, thus pointing to the importance of national educational programs. It does little good if governments abandon traditional economic growth, and specifically growth in GDP, if they replace it with equally fallacious measures that do not give all actors in society alternative objectives that are good for both people and Earth's climate system. It does little good if people come to realize that it is in their interest to stop consuming unhealthy (and environmentally unsustainable) foods or that there are alternatives to sitting in automobile traffic if governments and industry are not working to make healthy (and sustainable) foods and convenient public transport available and affordable for everyone.

A theme that runs throughout the prescriptions for climate governance is self-interest. The prescriptions need to protect and promote *genuine*, long-term national and human interests. Not every climate policy needs to be narrowly focused on promoting the interests of everyone affected by it, but that would be the ideal. Collectively, the policies that emanate from the prescriptions will have to do just that. One reason for this being so important is that it makes it far more likely that the actors affected by the prescriptions and policies will accept and implement them in the short amount of time that is available to alleviate the climate crisis and avert climate catastrophe. Naturally, making all of this work in the real world will, to a great extent, be determined by the extent to which states, individuals and enough other actors come to *perceive* their genuine interests as being tied to climate change. Perceiving one's genuine interests does not always guarantee the willingness to act in ways that protect and promote those interests – states, people and other actors do not always behave rationally – but it almost always helps.

10

Policies and Prospects
for Climate Governance

The climate crisis – the *worsening* climate crisis described in Chapter 2 – and the failure of governments and other actors to govern it effectively are very largely a consequence of the pathologies of international relations, national politics and human nature described in Chapters 3–7. These interacting, overlapping and self-reinforcing pathologies are extraordinarily persistent because they have deep historical, institutional and psychosocial roots. What is more, they are premised on anachronistic assumptions and perceptions of the interests of the actors whose behaviors cause and exacerbate the climate crisis, and whose changed behaviors are needed to mitigate climate change. As such, alleviating the pathologies of climate governance requires a variety of prescriptions, as considered and outlined in Chapters 8 and 9. The extent to which those (and other) types of prescriptions will be applied in the near and medium terms is an open question. Recent history implies that a certain amount of pessimism is warranted – and also that a great deal of hard work, and more than a little hope, will be essential. At the very least, the prescriptions point to the types of concrete policies for climate governance that will be required.

This chapter outlines what some of those policies might look like and considers the potential prospects for climate governance going forward. Whether the necessary policies will be formulated and implemented widely will substantially determine whether humanity will continue with business as usual, miraculously end the climate crisis sometime relatively soon, prosper amidst it or, perhaps most likely, doggedly cope with its impacts as climate governance gradually and belated confronts the pathologies with which it is afflicted.

From Prescriptions to Policies

What would climate governance look like if the prescriptions were to be adopted substantially? What policies, actions and behaviors would result?

Climate change and climate governance are such complex processes – probably more complex than anything else, whether environmental or governmental – that nobody can predict in detail how natural and human systems will respond. That said, it seems likely that if the prescriptions were to be implemented, the results would be closer to that which is intended and essential: at least major and relatively swift reductions in GHG pollution and, ideally, new measures to help people around the world adapt to unavoidable climate change. While it is possible that some policies for more effective climate governance would mostly be applicable at a single level of governance pathology – international, national or human – it is all but inevitable that they would intersect and interact, much as occurs with the pathologies that they are intended to alleviate (see Figure 1.1). As such, most policies should be viewed holistically as connected and overlapping components of a larger effort to make climate governance more effective.

The sample of 20 policy programs listed below is by no means comprehensive; many other types of policies can and should follow from the prescriptions. Most of these policies, at least in some form, have been proposed by others, including by some governments and international organizations. Importantly, many of these and similar policies are already being implemented to varying degrees around the world. Those actions are not happening on anything like the scale that will be required to address the climate crisis effectively, but the countries, communities and households that are taking them are role models for the rest of the world.

1. International agreement(s) and national policies for decarbonization and ending fossil-fuel production.

Without decarbonization, "there is no other real solution" to climate change (Ellis, Maslin and Lewis, 2020). Consequently, concrete international agreements and national policies will be required, first, to agree that rapid decarbonization is a concrete objective of the international community (currently this is only implied by agreements, and definitely not accepted by some parties) and, second, to agree on fixed dates for and concrete steps toward the objective of decarbonization. Specific policies would follow. A useful step would be agreement on an international treaty to eliminate coal mining and burning (Burke and Fishel, 2020). It would be necessary immediately to stop issuing new permits for fossil-fuel extraction and to decommission as quickly as possible the mining of fossil fuels – to keep carbon in the ground (except for hydrocarbons that are used sustainably to make important products). This will in turn require policies to aid those who will be affected by these actions. (See, e.g., Erickson, Lazarus and Piggot, 2018; Victor, 2020.)

2. International agreement(s) and national policies on energy subsidies and pricing.

Subsidies for fossil fuels will need to be phased out as rapidly as possible, and prices of fossil fuels will have to rise. It would be helpful to charge carbon fees at source, or nearly so, likely in combination with regulatory emissions caps and trading. For these measures to be effective, they will need to be implemented globally. Implementation would be facilitated, and grassroots opposition minimized or possibly even turned into support, by using some or most of the funds made available by them to provide financial assistance to individuals, families and small businesses most affected by the transition away from fossil-fuels. (See policies for carbon-dividend schemes below.) Other funds produced by such policies could be used to subsidize energy-demand management and alternative-energy development and deployment. (See, e.g., Bridle *et al.*, 2019; Guterres, 2019a.)

3. National (but ideally global) carbon-dividend schemes.

In addition to revenues arising from personal emissions accountability schemes (see below), some (or all) of the revenues from fees on fuels and products with substantial embodied GHG emissions (see below) should be transferred to individuals as dividends. The aim should be to both incentivize reductions in the direct and indirect use of energy that results in CO_2 pollution, to garner political support for doing so and to benefit the least well-off people in societies (Boyce, 2019). Funds could be delivered to individuals via an international financial scheme, national governments, NGOs or private banks, depending on the circumstances. (See, e.g., Kunkel and Kammen, 2011; Carattini, Kallbekken and Orlov, 2019.)

4. International cooperation and national policies for energy efficiency and conservation.

Energy efficiency improvements will be important to ensure that future alternative and renewable energy is ample to meet the needs of individuals, societies and national economies during and following decarbonization. This will require massive investment in energy-efficiency, renewable-energy and alternative-fuel research. International cooperation would be helpful to coordinate efforts and muster financial resources for national action, although it ought not be a substitute for the latter. Vitally, energy conservation will be essential to avoid repeating the historical trend of improved energy efficiency and price declines resulting in disproportionately higher increases in new demand for energy (i.e., Jevon's Paradox). The objective of policy should be to meet future energy needs while eliminating CO_2 pollution, and to do so in ways that are otherwise environmentally sustainable. (See, e.g., Foster, Clark and York, 2010; Moriarty and Honnery, 2019.)

5. New research-and-development funding focused on climate solutions.

Wealthy governments will have to individually and in cooperation (e.g., in the European Union) massively increase funding for R&D projects intended to identify and produce new knowledge, methodologies and technologies that will rapidly mitigate GHG pollution and facilitate adaptation to climate change around the world. This should be done to accelerate decarbonization, ease the transition away from fossil fuels and enable people and communities to cope with climate change. The objective should *not* be to extend the life of fossil fuels. Resulting policies and programs should not create new environmental problems, as might happen with the development of certain biofuels or from some geoengineering schemes. (See, e.g., Jones *et al.*, 2018; Nightingale *et al.*, 2019.)

6. National policies for, and international regional cooperation to make possible, electrification of everything that can be electrified.

To facilitate the rapid shift away from fossil fuels without requiring politically impossible changes in behaviors, electricity should become the dominant form of energy used by households, transportation and industry. As soon as possible, all electricity should be produced from non-carbon sources of energy, thus requiring massive scale up of solar, wind and other renewables. There may be a place for new nuclear and, very rarely, small hydroelectric power plants in some localities, but the urgency of electrification should not become an excuse to build such facilities unsustainably or unnecessarily, and certainly not when other options exist (including energy conservation). Significantly, electrified products and activities that contribute to environmentally harmful impacts, for example due to the manner in which they are manufactured (e.g., electric cars), should be consumed sparingly. (See, e.g., Roberts, 2017; Ram *et al.*, 2019.)

7. *International agreement(s) and national policies for climate security.*

The climate crisis is now the greatest threat to security, akin to the threat of global war (McKibben, 2016). It demands a diversion of resources and ingenuity away from preparation for armed conflict toward preventing the instability, scarcities and insecurities posed by climate change. The notion of long-term human security as a vital national interest should be melded into climate security, which should in turn be a primary mission of national security. Internationally, climate change should become a long-term mandate of the UN Security Council (Conca, Thwaites and Lee, 2017). Whenever possible, resources should be diverted away from military preparedness toward international poverty alleviation, development assistance and climate adaptation strategies that will reduce the likelihood of violent conflict within and among countries. Importantly, insofar as there is a securitization of climate change, it ought to be viewed in terms of promoting peace rather than prosecuting war. (See, e.g., Hussain, 2019; Pohl and Schaller, 2019; Guy *et al.*, 2020.)

8. *International agreement(s) and national policies to protect human rights and to realize justice in transition and adaptation.*

Agreements and policies to prevent human rights violations caused by climate change are required, as are those to provide remedies for individuals and communities whose rights have been violated (Duyck, *et al.*, 2018). These will require amendments to practices of international and domestic law (see Wewerinke-Singh, 2019). Policies will be needed to realize a *just* transition to a post-carbon world in which the causes and impacts of climate change are greatly mitigated (Robinson and Shine, 2018). This means fair schemes for compensation and assistance to the countries, small businesses, communities and individuals that will be affected by the process of mitigating GHG emissions, most importantly in the process of decarbonization. This does not mean bailing out the fossil-fuel industry or paying the world's wealthy countries and people, but some selected programs to minimize political opposition to more effective policies for climate governance may be required in the short and medium terms. (See, e.g., Schlosberg, 2012; Stanley Foundation, 2017; WBGU, 2018.)

9. Programs and policies for international organizations and national governments to supplant GDP growth with well-being objectives.

Existing policies that assume endless economic growth are not sustainable (Washington and Kopnina, 2018). New global and national economic policies suited to the climate crisis should supplant growth in material throughput and consumption. Those new policies should favor material and consumption *degrowth* globally except among those people whose needs in this respect have not been met. As part of this process, traditional measures of economic growth, specifically GDP, should be replaced by alternatives, such as GNH or other methodologies appropriate to national and local circumstances, that assist policymakers seeking to govern climate change more effectively. These shifts should result in national and international polices that ensure that every person's needs are met, and which maximize environmentally sustainable human well-being. (See, e.g., van den Bergh and Botzen, 2016; Gough, 2017; Rayworth, 2017.)

10. Regional and national transport and travel policies to minimize GHG emissions.

Transport policies will have to become much more assertive in rapidly removing carbon from all forms of transport insofar as technology allows, and in drastically reducing CO_2 emissions from those forms of transport that must continue to use fossil fuels while alternatives are being developed and deployed. Policies should provide the best possible public transport infrastructure, encourage alternatives to car ownership (e.g., car sharing), electrify transport insofar as possible, discourage all unnecessary air travel and require sustainable and permanent carbon offsetting for essential travel by air whenever possible. Development of alternative transport fuels should be done in ways that are truly sustainable (e.g., avoidance of biofuels that adversely impact biodiversity, sustainability and food production). (See, e.g., Schiller and Kenworthy, 2017; Garcia-Olivares, Sole and Osychenko, 2018.)

11. Housing policies and building codes that minimize GHG emissions from construction and eliminate emissions from heating, cooling and powering homes and other buildings.

The very large contribution of buildings to carbon emissions – approaching 40 percent of energy-related emissions globally (Stewart, Pugh and Jordan,

2019) – will have to be eliminated insofar as possible and as soon possible, not least because each building will be in use for many decades following its construction. This will require policies, such as R&D investments and building codes, that result in new homes and offices that are carbon-neutral or carbon-negative (e.g., solar-powered homes that generate more energy than they consume). Equally ambitious policies for making existing homes and buildings carbon neutral, whether through efficiency improvements or carbon-free electrification, or both, will be essential. The objective of such policies should be to enable people to live and work without adding to the climate burden or to energy demand. (See, e.g., Becque *et al.*, 2019; Aggarwal, 2020.)

12. Improved domestic social welfare and international aid and development programs.

Many people whose needs are not met will find the transition to a decarbonized world difficult. For this reason (and many others), improved and well-funded national social welfare and international assistance programs are needed. Developed countries will need to revamp existing welfare programs to make them consistent with climate governance objectives, while developing countries will require international assistance to implement and scale up welfare programs that simultaneously improve human well-being and address climate change-related challenges. Such programs should be guided by the CBDR principle, bearing in mind respective capabilities, meaning that resources for such programs should come from the most responsible and capable national governments *and* individuals. Institutions are already in place for international assistance, but new systems will be needed to greatly increase funding and to implement individualized CBDR (alongside personal emissions accountability schemes, as noted below). (See, e.g., Vanderheiden, 2015; IIED, 2020.)

13. Family planning policies to limit population where consumption rates are high.

Family planning policies and voluntary population management programs are needed to limit the impact of overconsumption until consumption can be disconnected from GHG emissions and environmental destruction. Because the objective is to eliminate unnecessary GHG pollution, the focus should be on communities and countries where consumption is already too high or likely to become too high. Because having fewer (or no) children is the most effective action a person can take to reduce individual long-term contributions to climate change, the best choice for many people may be to have no children (Wynes and Nicholas, 2017; see also Murtaugh and Schlax, 2009). Programs could include incentives in developed countries to have fewer (or no) children and greatly improved healthcare and welfare provision in developing countries to discourage high fertility rates. Policies should expressly avoid discriminating against the poor and powerless. (See, e.g., Gerlagh, Lupi and Marzio, 2018; Ripple *et al.*, 2020.)

14. *Dietary, agricultural and land-use policies to improve health while reducing GHG emissions from food production and consumption.*

New dietary and nutrition policies are needed to improve health and ensure food security while reducing GHG emissions. Policies should include new dietary guidelines that encourage healthier and more sustainable eating, and measures to limit (and eliminate where possible) the consumption of meat. Industry involvement in the formulation of official dietary guidelines should be ended. Another objective should be to eliminate non-essential livestock production, with very strict regulations put in place globally to assure animal welfare, health, hygiene and environmental sustainability whenever animals are used for food. Agricultural policies should be aimed at producing adequate food for everyone while reducing GHG emissions, maximizing sequestration of carbon and protecting biodiversity (Springmann *et al.*, 2018). Specific policies would include those to eliminate unnecessary waste of food and prevent the use of essential food-producing land and natural areas for biofuels. Governments should aim to keep or return half of all land to its natural state as a necessary step for achieving the Paris Agreement's objectives (Dinerstein *et al.*, 2019). (See, e.g., Willett *et al.*, 2019; Fesenfeld *et al.*, 2020; IPCC, 2020.)

15. *Regulation of advertising, fees on consumption and restrictions on dangerous products.*

The climate crisis demands new restrictions on commercial advertising of products whose unnecessary consumption results in GHG pollution, akin to existing bans on advertising of cigarettes in many countries, as well as public service advertising that discourages consumption of such products, similar to ads that discourage smoking and those that encourage consumption of healthy foods. It is likely that there will need to be quite strict measures to ensure that online social media are following advertising guidelines and not finding crafty ways around them. Assuming lingering demand for luxury products with high embodied GHG emissions, there will have to be very high fees levied on many such things, and regulation, potentially including restrictions and prohibitions, of some of the most-polluting products (e.g., petrol/gasoline and diesel SUVs, motor yachts and private jets) and on environmentally harmful luxury merchandise, throw-away products and appliances that cannot be repaired. (See, e.g., Corley, 2020; Peltier, 2020.)

16. National and ideally global personal emissions accountability schemes.

Policies are needed for the implementation of domestic and international carbon-accountability schemes for individuals. These schemes should account for consumption behaviors (i.e., direct and indirect consumption emissions) and should be designed to bring about action on the common but differentiated responsibilities and respective capabilities of individuals. The express purpose should be both to address the causes of climate change and to ensure that the most responsible (and capable) individuals compensate the least responsible (and capable) individuals. One option would be personal emissions trading schemes administered internationally and transferring resulting revenues from affluent individuals in all countries to poor individuals globally. To enhance the popularity of such schemes, recipients should be given information on the sources of these payments so that it is clear to poor people in the Global North that some of their benefits come from affluent people in the South. (See, e.g., Fawcett and Parag 2010; Parag and Fawcett, 2014.)

17. Policies of social influencers and religious leaders to promote the value and protection of climate and environment.

People often behave in ways advocated by celebrities, social influencers (e.g., film stars, online media personalities, music bands, popular authors) and religious leaders (and their organizations' teachings). The climate crisis requires that these individuals and their networks persuade their followers to adopt and support lifestyles and behaviors that are environmentally sustainable. Already, many popular personalities have become advocates for the environment; more of them need to do this proactively. The power of faith and religion means that churches, synagogues, mosques and other venues of worship need to work with policymakers and their communities to support aggressive action to mitigate climate change and ameliorate its injustices. (See, e.g., Harvey, 2018; Morton, 2019.)

18. Subnational, local and neighborhood initiatives to encourage community engagement in sustainability.

The climate crisis is so serious that it requires more than international agreements and national policies. It also requires public and private policies and initiatives in subnational regions, municipalities and neighborhoods that eliminate, insofar as possible, climate pollution and which mitigate the impacts and injustices of climate change. Regions such as Victoria in Australia, Maharashtra in India and Florida in the United States should initiate much more effective policies, in addition to those at the national level, based on their circumstances and needs related to climate change. City, town and village governments around the world will need resources to devise and carry out their own local schemes for addressing climate change. Neighborhood associations can and should share ideas and create conditions to encourage and support climate action. (See, e.g., Galarraga, Gonzalez-Eguino and Markandya, 2011; NewClimate Institute, 2019.)

19. Individual and household initiatives to reduce every capable individual's contribution to GHG pollution and to maximize individual contributions to climate solutions while promoting everyone's well-being.

Successfully implementing prescriptions for climate governance requires that people behave in certain ways. Those who overconsume need to consume less, and those with the capability to do so need to help those most affected and least responsible for climate action. All of these actions require that people do more to promote their own genuine interests and the interests of others by living in ways that are sustainable for Earth's climate system. Initiatives range from changing diets to ending overconsumption of products and looking for ways to simplify people's lives, especially among the affluent. All of this will require that more people be conscious of their own behaviors and the impacts of those behaviors on others, and that more people care about these causes and consequences. If more people do these things, climate governance will become far more effective. Guidance for specific steps that individuals and families can take is now abundant online and in books. (See, e.g., Wynes and Nicholas, 2017; Ortiz, 2018; Washington, 2019; Berners-Lee, 2019.)

20. International, national and local education policies and programs designed to promote climate citizenship.

The power of education cannot be overstated; it is the source of both lifelong skills and strong feelings, such as patriotism, that shape people's behaviors and their willingness to act in the common good. Thus, education may be the most important policy response to climate change in the long term. Climate-focused curricula, programs and initiatives, aided by international support in the developing world, will be needed in primary, secondary, tertiary and lifelong education. People need to understand the climate-change problem, care about it and comprehend fully the many ways in which it is related to their own behaviors and interests, as well as the genuine interests of their families, communities and countries. Such knowledge and sentiments, or the lack of them, will greatly determine whether other policies to address climate change will be effective. (See, e.g., Young, 2018; Filho and Hemstock, 2019.)

It must be acknowledged that it is far easier to propose climate governance policies in outline than to formulate them in detail, let alone to put them into practice. Several decades of climate governance has provided much evidence to demonstrate how difficult it will be to scale up these and other policy responses sufficiently to reverse dangerous climatic trends and to help people cope with them. But if policies such as these can be implemented in earnest, there may be a real opportunity to govern climate change effectively. Even if the climate crisis continues, implementing policies such as these would have added benefits that are of inestimable value: they would make people, communities and countries better off and more prepared to cope with climate change. They would also make the world more environmentally sustainable and just. In other words, if these and other policies end up being too little and too late, they would be very beneficial nonetheless.

Prospects for Climate Governance

What are the prospects for climate governance in the future? There is a spectrum of possibilities. One end of the spectrum sees climate governance going backwards and returning to business as usual. Such a future would entail following the prescriptions of climate denialists, populist politicians and laissez-faire economists who want to promote economic growth as the savior of humankind and to power that growth with coal, oil and other fossil fuels. At the other end of the spectrum is just the opposite: taking the pathologies of climate governance, and other causes of the climate crisis, extraordinarily seriously, and then robustly implementing prescriptions and policies for over-coming them. Such a future would entail transforming societies, economies, politics and indeed humanity to end the climate crisis in the near future. Neither of these futures is likely, but they bear thinking about because one reminds us of why the world is in the midst of a worsening climate crisis and the other points toward an ideal that, although unattainable soon, is worth striving toward because the process of doing so will mitigate the causes and impacts of climate change while making the world a better place. These unlikely futures for climate governance are considered briefly in turn before considering less dramatic, but more likely, prospects.

The Status Quo Ante and the Zombie of Business as Usual?

One potential future for climate governance is a return to the status quo ante when coal was king, oil production and consumption were expected always to be at the heart of the global economy, and global warming, when belatedly acknowledged, was a problem for the future that capitalist ingenuity would inevitably solve. Such a future would be plagued by the zombie of business as usual. It would be a future in which climate skeptics and denialists would dictate the policies of many governments, much as President Trump empowered them to do in the United States. It would be a world in which global GHG pollution would, at best, stabilize, ensuring eventual climate disaster, or perhaps continue to increase, all but guaranteeing climate apoca-lypse. It would be a future characterized by all of the most worrying impacts of global warming and climate change: deadly weather, rising seas, spreading disease, recurring famines and many millions of climate migrants.

Many of these impacts may be inevitable, and it is conceivable that the Trumps and Saudi Arabias of the world might prevail in the future. However, the prospect that the world will digress several decades to the mindset that was dominent before the advent of the climate regime seems to be very unlikely. Too much progress has been made since then – inadequate progress that has failed to avert the climate crisis, but still progress. Even as President Trump's minions assiduously dismantled his government's institutions for climate (and all environmental) protection, many other governments (including state and municipal governments in the United States, as noted in Chapter 4) have set their courses toward addressing the climate crisis with seriousness. Meanwhile, few industries are now following the lead of the climate denialists. A growing number of financial institutions are starting to minimize long-term risks to their portfolios by divesting from fossil fuels. Even some of the largest oil corporations seem to recognize that a growing share of their future profits will come from renewable forms of energy (Pickl, 2019), many of which are now less costly and more secure than fossil fuels. Climate governance seems to be too far developed, and too widely recognized as being important for humanity's future, for the carbon zombies to prevail. Could it be more likely that the Greta Thunbergs and vulnerable SIDS of the world – those calling for aggressive, forthright universal action to discard business as usual and decarbonize the global economy within a matter of years – might prevail instead?

Ending the Climate Crisis?

In an ideal world, it would be possible to end the climate crisis soon. With a wide-ranging and all-inclusive global response, it may be possible to decarbonize the global economy within a generation and undertake land-use changes and other activities that extract carbon from the atmosphere, thereby starting the process of reversing centuries of global GHG emissions. Doing just that – cutting GHG pollution *alongside* CO_2 removal (CDR) from the atmosphere – are assumed by the IPCC in their models for limiting global warming to 1.5°C (IPCC, 2018). Various strategies have been proposed for going about this. For example, planting billions of trees has the potential to sequester large amounts of CO_2, at least for some decades (Carrington, 2019). Geoengineering schemes, such as those that involve fertilization of the oceans to feed plankton, which might then sequester carbon in the deep seabed (Oliver and Tucker, 2019), and other negative-emissions technologies (NETs), such as direct-air capture (sucking CO_2 from the atmosphere and sequestering it somehow) have the potential to dial down global warming (Pearce, 2019), assuming that they are accompanied by decarbonization. Such schemes will surely be tried, and in an ideal world they would have the intended effect of greatly mitigating climate change while avoiding unforeseen adverse human and environmental impacts.

However, the potential of many CDR schemes and related approaches to reduce concentrations of carbon in the atmosphere and environment might not be realized (EASAC, 2018). For example, it is impossible to guarantee that those billions of trees would not become victims of, and fuel for, future wildfires, thereby rapidly returning their stored carbon to the atmosphere (Moura, 2019). (By way of example, CO_2 emissions from Australia's bushfires of September 2019 to February 2020 greatly exceeded the country's total annual emissions and surpassed the total annual emissions of all but the five largest national sources of carbon pollution – China, the United States, India, Russia and Japan [Morton, 2020].) What is more, CDR, geoengineering and NETs have risks (ETC Group and Heinrich Boll Foundation, 2017).

The promise of geoengineering solutions to climate change is a godsend to corporations that rely on fossil fuels for their profits; it could have the effect of reducing the perceived urgency of decarbonization. If not done very carefully, planting billions of trees for the purpose of addressing climate change could do harm to ecosystems and agriculture. Other potential risks include the threat of adverse changes to weather patterns, which might decimate agricultural productivity in famine-prone regions, arising from geoengineering projects, and the moral hazard of doing too little in the present – such as preventing rampant deforestation that is occurring in, say, Brazil – because NETs and other interventions are expected to solve the climate crisis in the future (Dunne, 2018).

Prospering and Coping amidst Climate Change?

We do not live in an ideal world. Achieving the Paris Agreement's aim of limiting global warming to 2°C, let alone achieving the agreement's aspiration of limiting it to 1.5°C, seems to be very unlikely (Raftery *et al.*, 2017). Greenhouse gas pollution that is already in Earth's atmosphere, coupled with the likely effects of positive feedback loops (e.g., GHG emissions from melting tundra contributing to more global warming and, in turn, more melting of tundra resulting in further GHG emissions, and so on), means that continued climate change is a certainty and continued worsening of it is highly probable. The problem will be with us for decades, likely throughout this century and beyond. Despite all of the action that is occurring around the world to mitigate the pollution causing climate change and to adapt to its impacts, many trends are going in the wrong direction. These include the growing aspirations of billions of people to have lifestyles that are still very much environmentally unsustainable. They include national politics that, in most countries, still do not elicit the robust action that is required to decarbonize economies quickly enough, often still doing exactly the opposite (e.g., continued fossil-fuel subsidies). They include the failure of countries to share enough of the resources that are needed to help the countries, communities and individuals most affected by climate change to cope effectively. Incredibly, despite all that is known about this problem, they include the persistence of climate denial, which, even when it ends (as it will do apart from a relatively small group of outliers that will always deny this and many other aspects of reality), will have left such a lasting legacy of environmental destruction that at least many decades will be needed to make up for lost ground. Put another way, ending climate change in the lifetimes of the readers of this book is very unlikely indeed.

That said, many of the necessary policies for alleviating the pathologies of climate governance will be put into practice, at least to some extent. The process of global decarbonization has started. The world's current addiction to fossil fuels will start to abate, perhaps at an accelerating pace in the coming years and decades. It seems likely that Green New Deals of different sorts will be implemented in various forms in more than a few countries, partly as a response to climate change and perhaps partly to stimulate economies left reeling by the global coronavirus pandemic, without in the process unnecessarily exacerbating the climate crisis. While these undertakings will be mostly focused nationally, they will have the effect of limiting global GHG pollution, at least compared to what it would be without such programs. The pressing question is whether, through these and other attempts at improved climate governance, it will be possible to end the *crisis* that will accompany the climate change that will not be avoided.

What seems most likely is that some wealthy countries and people will prosper despite the climate crisis. Many people will muddle along, much as they do today. And many millions of people will struggle to survive, let alone thrive. In short, climate governance in the near future may not make the climate crisis go away, but it is possible that it will do enough to prevent things from being as bad as they would be otherwise. That is not quite the same as overcoming the pathologies of climate governance, but it is moving in the right direction.

Conclusion

Climate change is becoming part of life around the world. Globally it is a crisis. In some places it is already an existential threat. In many others it will become so. Fundamental causes of the climate crisis are the pathologies of climate governance found in international relations, national politics and human nature. Fundamental to making climate governance more effective in slowing, and one day reversing, the worsening climate crisis are prescriptions and associated policies intended to alleviate those pathologies. The pathologies of climate governance arise, at least in large part, from widely misperceived conceptions of the interests of key actors at all levels, from the international to the individual. These misperceptions have often been manifested when the genuine long-term interests and well-being of people are overpowered by the narrow interests of other actors, often the corporations and their political enablers whose interests lie in continuing to pollute Earth's climate system. Too often, governments and corporations behave like illicit-drug dealers.

They encourage addiction to behaviors that, while providing temporary pleasure, are manifested in the feelings of dissatisfaction upon which much of today's capitalism is premised. Too often, people behave like those who are addicted to illicit drugs, wanting more of that which is bad for them (at least in the quantities consumed) and becoming preoccupied with getting more of it at the expense of those things in life that will make them happier and healthier. Much as addictions to illicit drugs often end very badly, so has the world's direct and indirect addictions to fossil fuels ended very badly for the climate system – and for those who are most vulnerable to its accelerating changes.

Prescriptions for the pathologies of climate governance, if they are to alleviate the climate crisis, should redirect perceptions of interests in ways that promote the long-term interests of the actors that matter most: people. (Apologies to those who believe that nonhumans and the environment matter the most. As suggested earlier, there is a case to be made for giving them priority, but there is also a case to be made that the climate crisis leaves too little time to convince enough people, governments and other actors to do so.) Climate governance that does this would involve doing more to reduce vulnerabilities to climate change, including the poverty and economic inequality that often make people incapable of coping with the impacts, and doing more to discourage the lifestyles and behaviors, not least overconsumption, that often reduce human well-being and the vitality of the climate system at the same time. It would involve recognition that the interests of the climate system, of the natural environment in general and of individuals, states and the international community are all interdependent and complementary. It would involve corresponding action internationally, nationally and among individuals.

The raison d'être of states is, by definition, to protect the interests of their citizens (without citizens, there are no states, after all). It is therefore in the interests of states to prevent dangerous climate change and its many impacts that harm the interests of those citizens, now and in the future. This will require much more effective agreements for international climate governance. It will also require that national governments recognize that responsibility for climate change lies not just with affluent states but also with affluent people. Acting on this recognition will require national policies that attribute that responsibility accordingly. For individuals, more effective climate governance means greater effort to promote well-being – long-term health, happiness and security. Doing that means changes in behavior, not least ending overconsumption and many of the voluntary but unnecessary actions that exacerbate climate change.

The burden to accept the need for such a change, and to put it into practice, is especially important – practically and morally – for the world's many capable people. They should be more conscious of the impact of their actions on themselves, others and the climate, now and in the future. Acting on that awareness, as good climate citizens – meaning not just in their lifestyle choices but also in their political choices – will be essential if climate governance is to make substantial progress. Doing these things will not end the climate crisis soon, but they will move the world closer to that objective while simultaneously improving the well-being of more people. They will set the world on course toward alleviating the pathologies of climate governance.

References

Note: Internet hyperlinks were operational at the time of publication. Corrections can be sent to the author via this webpage: https://paulgharris.net/contact. A comprehensive bibliography, including updated links to sources, can be found on the book's companion website: https://paulgharris.net/pathologies-of-climate-governance/.

Aamodt, S. (2018). The ability to influence: a comparative analysis of the role of advocacy coalitions in Brazilian climate politics. *Review of Policy Research* **35**: 372–97, https://onlinelibrary.wiley.com/doi/abs/10.1111/ropr.12282.

Acharya, A., and Buzan, B. (2019). *The Making of Global International Relations*. Cambridge: Cambridge University Press, https://doi.org/10.1017/9781108647670.

Adger, W. N., Pulhin, J. M., Barnett, J., *et al.* (2014). Human security. In C. B. Field, V. R. Barros, D. J. Dokken *et al.*, eds. *Climate Change 2014: Impacts, Adaptation and Vulnerability*. Cambridge: Cambridge University Press, pp. 755–91, www.ipcc.ch/report/ar5/wg2/.

AFP (Agence France-Press) (2020). Russia announces plan to "use the advantages" of climate change. *The Guardian*, January 5, www.theguardian.com/world/2020/jan/05/russia-announces-plan-to-use-the-advantages-of-climate-change.

Aggarwal, S. (2020). Pathways to net zero carbon buildings in reach around the world today. *Forbes*, January 29, www.forbes.com/sites/energyinnovation/2020/01/29/pathways-to-net-zero-carbon-buildings-in-reach-around-the-world-today/.

Albeck-Ripka, L., Tarabay, J., and Kwai, I. (2020). As fires rage, Australia sees its leader as missing in action. *New York Times*, January 4, www.nytimes.com/2020/01/04/world/australia/fires-scott-morrison.html.

Aldrich, D., Lipscy, P. Y., and McCarthy, M. M. (2019). Japan's opportunity to lead. *Nature Climate Change* **9**: 492, www.nature.com/articles/s41558-019-0510-0.

Alexandratos, N., and Bruinsma, J. (2012). World agriculture towards 2030/2050. ESA Working Paper No. 12-03, www.fao.org/fileadmin/templates/esa/Global_perspctives/world_ag_2030_50_2012_rev.pdf.

America's Pledge (2020). *America's Pledge*, www.americaspledgeonclimate.com/.

Andonova, L. B. (2009). The climate regime and domestic politics: the case of Russia. In P. G. Harris, ed., *The Politics of Climate Change: Environmental Dynamics in International Affairs*. London: Routledge, pp. 29–50, www.routledge.com/The-Politics-of-Climate-Change-Environmental-Dynamics-in-International/Harris/p/book/9780415518765.

Andresen, S. (2015). Regime effectiveness. In K. Backstrand and E. Lovbrand, eds., *Research Handbook on Climate Governance*. Cheltenham: Edward Elgar, pp. 425–34, www.elgaronline.com/view/edcoll/9781783470594/9781783470594 .00050.xml.

AP (Associated Press) (2020a). Canada court upholds Trans Mountain Pipeline expansion approval. *The Guardian*, February 4, www.theguardian.com/world/2020/feb/ 04/canada-trans-mountain-pipeline-expansion-approval-court-upholds.

AP (Associated Press) (2020b). Virginia lawmakers send "historic" energy bill to governor. *AP News*, March 7, https://apnews.com/c2c7dcd9132d496a9879cbccfd136a0d.

Askar, K. I. (2018). Environmental foreign policy as a soft power instrument: cases of China and India. *Journal of Contemporary Eastern Asia*, **17**(1): 5–26, www .academia.edu/37155319/Environmental_Foreign_Policy_as_a_Soft_Power_ Instrument_Cases_of_China_and_India.

Atsom, Y., Magni, M., Li, L., and Liao, W. (2012). Meet the 2020 Chinese consumer. *McKinsey Consumer and Shopper Insights*, www.mckinsey.com/~/media/mckin sey/featured%20insights/asia%20pacific/meet%20the%20chinese%20consumer% 20of%202020/mckinseyinsightschina%20meetthe2020chineseconsumer.ashx.

Atteridge, A., Shrivastava, M. K., Pahuja, N., and Upadhyay, H. (2012). Climate policy in India: what shapes international, national and state policy? *Ambio* **41**: 68–77, www.ncbi.nlm.nih.gov/pmc/articles/PMC3357885/.

Austin, A., and Phoenix, L. (2005). The neoconservative assault on the earth: the environmental imperialism of the Bush administration. *Capitalism Nature Socialism* **16**(2): 25–44, www.academia.edu/37012215/The_neoconservative_assault_on_the_Earth_ The_environmental_imperialism_of_the_Bush_administration.

Australia (2015). Australia's Intended Nationally Determined Contribution to a new Climate Change Agreement, www4.unfccc.int/sites/submissions/INDC/Published %20Documents/Australia/1/Australias%20Intended%20Nationally% 20Determined%20Contribution%20to%20a%20new%20Climate%20Change% 20Agreement%20-%20August%202015.pdf.

Backstrand, K., and Lovbrand, E. (2015). Climate governance after Copenhagen: research trends and policy practice. In K. Backstrand and E. Lovbrand, eds., *Research Handbook on Climate Governance*. Cheltenham: Edward Elgar, pp. xvii–xxx, www .elgaronline.com/view/edcoll/9781783470594/9781783470594.00007.xml.

Baer, P., Fieldman, G., Athanasiou, T., and Kartha, S. (2009). Greenhouse development rights: towards an equitable framework for global climate policy. In P. G. Harris, ed., *The Politics of Climate Change: Environmental Dynamics in International Affairs*. London: Routledge, pp. 192–212, www.routledge.com/The-Politics-of-Climate-Change-Environmental-Dynamics-in-International/Harris/p/book/9780415518765.

Bailey, I. (2019). National climate-mitigation policy: the spatial framing of (in)justice claims. In P. G. Harris, ed., *A Research Agenda for Climate Justice*. Cheltenham: Edward Elgard, pp. 52–63, www.elgaronline.com/view/edcoll/9781788118163/ 9781788118163.00010.xml.

Baker, P. (2017). Does Trump still think climate change is a hoax? No one can say. *New York Times*, June 2, www.nytimes.com/2017/06/02/us/politics/climate-change-trump-hoax-scott-pruitt.html.

Barkdull J., and Harris, P. G. (2015). Climate-induced conflict or hospice earth. *Global Change, Peace and Security* **27**(2): 237–43, www.tandfonline.com/doi/full/10.1080/14781158.2015.1019442.

Barnett, J. (2008). The worst of friends: OPEC and G-77 in the climate regime. *Global Environmental Politics* **8**(4): 1–8, www.researchgate.net/publication/23546961_The_Worst_of_Friends_OPEC_and_G-77_in_the_Climate_Regime.

Barton, D. (2013). Half a billion: China's middle-class consumers. *The Diplomat*, May 30, https://thediplomat.com/2013/05/half-a-billion-chinas-middle-class-consumers/.

BBC (2019a). Germany plans €54bn climate deal amid 500 protests. *BBC News*, September 20, www.bbc.com/news/world-europe-49767649.

BBC (2019b). UK Parliament declares climate change emergency. *BBC News*, May 1, www.bbc.com/news/uk-politics-48126677.

BBC (2020). Brazil's Amazon: deforestation high in January despite rainy season. *BBC News*, February 8, www.bbc.com/news/world-latin-america-51425408.

Becque, R., Weyl, D., Stewart, E., *et al.* (2019). Accelerating building decarbonization: eight attainable policy pathways to net zero carbon buildings for all. World Resources Institute working paper, https://wriorg.s3.amazonaws.com/s3fs-public/accelerating-building-decarbonization.pdf.

Benedict, R. E. (1998). *Ozone Diplomacy: New Directions in Safeguarding the Planet.* Cambridge, MA: Harvard University Press, www.hup.harvard.edu/catalog.php?isbn=9780674650039.

Berners-Lee, M. (2019). *There Is No Planet B: A Handbook for the Make or Break Years.* Cambridge: Cambridge University Press, https://doi.org/10.1017/9781108545969.

Berners-Lee, M., Hoolohan, C., Cammack, H., and Hewett, C. N. (2012). The relative greenhouse gas impacts of realistic dietary choices. *Energy Policy* **43**: 183–90, www.sciencedirect.com/science/article/abs/pii/S0301421511010603.

Betsill, M. (2016). The United States and the evolution of international climate change norms. In P. G. Harris, ed., *Climate Change and American Foreign Policy.* New York: Palgrave Macmillan, pp. 205–24, https://link.springer.com/chapter/10.1057/9781137120809_10.

Betzold, C. (2015). Adapting to climate change in small island developing states. *Climatic Change* **133**: 481–9, https://link.springer.com/article/10.1007/s10584-015-1408-0.

Black, R. (2009). China unveils emissions targets ahead of Copenhagen. *BBC News*, November 26, http://news.bbc.co.uk/2/hi/asia-pacific/8380106.stm.

BloombergNEF (2019). New energy outlook 2019, https://bnef.turtl.co/story/neo2019/.

Blyth, M. (2019) What will the world look like in 2030? *New York Times*, December 26, www.nytimes.com/interactive/2019/12/26/opinion/2020s-future-predictions.html.

Bodansky, D. (2007). Targets and timetables: good policy but bad politics? In J. E. Aldy and R. N. Stavins, eds., *Architectures for Agreement: Addressing Global Climate Change in the Post-Kyoto World.* Cambridge: Cambridge University Press, 2007, pp. 57–66, https://papers.ssrn.com/sol3/papers.cfm?abstract_id=1033550.

Bongaarts, J., and O'Neill, B. C. (2018). Global warming policy: is population left out in the cold? *Science* **361**(6403): 650–52, https://science.sciencemag.org/content/361/6403/650.

Boyce, J. K. (2019). *The Case for Carbon Dividends.* Cambridge: Polity, https://politybooks.com/?s=case+for+carbon+dividends.

BP (2018). *BP Statistical Review of World Energy 2018*. London: BP, www.bp.com/content/dam/bp/business-sites/en/global/corporate/pdfs/energy-economics/statistical-review/bp-stats-review-2018-full-report.pdf.

BP (2019). *BP Statistical Review of World Energy 2019*. London: BP, www.bp.com/content/dam/bp/business-sites/en/global/corporate/pdfs/energy-economics/statistical-review/bp-stats-review-2019-full-report.pdf.

Bradley, R. S. (2011). *Global Warming and Political Intimidation: How Politicians Cracked Down on Scientists as the Earth Heated Up*. Boston: University of Massachusetts Press, www.umass.edu/umpress/title/global-warming-and-political-intimidation.

Bradsher, K. (2020). Beijing renews its "Belt and Road" push for global sway. *New York Times*, January 15, www.nytimes.com/2020/01/15/business/china-belt-and-road.html.

Bradsher, K., and Kwai, I. (2020). Australia's fires test its winning growth formula. *New York Times*, January 13, www.nytimes.com/2020/01/13/business/australia-economy-wildfires.html.

Brand, U., and Wissen, M. (2021). *The Imperial Mode of Living: Everyday Life and the Ecological Crisis of Capitalism*. London: Verso, www.versobooks.com/books/3691-the-imperial-mode-of-living.

Brazil (2015). Intended Nationally Determined Contribution towards achieving the objective of the United Nations Framework Convention on Climate Change, www4.unfccc.int/sites/ndcstaging/PublishedDocuments/Brazil%20First/BRAZIL%20iNDC%20english%20FINAL.pdf.

Breakey, H., Popovski, V., and Maguire, R., eds. (2015). *Ethical Values and the Integrity of the Climate Change Regime*. London: Routledge, www.routledge.com/Ethical-Values-and-the-Integrity-of-the-Climate-Change-Regime-1st-Edition/Breakey-Popovski/p/book/9781472469595.

Brewer, T. L. (2015). *The United States in a Warming World: The Political Economy of Government, Business and Public Responses to Climate Change*. Cambridge: Cambridge University Press, https://doi.org/10.1017/CBO9781107706569.

Bridle, R., Sharma, S., Mostaf, M., and Geddes, A. (2019). Fossil fuel to clean energy subsidy swaps: how to pay for an energy revolution. International Institute for Sustainable Development Global Subsidies Initiative report, www.iisd.org/sites/default/files/publications/fossil-fuel-clean-energy-subsidy-swap.pdf.

Broberg, M. (2020). Interpreting the UNFCCC's provisions on "mitigation" and "adaptation" in light of the Paris Agreement's provision on "loss and damage." *Climate Policy*, April 7, https://doi.org/10.1080/14693062.2020.1745744.

Burke, A., and Fishel, S. (2020). A coal elimination treaty 2030: fast tracking climate change mitigation, global health and security. *Earth System Governance*, March 10, https://doi.org/10.1016/j.esg.2020.100046.

Canada (2015). Canada's INDC submission to the UNFCCC, www4.unfccc.int/sites/submissions/INDC/Published%20Documents/Canada/1/INDC%20-%20Canada%20-%20English.pdf.

Carattini, S., Kallbekken, S., and Orlov, A. (2019). How to win public support for a global carbon tax. *Nature* **565**: 289–91, www.nature.com/articles/d41586-019-00124-x.

Carrington, D. (2016). The Anthropocene epoch: scientists declare dawn of human-influenced age. *The Guardian*, August 29, www.theguardian.com/environment/

2016/aug/29/declare-anthropocene-epoch-experts-urge-geological-congress-human-impact-earth.

Carrington, D. (2019). Tree planting "has mind-blowing potential" to tackle climate crisis. *The Guardian*, July 4, www.theguardian.com/environment/2019/jul/04/planting-billions-trees-best-tackle-climate-crisis-scientists-canopy-emissions.

Casado, L., and Londono, E. (2019). Under Brazil's far-right leader, Amazon protections slashed and forests fall. *New York Times*, July 28, www.nytimes.com/2019/07/28/world/americas/brazil-deforestation-amazon-bolsonaro.html.

Cave, D. (2019). It was supposed to be Australia's climate change election: what happened? *New York Times*, May 19, www.nytimes.com/2019/05/19/world/australia/election-climate-change.html.

Centre for Bhutan Studies and GNH Research (2016). *A Compass towards a Just and Harmonious Society: 2015 GNH Survey Report*. Thimphu: Centre for Bhutan Studies and GNH Research, www.grossnationalhappiness.com/wp-content/uploads/2017/01/Final-GNH-Report-jp-21.3.17-ilovepdf-compressed.pdf.

Ceroni, M. (2014). Beyond GDP: US states have adopted genuine progress indicators. *The Guardian*, September 23, www.theguardian.com/sustainable-business/2014/sep/23/genuine-progress-indicator-gdp-gpi-vermont-maryland.

Chakravarty, S., Chikkatur, A., Coninck, H., *et al.* (2009). Sharing global CO_2 emissions among one billion high emitters. *PNAS* **106**(29): 11884–8, www.pnas.org/content/106/29/11884.

Chasek, P. S., Downie, D. L., and Brown, J. W. (2014). *Global Environmental Politics*, 6th ed. Boulder, CO: Westview Press, www.worldcat.org/title/global-environmental-politics/oclc/827119914.

Chemnic, J. (2018). U.S. stands with Russia and Saudi Arabia against climate science. *Scientific American*, December 10, www.scientificamerican.com/article/u-s-stands-with-russia-and-saudi-arabia-against-climate-science/.

Christoff, P. (2010). Cold climate in Copenhagen: China and the United States at COP15. *Environmental Politics* **19**(4): 637–56, www.tandfonline.com/doi/abs/10.1080/09644016.2010.489718.

Ciplet, D., Roberts, J. T., Khan, M. (2015). Geopolitics. In K. Backstrand and E. Lovbrand, eds., *Research Handbook on Climate Governance*. Cheltenham: Edward Elgar, pp. 109–20, www.elgaronline.com/view/edcoll/9781783470594/9781783470594.00019.xml.

Climate Action Tracker (2020). Countries, https://climateactiontracker.org/countries/.

Climate Council (2019). *Compound Costs: How Climate Change is Damaging Australia's Economy*. Potts Point, Australia: Climate Council of Australia, www.climatecouncil.org.au/wp-content/uploads/2019/05/costs-of-climate-change-report-v3.pdf.

Climate Investigations Center (2019). Thousands of fossil fuel "observers" attended climate negotiations: UNFCCC data 2005-2018 COP1-COP24. Climate Investigations Center, June 21, https://climateinvestigations.org/thousands-of-fossil-fuel-observers-attended-climate-negotiations-unfccc-data-2005-2018-cop1-cop24/.

Coady, D., Parry, I., Le, N. P., and Shang, B. (2019). Global fossil fuel subsidies remain large: an update based on country-level estimates. IMF Working Paper, WP/19/89, www.imf.org/en/Publications/WP/Issues/2019/05/02/Global-Fossil-Fuel-Subsidies-Remain-Large-An-Update-Based-on-Country-Level-Estimates-46509.

Cochrane, E., and Friedman, L. (2020). House Democrats push environmental bills, but victories are few. *New York Times*, January 10, www.nytimes.com/2020/01/10/us/politics/environment-climate-democrats-congress.html.

Colman, Z. (2019). Trump deepens legal war against California, automakers. *Politico*, September 6, www.politico.com/story/2019/09/06/doj-auto-trump-fuel-efficiency-1483589.

Conca, K., Thwaites, J., and Lee, G. (2017). Climate change and the UN Security Council: bully pulpit or bull in a china shop? *Global Environmental Politics* **17**(2): 1–20, www.mitpressjournals.org/doi/10.1162/GLEP_a_00398.

Cook, J. (2020). Global warming & climate change myths. *Skeptical Science: Getting Skeptical about Global Warming Skepticism*, www.skepticalscience.com/argument.php.

Cook, J., Oreskes, N., Doran, P.T., *et al.* (2016). Consensus on consensus: a synthesis of consensus estimates on human-caused global warming. *Environmental Research Letters* **11**(4): 1–7, https://iopscience.iop.org/article/10.1088/1748-9326/11/4/048002/pdf.

Corley, R. (2020). What if the restrictions on tobacco ads applied to climate-polluting products? *Corporate Knights* (Winter), www.corporateknights.com/channels/climate-and-carbon/restrictions-tobacco-ads-applied-climate-polluting-products-15798748/.

Corneloup, I. A., and Mol, A. P. J. (2014). Small island developing states and international climate change negotiations: the power of moral "leadership." *International Environmental Agreements* **14**: 281–97, www.researchgate.net/publication/271658504_Small_island_developing_states_and_international_climate_change_negotiations_the_power_of_moral_leadership.

Crippa, M., Oreggioni, G., Guizzardi, D., *et al.* (2019). *Fossil CO2 and GHG Emissions of All World Countries.* Luxembourg: Publication Office of the European Union, https://ec.europa.eu/jrc/en/publication/eur-scientific-and-technical-research-reports/fossil-co2-and-ghg-emissions-all-world-countries-0.

Crist, M. (2020). What the coronavirus means for climate change. *New York Times*, March 27, www.nytimes.com/2020/03/27/opinion/sunday/coronavirus-climate-change.html.

Daly, H. E. (1991). *Steady-State Economics*, 2nd ed. Washington, DC: Island Press, https://islandpress.org/books/steady-state-economics.

Dargay, J., Gately, D., and Sommer, M. (2007). Vehicle ownership and income growth, worldwide: 1960-2030. *Energy Journal* **28**(4): 143–70, www.jstor.org/stable/41323125?seq=1.

Dauvergne, P. (2008). *The Shadows of Consumption: Consequences for the Global Environment.* Cambridge, MA: MIT Press, https://mitpress.mit.edu/books/shadows-consumption.

Davenport, C., and Landler, M. (2019). Trump administration hardens its attack on climate science. *New York Times*, May 27, www.nytimes.com/2019/05/27/us/politics/trump-climate-science.html.

Davydova, A. (2017). From floods to fires, Russia sees stronger climate impacts – but efforts to adapt lag. *Reuters*, June 8, www.reuters.com/article/us-russia-climate-change-impacts-idUSKBN18Z04Z.

DeAngelis, T. (2004). Consumerism and its discontents. *Monitor on Psychology* **35**(6): 52, www.apa.org/monitor/jun04/discontents.

De Graaf, J., Wann, D., and Naylor, T. H. (2014). *Affluenza: How Overconsumption Is Killing Us – and How We Can Fight Back*. San Francisco: Barrett-Koehler, www .worldcat.org/title/affluenza-how-overconsumption-is-killing-us-and-how-we-can-fight-back/oclc/844728863.

Depledge, J. (2008). Striving for no: Saudi Arabia in the climate change regime. *Global Environmental Politics* **8**(4): 9–35, www.mitpressjournals.org/doi/10.1162/glep .2008.8.4.9.

Dessler, A. E., and Parson, E. A. (2020). *The Science and Politics of Global Climate Change: A Guide to the Debate*, 3rd ed. Cambridge: Cambridge University Press, https://doi.org/10.1017/CBO9780511790430.

Devlin, H. (2018). Rising global meat consumption "will devastate environment." *The Guardian*, July 19, www.theguardian.com/environment/2018/jul/19/rising-global-meat-consumption-will-devastate-environment.

Diamond, J. (2008). What's your consumption factor? *New York Times*, January 2, http://jareddiamond.org/Jared_Diamond/Further_Reading_files/Diamond %202008.pdf.

Dietzel, A., and Harris, P. G. (2019). A cosmopolitan agenda for climate justice: embracing non-state actors. In P. G. Harris, ed., *A Research Agenda for Climate Justice*. Cheltenham: Edward Elgard, pp. 77–90, www.elgaronline.com/view/ edcoll/9781788118163/9781788118163.00012.xml.

Dinerstein, E., Vynne, C., Sala, E., *et al.* (2019). A global deal for nature: guiding principles, milestones and targets. *Science Advances* **5**(4): 1–17, https://advances .sciencemag.org/content/5/4/eaaw2869/tab-pdf.

Dimitrov, R. S. (2019). Empty institutions in global environmental politics. *International Studies Review*, **22**(3): 626–50, https://doi.org/10.1093/isr/viz029.

Dorsey, K. (2014). Crossing boundaries: the environment in international relations. In A. C. Isenberg, ed., *The Oxford Handbook of Environmental History*. Oxford: Oxford University Press, pp. 688–715, www.oxfordhandbooks.com/view/10 .1093/oxfordhb/9780195324907.001.0001/oxfordhb-9780195324907-e-024.

Downie, C. (2017). Fighting for King Coal's crown: business actors in the US coal and utility industries. *Global Environmental Politics* **17**(1): 21–39, www .mitpressjournals.org/doi/10.1162/GLEP_a_00388.

Doyle, M. (2011). International ethics and the responsibility to protect. *International Studies Review* **13**(1): 72–84, www.jstor.org/stable/23016142.

Drexhage, J., and Murphy, D. (2009). Copenhagen: a memorable time for all the wrong reasons? An IISD Commentary, International Institute for Sustainable Development, www.iisd.org/articles/copenhagen-memorable-time-all-wrong-reasons.

Drollette, D. (2020). Trump, coronavirus and climate change: using a pandemic to gut the EPA. *Bulletin of the Atomic Scientists*, April 21, https://thebulletin.org/2020/ 04/trump-coronavirus-and-climate-change-using-a-pandemic-to-gut-the-epa/.

Dryzek, J. S., and Pickering, J. (2019). *The Politics of the Anthropocene*. Oxford: Oxford University Press, pp. 27–43, https://global.oup.com/academic/product/the-politics-of-the-anthropocene-9780198809623.

Dubash, N. K. (2019). *India in a Warming World: Integrating Climate Change and Development*. New Delhi: Oxford University Press, https://global.oup.com/aca demic/product/india-in-a-warming-world-9780199498734.

Dubois, D., and Ordabayeva, N. (2015). Social hierarchy, social status and status consumption. In M. I. Norton, D. D. Rucker and C. Lamberton, eds., *The Cambridge Handbook of Consumer Psychology*. Cambridge: Cambridge University Press, pp. 332–67, https://doi.org/10.1017/CBO9781107706552.013.

Dubois, G., Sovacool, B., Aall, C., *et al.* (2019). It starts at home? Climate policies targeting household consumption and behavioral decisions are key to low-carbon futures. *Energy Research & Social Science* 52: 144–58, www.sciencedirect.com/science/article/pii/S2214629618310314.

Dunne, D. (2018). Geoengineering carries "large risks" for natural world, studies show. *Carbon Brief*, January 22, www.carbonbrief.org/geoengineering-carries-large-risks-for-natural-world-studies-show.

Dupont, C., and Oberthur, S. (2015). The European Union. In K. Backstrand and E. Lovbrand, eds., *Research Handbook on Climate Governance*. Cheltenham: Edward Elgar, pp. 224–36, www.elgaronline.com/view/edcoll/9781783470594/9781783470594.00030.xml.

Durning, A. (1992). *How Much Is Enough: The Consumer Society and the Future of the Earth*. New York: W. W. Norton, www.worldcat.org/title/how-much-is-enough-the-consumer-society-and-the-future-of-the-earth/oclc/25916891.

Duyck, S, Lennon, E., Obergassel, W., and Savaresi, A. (2018). Human rights and the Paris Agreement's implementation guidelines: opportunities to develop a rights-based approach. *Carbon and Climate Law Review* 12(3): 191–202, https://cclr.lexxion.eu/article/CCLR/2018/3/5.

Dyer, H. (2017). Challenges to traditional international relations theory posed by environmental change. *Oxford Research Encyclopedias: International Studies*, https://oxfordre.com/internationalstudies/view/10.1093/acrefore/9780190846626.001.0001/acrefore-9780190846626-e-108.

EASAC (2018). Negative emission technologies: what role in meeting Paris Agreement targets? EASC policy report 35, https://easac.eu/fileadmin/PDF_s/reports_statements/Negative_Carbon/EASAC_Report_on_Negative_Emission_Technologies.pdf.

Easterlin, R. A. (2016) *Happiness, Growth and the Life Cycle*. Oxford: Oxford University Press, https://global.oup.com/academic/product/happiness-growth-and-the-life-cycle-9780199597093.

Easterlin, R. A. (2017). Paradox lost? USC-INET Research Paper No. 16-02, https://papers.ssrn.com/sol3/papers.cfm?abstract_id=2714062.

Easterlin, R. A., McVey, L. A., Switek, M., Sawangfa, O., and Zweig, J. S. (2010). The happiness-income paradox revisited. *PNAS* 107(52): 22463–8, www.pnas.org/content/107/52/22463.

Easterlin, R. A., Morgan, R., Switek, M., and Wang, F. (2012). China's life satisfaction, 1990–2010. *PNAS* 109(25): 9775–80, www.pnas.org/content/109/25/9775.

Ebinger, C. K. (2016). *India's Energy and Climate Policy: Can India Meet the Challenge of Industrialization and Climate Change?* Brookings Policy Brief 16-01. Washington, DC: Brookings Institution, www.brookings.edu/research/indias-energy-and-climate-policy-can-india-meet-the-challenge-of-industrialization-and-climate-change/.

EcoEquity and Stockholm Environment Institute (2018). After Paris: inequality, fair shares and the climate emergency. Climate Equity Project report, http://civilsocietyreview.org/files/COP24_CSO_Equity_Review_Report.pdf.

Ecola, L., Rohr, C., Zmud, J. *et al.* (2014). *The Future of Driving in Developing Countries*. Santa Monica, CA: RAND Corporation, www.rand.org/pubs/research_reports/RR636.html.

Elgin, D. (2010). *Voluntary Simplicity, 2nd edition*. New York: HarperCollins, www.harpercollins.com/9780061779268/voluntary-simplicity-second-revised-edition/.

Elliott, B. (2016). *Natural Catastrophe: Climate Change and Neoliberal Governance*. Edinburgh: Edinburgh University Press, https://edinburghuniversitypress.com/book-natural-catastrophe.html.

Ellis, E. C., Maslin, M., and Lewis, S. (2020). Planting trees won't save the world. *New York Times*, February 12, www.nytimes.com/2020/02/12/opinion/trump-climate-change-trees.html.

Elmer-Dewitt, P. (2019). Summit to save the earth: rich vs. poor. *Time*, June 1, http://content.time.com/time/magazine/article/0,9171,975656,00.html.

Elzen, M. G. J., Olivier, J. G. J., Hohne, N., and Janssens-Maenhout, G. (2013). Countries' contributions to climate change: effect of accounting for all greenhouse gases, recent trends, basic needs and technological progress. *Climatic Change* **121**: 397–412, www.academia.edu/22257985/Countries_contributions_to_climate_change_effect_of_accounting_for_all_greenhouse_gases_recent_trends_basic_needs_and_technological_progress.

Embassy of the Federative Republic of Brazil (2010). Letter to the United Nations Framework Convention on Climate Change, January 29, https://unfccc.int/files/meetings/cop_15/copenhagen_accord/application/pdf/brazilcphaccord_app2.pdf.

Environment and Climate Change Canada (2019). Canadian environmental sustainability indicators: greenhouse gas emissions, www.canada.ca/content/dam/eccc/documents/pdf/cesindicators/ghg-emissions/2019/national-GHG-emissions-en.pdf.

EPA (2015). Overview of the Clean Power Plan: cutting carbon pollution from power plants. EPA Factsheet, https://19january2017snapshot.epa.gov/sites/production/files/2015-08/documents/fs-cpp-overview.pdf.

Erickson, P., Lazarus, M., and Piggot, G. (2018). Limiting fossil fuel production as the next big step in climate policy. *Nature Climate Change* **8**(12): 1037–43, www.nature.com/articles/s41558-018-0337-0.

Ehrlich, P. R. (1968). *The Population Bomb*. New York: Sierra Club/Ballantine, www.worldcat.org/title/population-bomb/oclc/170688.

Ehrlich, P. R., and Ehrlich, A. H. (2009). The Population Bomb revisited. *Electronic Journal of Sustainable Development* **1**(3): 5–13, https://geog.utm.utoronto.ca/desrochers/The_Population_Bomb.pdf.

ETC Group and Heinrich Boll Foundation (2017). A civil society briefing on geoengineering: climate change, smoke and mirrors. Briefing paper, www.etcgroup.org/sites/www.etcgroup.org/files/files/etc_geoeng_briefing_usletter_sept2017_v2.pdf.

European Commission (2019a). A European Green Deal: striving to be the first climate-neutral continent, https://ec.europa.eu/info/strategy/priorities-2019-2024/european-green-deal_en.

European Commission (2019b). What is the European Green Deal? https://ec.europa.eu/commission/presscorner/detail/en/fs_19_6714.

European Commission (n.d.). Reducing emissions from aviation, https://ec.europa.eu/clima/policies/transport/aviation_en.

Fang, L., and Lerner, S. (2019). Saudi Arabia denies its key role in climate change even as it prepares for the worst. *The Intercept*, September 18, https://theintercept.com/2019/09/18/saudi-arabia-aramco-oil-climate-change/.

Farand, C. (2019a). Nationalism could sink the Paris Agreement. The UN chief is fighting back. *Climate Home News*, June 28, www.climatechangenews.com/2019/06/28/antonio-guterres-fights-climate-un/.

Farand, C. (2019b). UN report on 1.5C blocked from climate talks after Saudi Arabia disputes science. *Climate Home News*, June 27, www.climatechangenews.com/2019/06/27/un-report-1-5c-blocked-climate-talks-saudi-arabia-disputes-science/.

Farand, C. (2020). Coronavirus may toughen airlines' goals for curbing emissions in 2020s. *Climate Home News*, March 13, www.climatechangenews.com/2020/03/13/coronavirus-may-toughen-airlines-goals-curbing-emissions-2020s/.

Fawcett, T., and Parag, Y. (2010). An introduction to personal carbon trading. *Climate Policy* 10: 329–38, www.tandfonline.com/doi/abs/10.3763/cpol.2010.0649.

Fearnside, P. M., and Pueyo, S. (2012). Greenhouse-gas emissions from tropical dams. *Nature Climate Change* 2: 382–4, www.nature.com/articles/nclimate1540.

Fesenfeld, L. P., Wicki, M., Sun, Y., and Bernauer, T. (2020). Policy packaging can make food system transformation feasible. *Nature Food* 1: 173–82, www.nature.com/articles/s43016-020-0047-4.

Fiji (2017). Talanoa Dialogue for Climate Ambition, https://cop23.com.fj/talanoa-dialogue/.

Filho, W. L., and Hemstock, S. L., eds. (2019). *Climate Change and the Role of Education*. Cham, Switzerland: Springer, www.springer.com/gp/book/9783030328979.

Fitzpatrick, T. (2014). *Climate Change and Poverty: A New Agenda for Developed Nations*. Bristol: Policy Press, https://policy.bristoluniversitypress.co.uk/climate-change-and-poverty.

Flannery, T. (2007). *The Weather Makers: Our Changing Climate and What It Means for Life on Earth*. London: Penguin, www.worldcat.org/title/weather-makers-our-changing-climate-and-what-it-means-for-life-on-earth/oclc/144595389.

Forbes (2018). Saudi Arabia: profile, www.forbes.com/places/saudi-arabia/.

Foster, J. B., Clark, B., and York, R. (2010). Capitalism and the curse of energy efficiency: the return of Jevons Paradox. *Monthly Review*, November 1, https://monthlyreview.org/2010/11/01/capitalism-and-the-curse-of-energy-efficiency/.

Fountain, H. (2020). 2019 was second hottest year on record. *New York Times*, January 8, www.nytimes.com/2020/01/08/climate/2019-temperatures.html.

Fox, M. J., and Erickson, J. D. (2020). Design and meaning of the genuine progress indicator: a statistical analysis of the U.S. fifty-state model. *Ecological Economics* 167: 106441, www.sciencedirect.com/science/article/pii/S0921800919302411.

Friedlingstein, P., Jones, M. W., O'Sullivan, M., *et al.* (2019). Global carbon budget 2019. *Earth System Science Data* 11: 1783–1838, www.earth-syst-sci-data.net/11/1783/2019/.

Galarraga, I., Gonzalez-Eguino, M., and Markandya, A. (2011). The role of regional governments in climate change policy. *Environmental Policy and Governance* 21 (3): 164–82, https://doi.org/10.1002/eet.572.

Gallagher, K. S., Zhang, F., Orvis, R., Rissman, J., and Liu, Q. (2019). Assessing the policy gaps for achieving China's climate targets in the Paris Agreement. *Nature Communications* 10: 1256, www.nature.com/articles/s41467-019-09159-0.

Galvin, R., and Healy, N. (2020). The Green New Deal in the United States: what it is and how to pay for it. *Energy Research and Social Science* **67**: 1–9, https://doi.org/10.1016/j.erss.2020.101529.

Garcia-Olivares, A., Sole, J., and Osychenko, O. (2018). Transportation in a 100% renewable energy system. *Energy Conversion and Management* **158**: 266–85, https://reader.elsevier.com/reader/sd/pii/S0196890417312050.

Gerlagh, R., Lupi, V., and Galeotti, M. (2018). Family planning and climate change. CESifo Working Paper No. 7421, https://ssrn.com/abstract=3338775.

Gershkovich, E. (2019). How does a powerful Russian lobby plan to halt climate change? With coal, oil and gas. *The Moscow Times*, November 15, www.themoscowtimes.com/2019/11/15/how-does-a-powerful-russian-lobby-plan-to-halt-climate-change-with-coal-oil-and-gas-a68173.

Gerth, K. (2010). *As China Goes, So Goes the World: How Chinese Consumers are Transforming Everything.* New York: Hill and Wang, www.worldcat.org/title/as-china-goes-so-goes-the-world-how-chinese-consumers-are-transforming-every thing/oclc/751796120.

Ghebreyesus, T. A. (2019). Climate change is already killing us: how our warmer and wetter planet is getting sicker and deadlier by the day. *Foreign Affairs*, September 23, www.foreignaffairs.com/articles/2019-09-23/climate-change-already-killing-us.

Gilding, P. (2012). *The Great Disruption: How the Climate Crisis Will Transform the Global Economy.* London: Bloomsbury, www.bloomsbury.com/uk/the-great-disruption-9781408817513/.

Global Carbon Project (2020). *Global Carbon Atlas*, http://globalcarbonatlas.org/en/content/welcome-carbon-atlas.

Global Footprint Network (2017). How ecological footprint accounting helps us to recognize that engaging in meaningful climate action is critical for our own success. Blog post, November 9, www.footprintnetwork.org/2017/11/09/ecological-footprint-climate-change/.

Global Footprint Network (2020). Ecological footprint, www.footprintnetwork.org/our-work/ecological-footprint/.

Global Energy Monitor (2020). In tougher times China falls back on coal, January 13, https://globalenergymonitor.org/gem-in-the-news/in-tougher-times-china-falls-back-on-coal/.

Global Humanitarian Forum (2009). *Human Impact Report: Climate Change – The Anatomy of a Silent Crisis.* Geneva: Global Humanitarian Forum, www.ghf-ge.org/human-impact-report.pdf.

Godfray, H. C. J., Aveyard, P., Garnett, T., *et al.* (2018). Meat consumption, health and the environment. *Science* **361**(6399): 1–8, https://science.sciencemag.org/content/sci/361/6399/eaam5324.full.pdf.

Goldberg, M., Gustafson, A., Rosenthal, S., *et al.* (2020). For the first time, the Alarmed are now the largest of global warming's six Americas. Yale Program on Climate Change Communication, https://climatecommunication.yale.edu/publications/for-the-first-time-the-alarmed-are-now-the-largest-of-global-warmings-six-americas/.

Gondor, D. (2009). Why do we over-consume? *Our World*, December 14, https://ourworld.unu.edu/en/why-do-we-over-consume.

Gore, T. (2015). Extreme carbon inequality: why the Paris climate deal must put the poorest, lowest emitting and most vulnerable people first. Oxfam media briefing, December 2, www.oxfam.org/en/research/extreme-carbon-inequality.

Gotmark, F., Cafaro, P., and O'Sullivan, J. (2018). Ageing human populations: good for us, good for the earth. *Trends in Ecology & Evolution* **33**(11): 851–62, https://doi.org/10.1016/j.tree.2018.08.015.

Gough, I. (2017). *Heat, Greed and Human Need: Climate Change, Capitalism and Sustainable Wellbeing*. Cheltenham: Edward Elgar, www.elgaronline.com/view/9781785365102/9781785365102.xml.

Gregoire, C. (2017). The psychology of materialism, and why it's making you unhappy. *Huffington Post*, December 6, www.huffpost.com/entry/psychology-materialism_n_4425982.

Griffin, P. (2017). CDP carbon majors report 2017. CDP Report (July), www.cdp.net/en/articles/media/new-report-shows-just-100-companies-are-source-of-over-70-of-emissions.

Griffiths, S. (2020). Why your internet habits are not as clean as you think. *BBC Future*, March 6, www.bbc.com/future/article/20200305-why-your-internet-habits-are-not-as-clean-as-you-think.

Gupta, H., Kohli, K. K., and Ahluwalia, A. S. (2015). Mapping "consistency" in India's climate change position: dynamics and dilemmas of science diplomacy. *Ambio* **44**: 592–99, https://link.springer.com/article/10.1007/s13280-014-0609-5.

Guterres, A. (2019a). End fossil fuel subsidies, and stop using taxpayers' money to destroy the world: Guterres. *UN News*, May 28, https://news.un.org/en/story/2019/05/1039241.

Guterres, A. (2019b). Remarks at the opening ceremony of the UN Climate Change Conference COP25, www.un.org/sg/en/content/sg/speeches/2019-12-02/remarks-opening-ceremony-of-cop25.

Guy, K. A., Femia, F., Werrell, C., *et al.* (2020). A security threat assessment of global climate change: how likely warming scenarios indicate a catastrophic security future. Product of the National Security, Military and Intelligence Panel on Climate Change, https://climateandsecurity.files.wordpress.com/2020/03/a-security-threat-assessment-of-climate-change.pdf.

Hamilton, C. (2015). *Requiem for a Species: Why We Resist the Truth about Climate Change*. London: Earthscan, www.routledge.com/Requiem-for-a-Species/Hamilton/p/book/9781138928084.

Hansen, C. O., Gronsedt, P., Graversen, C. L., and Hendricksen, C. (2016). *Arctic Shipping: Commercial Opportunities and Challenges*. Copenhagen: CBS Maritime, https://services-webdav.cbs.dk/doc/CBS.dk/Arctic%20Shipping%20-%20Commercial%20Opportunities%20and%20Challenges.pdf.

Hantula, D. A. (2003). Evolutionary psychology and consumption. *Psychology and Marketing* **20**(9): 757–63, https://onlinelibrary.wiley.com/doi/abs/10.1002/mar.10095.

Harris, P. G. (2001a). *International Equity and Global Environmental Politics: Power and Principles in U.S. Foreign Policy*. London: Routledge, 2001, www.routledge.com/International-Equity-and-Global-Environmental-Politics-Power-and-Principles/Harris/p/book/9781138735668.

Harris, P. G., ed. (2001b). *The Environment, International Relations, and U.S. Foreign Policy*. Washington, DC: Georgetown University Press, http://press.georgetown.edu/book/georgetown/environment-international-relations-and-us-foreign-policy.

Harris, P. G., ed. (2002). *International Environmental Cooperation: Politics and Diplomacy in Pacific Asia*. Boulder: University Press of Colorado, https://

paulgharris.files.wordpress.com/2018/10/p-g-harris-ed-international-environmental-cooperation.pdf.

Harris, P. G., ed. (2003). *Global Warming and East Asia: The Domestic and International Politics of Climate Change.* London: Routledge, www.routledge .com/Global-Warming-and-East-Asia-The-Domestic-and-International-Politics-of/Harris/p/book/9780415315449.

Harris, P. G., ed. (2005). *Confronting Environmental Change in East and Southeast Asia: Eco-Politics, Foreign Policy, and Sustainable Development.* New York: Earthscan/ United Nations University Press, www.routledge.com/Confronting-Environmental-Change-in-East-and-Southeast-Asia-Eco-politics/Harris/p/book/9781853839726.

Harris, P. G., ed. (2007a). *Europe and Global Climate Change: Politics, Foreign Policy, and Regional Cooperation.* Cheltenham: Edward Elgar, www.elgaronline .com/view/9781845429447.xml.

Harris, P. G. (2007b). Sharing the burdens of global climate change: international equity and justice in European policy. In P. G. Harris, ed., *Europe and Global Climate Change: Politics, Foreign Policy, and Regional Cooperation.* Cheltenham: Edward Elgar, 2007, pp. 349–90, www.elgaronline.com/view/ 9781845429447.00026.xml.

Harris, P. G. (2009a). Beyond Bush: environmental politics and prospects for US climate policy. *Energy Policy* **37**(3): 966–71, www.sciencedirect.com/science/ article/abs/pii/S0301421508006587.

Harris, P. G., ed. (2009b). *Climate Change and Foreign Policy: Case Studies from East to West.* London: Routledge, www.routledge.com/Climate-Change-and-Foreign-Policy-Case-Studies-from-East-to-West/Harris/p/book/9780415846615.

Harris, P. G., ed. (2009c). *Environmental Change and Foreign Policy: Theory and Practice.* London: Routledge, www.routledge.com/Environmental-Change-and-Foreign-Policy-Theory-and-Practice/Harris/p/book/9780415522038.

Harris, P. G., ed. (2009d). *The Politics of Climate Change: Environmental Dynamics in International Affairs.* London: Routledge, www.routledge.com/The-Politics-of-Climate-Change-Environmental-Dynamics-in-International/Harris/p/book/9780415518765.

Harris, P. G. (2010a). Misplaced ethics of climate Change: political vs. environmental geography. *Ethics, Place & Environment* **13**(2): 215–22, www.tandfonline.com/ doi/abs/10.1080/13668791003778875.

Harris, P. G. (2010b). *World Ethics and Climate Change: From International to Global Justice.* Edinburgh: Edinburgh University Press, www.worldcat.org/title/world-ethics-and-climate-change-from-international-to-global-justice/oclc/317524961.

Harris, P. G., ed. (2011a). *China's Responsibility for Climate Change: Ethics, Fairness and Environmental Policy.* Bristol: Policy Press, https://policy .bristoluniversitypress.co.uk/chinas-responsibility-for-climate-change.

Harris, P. G., ed. (2011b). *Ethics and Global Environmental Policy: Cosmopolitan Conceptions of Climate Change.* Cheltenham: Edward Elgar, www.elgaronline .com/abstract/9780857931603.xml.

Harris, P. G. (2012). *Environmental Policy and Sustainable Development in China.* Bristol: Bristol University Press/Policy Press https://policy.bristoluniversitypress .co.uk/environmental-policy-and-sustainable-development-in-china.

Harris, P. G. (2013). *What's Wrong with Climate Politics and How to Fix It.* Cambridge: Polity, https://politybooks.com/bookdetail/?isbn=9780745652511.

Harris, P. G., ed. (2014). *Routledge Handbook of Global Environmental Politics*. London: Routledge, www.routledge.com/Routledge-Handbook-of-Global-Environmental-Politics/Harris/p/book/9781138953611.

Harris, P. G. (2015). The future. In K. Backstrand and E. Lovbrand, eds., *Research Handbook on Climate Governance*. Cheltenham: Edward Elgar, pp. 566–77, www.elgaronline.com/view/edcoll/9781783470594/9781783470594.xml.

Harris, P. G., ed. (2016a). *Climate Change and American Foreign Policy*, updated edition. New York: Palgrave Macmillan, https://link.springer.com/book/10.1057%2F9781137120809.

Harris, P. G., ed. (2016b). *Ethics, Environmental Justice and Climate Change*. Cheltenham: Edward Elgar, www.elgaronline.com/view/Research_Reviews/9781783477135/intro.xml.

Harris, P. G. (2016c). *Global Ethics and Climate Change*. Edinburgh: Edinburgh University Press, https://edinburghuniversitypress.com/book-global-ethics-and-climate-change.html.

Harris, P. G. (2017). China's Paris pledge on climate change: inadequate and irresponsible. *Journal of Environmental Studies and Sciences* **7**: 102–7, https://link.springer.com/article/10.1007/s13412-017-0422-0.

Harris, P. G. (2018). Climate change: science, international cooperation and global environmental politics. In G. Kutting and K. Herman, eds., *Global Environmental Politics: Concepts, Theories and Case Studies*. London: Routledge, pp. 123–42, www.routledge.com/Global-Environmental-Politics-Concepts-Theories-and-Case-Studies-2nd/Kutting-Herman/p/book/9781138895355.

Harris, P. G., ed. (2019a). *A Research Agenda for Climate Justice*. Cheltenham: Edward Elgar, www.elgaronline.com/view/edcoll/9781788118163/9781788118163.xml.

Harris, P. G., ed. (2019b) *Climate Change and Ocean Governance: Politics and Policy for Threatened Seas*. Cambridge, Cambridge University Press, https://doi.org/10.1017/9781108502238.

Harris, P. G. (2019c). Climate change at sea: interactions, impacts and governance. In P. G. Harris, ed., *Climate Change and Ocean Governance: Politics and Policy for Threatened Seas*. Cambridge: Cambridge University Press, pp. 1–26, https://doi.org/10.1017/9781108502238.001.

Harris, P. G., and Symons, J. (2010). Justice in adaptation to climate change: cosmopolitan implications for international institutions. *Environmental Politics* **19**(4): 617–36, www.tandfonline.com/doi/abs/10.1080/09644016.2010.489716.

Harrison, K., and Sundstrom, L. M., eds. (2010). *Global Commons, Domestic Decisions: The Comparative Politics of Climate Change*. Cambridge, MA: MIT Press, https://mitpress.mit.edu/books/global-commons-domestic-decisions.

Hartmann, B. (2011). Population alarmism is dangerous. *Sustainability Forum: The Population and Sustainability Debate*, Carnegie Council for Ethics and International Affairs, September 15, www.carnegiecouncil.org/publications/articles_papers_reports/0107.

Harvard Medical School (2020). What's the beef with red meat? *Harvard Men's Health Watch*, www.health.harvard.edu/staying-healthy/whats-the-beef-with-red-meat.

Harvey, F. (2019). One climate crisis disaster happening every week, UN warns. *The Guardian*, July 7, www.theguardian.com/environment/2019/jul/07/one-climate-crisis-disaster-happening-every-week-un-warns.

Harvey, M. (2018). *Celebrity Influence: Politics, Persuasion and Issue-Based Advocacy.* Lawrence: University Press of Kansas, https://kansaspress.ku.edu/978-0-7006-2498-0.html.

Harwatt, H., Ripple, W. J., Chaudhary, A., Betts, M. G., and Hayek, M. N. (2020). Scientists call for renewed Paris pledges to transform agriculture. *The Lancet Planetary Health* **4**(1): E9–E10, www.thelancet.com/journals/lanplh/article/PIIS2542-5196(19)30245-1/fulltext.

Hausfather, Z. (2019). Analysis: global fossil-fuel emissions up 0.6% in 2019 due to China. *Carbon Brief*, December 4, www.carbonbrief.org/analysis-global-fossil-fuel-emissions-up-zero-point-six-per-cent-in-2019-due-to-china.

Henly, J. (2019). Finland pledges to become carbon neutral by 2035. *The Guardian*, June 4, www.theguardian.com/world/2019/jun/04/finland-pledges-to-become-carbon-neutral-by-2035.

Henry, L. A., and Sundstrom, L. M. (2007). Russia and the Kyoto Protocol: seeking an alignment of interests and image. *Global Environmental Politics* **7**(4): 47–69, www.researchgate.net/publication/241688820_Russia_and_the_Kyoto_Protocol_Seeking_an_Alignment_of_Interests_and_Image_with_Lisa_McIntosh_Sundstrom_Global_Environmental_Politics_7_4_November_2007_47-69.

Herring, J. (2020). "We're not willing to cave": UCP restates opposition to carbon tax. *Calgary Herald*, January 1, https://calgaryherald.com/news/local-news/ucp-outline-plan-to-fight-carbon-tax-as-new-year-brings-federal-levy.

Highfield, R. (2007). Relative wealth "makes you happier." *The Telegraph*, November 22, www.telegraph.co.uk/news/science/science-news/3315638/Relative-wealth-makes-you-happier.html.

Hilton, I (2019). How China's big overseas initiative threatens global climate progress. *YaleEnvironment360*, January 3, https://e360.yale.edu/features/how-chinas-big-overseas-initiative-threatens-climate-progress.

Ho, M. (2018). A simple guide to Xi Jinping Thought? Here's how China's official media tried to explain it. *South China Morning Post*, October 18, www.scmp.com/news/china/politics/article/2169151/simple-guide-xi-jinping-thought-heres-how-chinas-offi cial-media.

Howlett, M. (2014). Why are policy innovations rare and so often negative? Blame avoidance and problem denial in climate change policy-making. *Global Environmental Change* **29**: 395–403, www.sciencedirect.com/science/article/abs/pii/S0959378013002392?via%3Dihub.

Hulac, B. (2018). Every president since JFK was warned about climate change. *E&E News*, November 6, www.eenews.net/stories/1060105233.

Hussain, M. (2019). War on the world: industrialized militaries are a bigger part of the climate emergency than you know. *The Intercept*, September 15, https://theintercept.com/2019/09/15/climate-change-us-military-war/.

ICAO (n.d.). Carbon offsetting and reduction for international aviation, www.icao.int/environmental-protection/CORSIA/Pages/default.aspx.

India (2015). India's intended nationally determined contribution: working towards climate justice, www4.unfccc.int/sites/ndcstaging/PublishedDocuments/India%20First/INDIA%20INDC%20TO%20UNFCCC.pdf.

Ingraham, C. (2019). Americans are getting more miserable, and there's data to prove it. *Washington Post*, March 22, www.washingtonpost.com/business/2019/03/22/americans-are-getting-more-miserable-theres-data-prove-it/.

IEA (2019a). *Global Energy & CO2 Status Report 2019*. Paris: IEA, www.iea.org/geco/.

IEA (2019b). *World Energy Outlook 2019*. Paris: IEA, www.iea.org/reports/world-energy-outlook-2019.

IEA (2020a). *Aviation: More Efforts Needed*. Paris: IEA, www.iea.org/reports/aviation.

IEA (2020b). *Global Energy Review*. Paris: IEA, www.iea.org/reports/global-energy-review-2020.

IIED (2020). Call for business unusual: mechanisms for delivery change. IIED Briefing, https://pubs.iied.org/pdfs/17749IIED.pdf.

IISD (1998). Report of the Fourth Conference of the Parties to the UN Framework Convention on Climate Change: 2–13 November 1998. *Earth Negotiations Bulletin* **12**(97): 1–14, https://enb.iisd.org/download/pdf/enb1297e.pdf.

IISD (2000). Summary of the Sixth Conference of the Parties to the Framework Convention on Climate Change: 13–25 November 2000. *Earth Negotiations Bulletin* **12**(163): 1–19, http://enb.iisd.org/download/pdf/enb12163e.pdf.

IISD (2001). Summary of the Resumed Sixth Conference of the Parties to the UN Framework Convention on Climate Change Resumed Session, Bonn, Germany: 16–27 July 2001. *Earth Negotiations Bulletin* **12**(176): 1–15, http://enb.iisd.org/download/pdf/enb12176e.pdf.

IISD (2003). Summary of the Ninth Conference of the Parties to the UN Framework Convention on Climate Change: 1–12 December 2003. *Earth Negotiations Bulletin* **12**(231): 1–19, http://enb.iisd.org/vol12/enb12231e.html.

IISD (2004). Summary of the Tenth Conference of the Parties to the UN Framework Convention on Climate Change: 6–18 December 2004. *Earth Negotiations Bulletin* **12**(260): 1–16, https://enb.iisd.org/download/pdf/enb12260e.pdf.

IISD (2005). Summary of the Eleventh Conference of the Parties to the UN Framework Convention on Climate Change and First Conference of the Parties Serving as the Meeting of the Parties to the Kyoto Protocol: 28 November – 10 December 2005. *Earth Negotiation Bulletin* **12**(291): 1–20, http://enb.iisd.org/download/pdf/enb12291e.pdf.

IISD (2006). Summary of the Twelfth Conference of the Parties to the UN Framework Convention on Climate Change and Second Meeting of the Parties to the Kyoto Protocol: 6–17 November 2006. *Earth Negotiation Bulletin* **12**(318): 1–22, http://enb.iisd.org/download/pdf/enb12318e.pdf.

IISD (2007). Summary of the Thirteenth Conference of the Parties to the UN Framework Convention on Climate Change and Third Meeting of the Parties to the Kyoto Protocol: 3–15 December 2007. *Earth Negotiation Bulletin* **12**(354): 1–22, http://enb.iisd.org/download/pdf/enb12354e.pdf.

IISD (2008). Summary of the Fourteenth Conference of the Parties to the UN Framework Convention on Climate Change and Fourth Meeting of the Parties to the Kyoto Protocol: 1–12 December 2008. *Earth Negotiation Bulletin* **12**(395): 1–20, http://enb.iisd.org/download/pdf/enb12395e.pdf.

IISD (2009). *A Brief Analysis of the Copenhagen Climate Change Conference*: An IISD Comentary, www.iisd.org/sites/default/files/publications/enb_copenhagen_commentary.pdf.

IISD (2010). Summary of the Cancun Climate Change Conference: 19 November – 11 December 2010. *Earth Negotiations Bulletin* **12**(498): 1–30, http://enb.iisd.org/download/pdf/enb12498e.pdf.

IISD (2011). Summary of the Durban Climate Change Conference: 28 November – 11 December 2011. *Earth Negotiations Bulletin* **12**(534): 1–34, http://enb.iisd.org/download/pdf/enb12534e.pdf.

IISD (2012). Summary of the Doha Climate Change Conference: 26 November – 8 December 2012. *Earth Negotiations Bulletin* **12**(567): 1–30, http://enb.iisd.org/download/pdf/enb12567e.pdf.

IISD (2013). Summary of the Warsaw Climate Change Conference: 11–23 November 2013. *Earth Negotiations Bulletin* **12**(594): 1–32, http://enb.iisd.org/download/pdf/enb12594e.pdf.

IISD (2014). Summary of the Lima Climate Change Conference: 1–14 December 2014. *Earth Negotiations Bulletin* **12**(619): 1–46, http://enb.iisd.org/download/pdf/enb12619e.pdf.

IISD (2015). Summary of the Paris Climate Change Conference: 29 November – 13 December 2015. *Earth Negotiations Bulletin* **12**(663): 1–47, http://enb.iisd.org/download/pdf/enb12663e.pdf.

IISD (2016). Summary of the Marrakech Climate Change Conference: 7–19 November 2016. *Earth Negotiations Bulletin* **12**(689): 1–39, https://enb.iisd.org/download/pdf/enb12689e.pdf.

IISD (2017). Summary of the Fiji/Bonn Climate Change Conference: 6–17 November 2017. *Earth Negotiations Bulletin* **12**(714): 1–33, https://enb.iisd.org/download/pdf/enb12714e.pdf.

IISD (2018). Summary of the Katowice Climate Change Conference: 2–15 December 2018. *Earth Negotiations Bulletin* **12**(747): 1–34, http://enb.iisd.org/download/pdf/enb12747e.pdf.

IISD (2019). Summary of the Chile/Madrid Climate Change Conference: 2–15 December 2019. *Earth Negotiations Bulletin* **12**(775): 1–28, https://enb.iisd.org/download/pdf/enb12775e.pdf.

International Organization for Migration (2014). *IOM Outlook on Migration, Environment and Climate Change*. Geneva: IOM, https://publications.iom.int/system/files/pdf/mecc_outlook.pdf.

IPCC (1996). *Climate Change 1995: The Science of Climate Change*. Cambridge: Cambridge University Press, www.ipcc.ch/report/ar2/wg1/.

IPCC (2007). *Climate Change 2007: Synthesis Report*. Cambridge: Cambridge University Press, www.ipcc.ch/report/ar4/syr/.

IPCC (2013). *Climate Change 2013: The Physical Science Basis*. Cambridge: Cambridge University Press, www.ipcc.ch/report/ar5/wg1/.

IPCC (2014a). *Climate Change 2014: Impacts, Adaptation and Vulnerability – Part B: Regional Aspects*. Geneva: IPCC, www.ipcc.ch/report/ar5/wg2/.

IPCC (2014b). *Climate Change 2014: Synthesis Report*. Geneva: IPCC, www.ipcc.ch/report/ar5/syr/.

IPCC (2018). *Global Warming of 1.5°C*. Geneva: IPCC, www.ipcc.ch/sr15/.

IPCC (2019). *Climate Change and Land*. Geneva: IPCC, www.ipcc.ch/srccl/.

Isaksen, K. A., and Stokke, K. (2014). Climate change discourse and politics in India: climate change as a challenge and opportunity for diplomacy and development. *Geoforum* **57**: 110–19, www.sciencedirect.com/science/article/abs/pii/S0016718514001948.

Iskyan, K. (2016). China's middle class is exploding. *Business Insider*, August 28, www.businessinsider.com/chinas-middle-class-is-exploding-2016-8?op=1.

Ives, M. (2018). Rich nations vowed billions for climate change; poor countries are waiting. *New York Times*, September, 9, www.nytimes.com/2018/09/09/world/asia/green-climate-fund-global-warming.html.

Jackson, R. B., Le Quere, C., Andrew, R. M., *et al.* (2019). Global energy growth is outpacing decarbonization. Special report for the United Nations Climate Action Summit, Global Carbon Project, www.globalcarbonproject.org/global/pdf/GCP_2019_Global%20energy%20growth%20outpace%20decarbonization_UN%20Climate%20Summit_HR.pdf.

Jackson, T. (2009). *Prosperity without Growth: Economics for a Finite Planet.* London: Earthscan, www.worldcat.org/title/prosperity-without-growth-economics-for-a-finite-planet/oclc/320800523.

Jevnaker, T., and Wettestad, J. (2017). Ratcheting up carbon trade: the politics of reforming EU emissions trading. *Global Environmental Politics* **17**(2): 105–24, www.mitpressjournals.org/doi/abs/10.1162/GLEP_a_00403?journalCode=glep.

Johnson, L. B. (1965). Special message to the Congress on conservation and restoration of natural beauty, February 8. LBJ Presidential Library, www.lbjlibrary.net/collections/selected-speeches/1965/02-08-1965.html.

Joint Research Centre (European Commission) (2017). CO2 time series 1990-2015 per region/country, https://edgar.jrc.ec.europa.eu/overview.php?v=CO2ts1990-2015.

Jolly, J., and Ambrose, J. (2019). Saudi Aramco become most valuable listed company in history. *The Guardian*, December 11, www.theguardian.com/business/2019/dec/11/saudi-aramco-shares-soar-as-it-becomes-world-largest-listed-company.

Jones, L., Harvey, B., Cochrane, L., *et al.* (2018). Designing the next generation of climate adaptation research for development. *Regional Environmental Change* **18**: 297–304, https://link.springer.com/article/10.1007/s10113-017-1254-x.

Jotzo, F., Depledge, J., and Winkler, H. (2018). US and international climate policy under President Trump. *Climate Policy* **18**(7): 813–17, https://doi.org/10.1080/14693062.2018.1490051.

Kahn, B. (2017). We just breached the 410 ppm threshold for CO_2. *Scientific American*, April 21, www.scientificamerican.com/article/we-just-breached-the-410-ppm-threshold-for-co2/.

Kaneti, M. (2020). China's climate diplomacy 2.0. *The Diplomat*, January 2, https://thediplomat.com/2020/01/chinas-climate-diplomacy-2-0/.

Kato, Y. (2019). What is Xi Jinping's major power diplomacy? *AsiaGlobal Online*, March 7, www.asiaglobalonline.hku.hk/xi-jinping-china-major-power-diplomacy/.

Kaufman, A. A. (2010). The "Century of Humiliation" then and now: Chinese perceptions of the international order. *Pacific Focus* **25**(1): 1–33, https://onlinelibrary.wiley.com/doi/abs/10.1111/j.1976-5118.2010.01039.x.

Kelley, C. P. Mohtadi, S., Cane, M. A., Seager, R., and Kushnir, Y. (2015). Climate change in the Fertile Crescent and implications of the recent Syrian drought. *PNAS* **112**(11): 3241–6, www.pnas.org/content/112/11/3241.

Kenner, D. (2019). *Carbon Inequality: The Role of the Richest in Climate Change.* London: Routledge, www.routledge.com/Carbon-Inequality-The-Role-of-the-Richest-in-Climate-Change/Kenner/p/book/9780815399223.

Kharas, H. (2017). The unprecedented expansion of the global middle class: an update. Brookings Global Economy and Development working paper 100, www.brookings.edu/wp-content/uploads/2017/02/global_20170228_global-middle-class.pdf.

Kharas, H., and Hamel, K. (2018). A global tipping point: half the world is now middle class or wealthier. Brookings "Future Development" blog, September 27, www .brookings.edu/blog/future-development/2018/09/27/a-global-tipping-point-half-the-world-is-now-middle-class-or-wealthier/.

Khatiwala, S., Tanhua, T., Mikaloff Fletcher, S., *et al.* (2013). Global ocean storage of anthropogenic carbon. *Biogeosciences* **10**: 2169–91, http://oceanrep.geomar.de/21469/1/bg-10-2169-2013.pdf.

Kintisch, E. (2015). Amazon rainforest ability to soak up carbon dioxide is falling. *Science*, March 18, www.sciencemag.org/news/2015/03/amazon-rainforest-ability-soak-carbon-dioxide-falling.

Klein, N. (2014). *This Changes Everything: Capitalism vs. the Climate.* New York: Simon and Schuster, www.worldcat.org/title/this-changes-everything-capitalism-vs-the-climate/oclc/894746822.

Kokorin, A., and Korppoo, A. (2017). Russia's ostrich approach to climate change and the Paris Agreement. *CEPS Policy Insights* 2017/40 (November), www.ceps.eu/ceps-publications/russias-ostrich-approach-climate-change-and-paris-agreement/.

Kommenda, N. (2019). How your flight emits as much CO2 as many people do in a year. *The Guardian*, July 19, www.theguardian.com/environment/ng-interactive/2019/jul/19/carbon-calculator-how-taking-one-flight-emits-as-much-as-many-people-do-in-a-year.

Kopra, S. (2019). *China and Great Power Responsibility for Climate Change.* London: Routledge, www.routledge.com/China-and-Great-Power-Responsibility-for-Climate-Change/Kopra/p/book/9781138557604.

Korppoo, A., Tynkkynen, N., and Honneland, G. (2015). *Russia and the Politics of International Environmental Regimes.* Cheltenham: Edward Elgar www .elgaronline.com/view/9781782548638.xml.

Krasner, S. D. (1982). Structural causes and regime consequences: regimes as intervening variables. *International Organization* **36**(2): 185–205, www.jstor.org/stable/2706520.

Krogman, N. (2020). Consumer values and consumption. In A. Kalfagianni, D. Fuchs and A. Hayden, eds., *Routledge Handbook of Global Sustainability and Governance.* London: Routledge, pp. 242–53, www.routledge.com/Routledge-Handbook-of-Global-Sustainability-Governance-1st-Edition/Kalfagianni-Fuchs-Hayden/p/book/9781138048287.

Krugman, P. (2020). This land of denial and death. *New York Times*, March 30, www .nytimes.com/2020/03/30/opinion/republicans-science-coronavirus.html.

Kugel, S. (2020). Are frequent flier miles killing the planet? *New York Times*, March 5, www.nytimes.com/2020/03/05/travel/loyalty-programs-climate-change.html.

Kunkel, C. M., and Kammen, D. M. (2011). Design and implementation of carbon cap and dividend policies. *Energy Policy* **39**(1): 477–86, https://rael.berkeley.edu/wp-content/uploads/2015/04/Kunkel-Kammen-CapDividend-2010.pdf.

Kutting, G. (2016). Consumption: institutions and actors. In P. G. Harris, ed., *Routledge Handbook of Global Environmental Politics.* London: Routledge, pp. 205–14, www.routledge.com/Routledge-Handbook-of-Global-Environmental-Politics/Harris/p/book/9781138953611.

Lamb, W. F., and Steinberger, J. K. (2017). Human well-being and climate change mitigation. *WIREs Climate Change* **8**(6): 1–16, https://doi.org/10.1002/wcc.485.

Latvian Presidency of the Council of the European Union (2015). Submission by Latvia and the European Commission on behalf of the European Union and its member states, March 6, www4.unfccc.int/sites/submissions/INDC/Published%20Documents/Latvia/1/LV-03-06-EU%20INDC.pdf.

Lenton, T. M., Rockstrom, J., Gaffney, O., *et al.* (2019). Climate tipping points: too risky to bet against. *Nature* **575**: 592–5, www.nature.com/articles/d41586-019-03595-0.

Le Page, M., and Ananthaswamy, A. (2012). Power paradox: clean might not be green forever. *New Scientist* 2849, www.newscientist.com/article/mg21328491-700-power-paradox-clean-might-not-be-green-forever/.

Lewis, J. I., and Gallagher, K. S. (2011) Energy and environment in China: achievements and enduring challenges. In R. S. Axelrod, S. D. Vandeveer, and D. L Downie, eds., *The Global Environment: Institutions, Law and Policy*. Washington, DC: CQ Press, pp. 259–84, www.worldcat.org/title/global-environment-institutions-law-and-policy/oclc/458890800.

Li, Y., and Shapiro, J. (2020). *China Goes Green: Coercive Environmentalism for a Planet on the Brink*. Cambridge: Polity, https://politybooks.com/bookdetail/?isbn=9781509543113.

Lieven, A. (2020). *Climate Change and the Nation State: The Realist Case*. London: Allen Lane, www.penguin.com.au/books/climate-change-and-the-nation-state-9780241394076.

Lin, K. (2016). Rising inequality and its discontents in China. *New Labor Forum*, December, https://newlaborforum.cuny.edu/2016/12/08/rising-inequality-and-its-discontents-in-china/.

Lombrana, L. M., and Krukowska, E. (2020). How fighting climate change gave the EU a new reason to exist. *Bloomberg Green*, February 26, www.bloomberg.com/news/articles/2020-02-26/behind-europe-s-green-deal-a-quiet-campaign-by-hidden-powerbrokers.

Londono, E., and Casado, L. (2019). Amazon deforestation in Brazil rose sharply on Bolsonaro's watch. *New York Times*, November 18, www.nytimes.com/2019/11/18/world/americas/brazil-amazon-deforestation.html.

Lovejoy, T. (2011). Stemming population growth is a cheap way to limit climate change. *The Guardian*, October 31, www.theguardian.com/environment/2011/oct/31/stemming-population-growth-climate-change.

Luomi, M. (2014). Mainstreaming climate policy in the Gulf Cooperation Council states. Oxford Institute for Energy Studies paper no. MEP7, www.oxfordenergy.org/wpcms/wp-content/uploads/2014/02/MEP-7.pdf.

MacFarquhar, N. (2019). Russian land of permafrost and mammoths is thawing. *New York Times*, August 4, www.nytimes.com/2019/08/04/world/europe/russia-siberia-yakutia-permafrost-global-warming.html.

Maisonnave, F. (2018). Amazon at risk from Bolsonaro's grim attack on the environment. *The Guardian*, October 9, www.theguardian.com/environment/2018/oct/09/brazils-bolsonaro-would-unleash-a-war-on-the-environment.

Maltais, A., and McKinnon, C., eds. (2015). *The Ethics of Climate Governance*. London: Rowman and Littlefield, https://rowman.com/ISBN/9781783482153/The-Ethics-of-Climate-Governance.

Malthus, T. (2015). *An Essay on the Principle of Population and Other Writings.* London: Penguin Classics, www.penguin.com.au/books/an-essay-on-the-principle-of-population-and-other-writings-9780141392820.

Mann, M. @MichaelEMann. (2018). There IS an axis of evil in the world. Twitter post, December 9, https://twitter.com/michaelemann/status/1071541747388428289.

Marengo, J. A., Nobre, C. A., Sampaio, G., Salazar, L. F., and Borma, L. S. (2011). Climate change in the Amazon Basin: tipping points, changes in extremes, and impacts on natural and human systems. In M. B. Bush, J. R. Flenley and W. D. Gosling, eds., *Tropical Rainforest Responses to Climatic Change,* 2nd ed. Berlin: Springer-Verlag, pp. 259–83, www.researchgate.net/publication/227147212_Climate_change_in_the_Amazon_Basin_Tipping_points_changes_in_extremes_and_impacts_on_natural_and_human_systems.

Marsa, L. (2013). *Fevered: Why a Hotter Planet Will Hurt Our Health – and How We Can Save Ourselves.* New York: Rodale, www.worldcat.org/title/fevered-why-a-hotter-planet-will-hurt-our-health-and-how-we-can-save-ourselves/oclc/830206295.

Marsden, W. (2012). *Fools Rule: Inside the Failed Politics of Climate Change.* Toronto: Vintage Canada, www.penguinrandomhouse.com/books/208714/fools-rule-by-william-marsden/.

Mason, M. (2015). Climate change and human security: the international governance architecture, policies and instruments. *LSE Research Online,* http://eprints.lse.ac.uk/64751/.

Masood, E. (1995). Climate panel confirms human role in warming, fights off oil states. *Nature* **378**: 524, www.nature.com/articles/378524a0.

Mathiesen, K. (2016). India to halt building new coal plants in 2022. *Climate Home News,* December 16, www.climatechangenews.com/2016/12/16/india-to-halt-building-new-coal-plants-in-2022/.

Mathiesen, K. (2017). Coal to power India for "decades to come," says government planning body. *Climate Home News,* August 28, www.climatechangenews.com/2017/08/28/coal-power-india-decades-come-says-government-planning-body/.

McGrath, M. (2019). UN climate talks: delegates back IPCC report without targets. *BBC News,* June 27, www.bbc.com/news/science-environment-48786296.

McGrath, M. (2020). Coronavirus: air pollution and CO2 fall rapidly as virus spreads. *BBC News,* March 19, www.bbc.com/news/science-environment-51944780.

McKibben, B. (2016). A world at war. *The New Republic,* August 15, https://newrepublic.com/article/135684/declare-war-climate-change-mobilize-wwii.

McKibben, B. (2018). How extreme weather is shrinking the planet. *The New Yorker,* November, 26, www.newyorker.com/magazine/2018/11/26/how-extreme-weather-is-shrinking-the-planet.

Meadows, D. H., Meadows, D. L., Randers, J. (1992). *Beyond the Limits: Confronting Global Collapse, Envisioning a Sustainable Future.* White River Junction, VT: Chelsea Green, www.worldcat.org/title/beyond-the-limits-confronting-global-collapse-envisioning-a-sustainable-future/oclc/48886446.

Meadows, D. H., Meadows, D. L., Randers, J., and Behrens, W. W. (1972). *The Limits to Growth.* New York: Universe, www.worldcat.org/title/limits-to-growth-a-report-for-the-club-of-romes-project-on-the-predicament-of-mankind/oclc/307838.

Met Office (2011). *Climate Observations, Projections and Impacts: Saudi Arabia*. Exeter: Met Office, https://docplayer.net/24236056-Climate-observations-projec tions-and-impacts-saudi-arabia.html.

Meyer, A. (2004). Briefing: contraction and convergence. *Proceedings of the Institution of Civil Engineers: Engineering Sustainability* **157**: 189–92, www .icevirtuallibrary.com/doi/abs/10.1680/ensu.2004.157.4.189.

Meyer, R. (2020). The oil industry is quietly winning local climate fights. *The Atlantic*, February 20, www.theatlantic.com/science/archive/2020/02/oil-industry-fighting-climate-policy-states/606640/.

Michaelowa, A. (1998). Climate policy and interest groups: a public choice analysis. *Intereconomics* **33**(6): 251–9, www.intereconomics.eu/pdf-download/year/1998/ number/6/article/climate-policy-and-interest-groups-a-public-choice-analysis.html.

Milman, O. (2019). US is hotbed of climate change denial, major global survey finds. *The Guardian*, May 8, www.theguardian.com/environment/2019/may/07/us-hotbed-climate-change-denial-international-poll.

Ministry of the Environment of Japan (2014). *Japan's Climate Change Policies*, www .env.go.jp/en/focus/docs/files/20140318-83.pdf.

MOFA (2016). Intended Nationally Determined Contributions (INDC): Greenhouse Gas Emission Reduction Target in FY2030, www.mofa.go.jp/ic/ch/page1we_ 000104.html.

Monroe, R. (2019). Carbon dioxide levels hit record peak in May. *The Keeling Curve*, June 4, https://scripps.ucsd.edu/programs/keelingcurve/2019/06/04/carbon-diox ide-levels-hit-record-peak-in-may/.

Moore, S. D. (2012). Climate change and environmental citizenship: transition to a post-consumerist future? PhD thesis, University of Tasmania, https://eprints.utas .edu.au/15930/.

Mora, C., Spirandelli, D., Franklin, E. C., *et al.* (2018). Broad threat to humanity from cumulative climate hazards intensified by greenhouse gas emissions. *Nature Climate Change* **8**: 1062–71, www.nature.com/articles/s41558-018-0315-6.

Moran, D., Hasanbeigi, A., and Springer, C. (2018). The carbon loophole in climate policy: quantifying the embodied carbon in traded products. Climate Works Foundation report, www.climateworks.org/wp-content/uploads/2018/09/Carbon-Loophole-in-Climate-Policy-Final.pdf.

Moriarty, P., and Honnery, D. (2019). Energy efficiency or conservation for mitigating climate change? *Energies* **12**(18): 1–17, www.researchgate.net/publication/ 335842805_Energy_Efficiency_or_Conservation_for_Mitigating_Climate_Change.

Morton, A. (2019). "No faith in coal": religious leaders urge Scott Morrison to take climate action. *The Guardian*, June 25, www.theguardian.com/environment/2019/ jun/25/no-faith-in-coal-religious-leaders-urge-scott-morrison-to-take-climate-action.

Morton, A. (2020). Summer bushfires released more carbon dioxide than Australia does in a year. *The Guardian*, April 21, www.theguardian.com/australia-news/2020/ apr/21/summers-bushfires-released-more-carbon-dioxide-than-australia-does-in-a-year.

Moura, P. (2019). An even more inconvenient truth: why carbon credits for forest preservation may be worse than nothing. *ProPublica*, May 22, https://features .propublica.org/brazil-carbon-offsets/inconvenient-truth-carbon-credits-dont-work-deforestation-redd-acre-cambodia/.

Mufson, S., and Freedman, A. (2019). What you need to know about the Amazon rainforest fires. *Washington Post*, August 27, https://www.washingtonpost.com/climate-environment/what-you-need-to-know-about-the-amazon-rainforest-fires/2019/08/27/ac82b21e-c815-11e9-a4f3-c081a126de70_story.html.

Murtaugh, P. A., and Schlax, M. G. (2009). Reproduction and carbon legacies of individuals. *Global Environmental Change* **19**(1): 14–20, https://doi.org/10.1016/j.gloenvcha.2008.10.007.

Myers, N., and Kent, J. (2003). New consumers: the influence of affluence on the environment. *Proceedings of the National Academy of Sciences* **100**(8): 4963–8, www.pnas.org/content/pnas/100/8/4963.full.pdf.

Myllyvirta, L. (2020). Analysis: coronavirus has temporarily reduced China's CO2 emissions by a quarter. *Carbon Brief*, February 19, www.carbonbrief.org/analysis-coronavirus-has-temporarily-reduced-chinas-co2-emissions-by-a-quarter?utm_content=bufferae67b&utm_medium=social&utm_source=twitter.com&utm_campaign=buffer.

NASA (2013). NASA scientists react to 400 ppm carbon milestone, https://climate.nasa.gov/400ppmquotes/.

NASA (2020). World of change: global temperatures, https://earthobservatory.nasa.gov/world-of-change/global-temperatures.

Natural Resources Canada (2019). *Energy Fact Book 2019-2020*, www.nrcan.gc.ca/sites/www.nrcan.gc.ca/files/energy/pdf/Energy%20Fact%20Book_2019_2020_web-resolution.pdf.

NDRC (2015). Enhanced Actions on Climate Change: China's Intended Nationally Determined Contributions. Beijing, NDRC Department of Climate Change, www.fao.org/faolex/results/details/en/c/LEX-FAOC186560/.

Netherlands Environmental Assessment Agency (2007). China now no. 1 in CO_2 emissions; USA in second position, www.pbl.nl/en/Chinanowno1inCO2emissionsUSAinsecondposition.

NewClimate Institute (2019). Global climate action from cities, regions and businesses. Research report, https://newclimate.org/wp-content/uploads/2019/09/Report-Global-Climate-Action-from-Cities-Regions-and-Businesses_2019.pdf.

New Economics Foundation (2016). The Happy Planet Index 2016: A global index of sustainable wellbeing, https://static1.squarespace.com/static/5735c421e321402778ee0ce9/t/57e0052d440243730fdf03f3/1474299185121/Briefing+paper+-+HPI+2016.pdf.

Newell, P. (2012). The political ecology of globalization. In P. Dauvergne, ed., *Handbook of Global Environmental Politics*, 2nd ed. Cheltenham: Edward Elgar, pp. 263–74, www.elgaronline.com/view/9781849809405.00031.xml.

Nightingale, A. J., Eriksen, S., Taylor, M., *et al.* (2019). Beyond technical fixes: climate solutions and the great derangement. *Climate and Development* **12**(4): 343–52, www.tandfonline.com/doi/pdf/10.1080/17565529.2019.1624495.

NOAA (2013) CO_2 at NOAA's Mauna Loa Observatory reaches new milestone: tops 400 ppm, www.esrl.noaa.gov/gmd/news/pdfs/7074.pdf.

NOAA (2020). Trends in atmospheric carbon dioxide, www.esrl.noaa.gov/gmd/ccgg/trends/mlo.html.

NRDC (2017). The road from Paris: Japan's progress toward its climate pledge. Issue Brief (17-11-B), www.nrdc.org/sites/default/files/paris-climate-agreement-progress-2017-japan-ib.pdf.

NRDC and Climate Observatory (2017). The road from Paris: Brazil's progress toward its climate pledge. Issue Brief (17-11-F), www.nrdc.org/sites/default/files/paris-climate-conference-Brazil-IB.pdf.

NRDC, ASCI, SEWA, *et al.* (2017). The road from Paris: India's progress toward its climate pledge. Issue Brief (17-11-E), www.nrdc.org/sites/default/files/paris-cli mate-conference-India-IB.pdf.

Nursey-Bray, M. (2009). Australia at the crossroads: climate change and foreign policy. In P. G. Harris, ed. *Climate Change and Foreign Policy: Case Studies from East to West*. London: Routledge, pp. 18–35, www.routledge.com/Climate-Change-and-Foreign-Policy-Case-Studies-from-East-to-West/Harris/p/book/9780415846615.

OHCHR (2015). Understanding human rights and climate change. Submission of to the 21st Conference of the Parties to the United Nations Framework Convention on Climate Change, www.ohchr.org/Documents/Issues/ClimateChange/COP21.pdf.

Ohta, H. (2009). Japanese foreign policy on climate change: diplomacy and domestic politics. In P. G. Harris, ed., *Climate Change and Foreign Policy: Case Studies from East to West*. London: Routledge, pp. 36–52, www.routledge.com/Climate-Change-and-Foreign-Policy-Case-Studies-from-East-to-West/Harris/p/book/9780415846615.

Oldenborgh, G. J. V., Krikken, F., Lewis, S., *et al.* (2020). Attribution of the Australian bushfire risk to anthropogenic climate change. *World Weather Attribution*, March, www.worldweatherattribution.org/wp-content/uploads/WWA-attribution_bush fires-March2020.pdf.

O'Lear, S. (2010). *Environmental Politics: Scale and Power*. Cambridge: Cambridge University Press, https://doi.org/10.1017/CBO9780511779428.

Oliver, J. T., and Tucker, S. M. (2019). Geoengineering at sea: ocean fertilization as a policy option. In P. G. Harris, ed., *Climate Change and Ocean Governance: Politics and Policy for Threatened Seas*. Cambridge: Cambridge University Press, pp. 424–36, https://doi.org/10.1017/9781108502238.026.

Oreskes, N., and Conway, E. M. (2010). *Merchants of Doubt: How a Handful of Scientists Obscured the Truth on Issues from Tobacco Smoke to Global Warming*. New York: Bloomsbury, www.bloomsbury.com/uk/merchants-of-doubt-9781596916104/.

Oreskes, N., Oppenheimer, M., and Jamieson, D. (2019). Scientists have been under-estimating the pace of climate change. *Scientific American*, August 19, https://blogs.scientificamerican.com/observations/scientists-have-been-underestimating-the-pace-of-climate-change/.

Ortiz, D. A. (2018). Ten simple ways to act on climate change. *BBC Future*, November 5, www.bbc.com/future/article/20181102-what-can-i-do-about-cli mate-change.

Otto, I. M., Kim, K. M., Dubrovsky, N., and Lucht, W. (2019). Shift the focus from the super-poor to the super-rich. *Nature Climate Change* **9**: 82–4, www.nature.com/articles/s41558-019-0402-3.

Pan, C., and Sherrard, J. (2017). China's animal protein outlook to 2020: growth in demand, supply and trade. Rabobank research report, https://research.rabobank.com/far/en/sectors/animal-protein/china_animal_protein_outlook_2020.html.

Parag, Y., and Fawcett, T. (2014). Personal carbon trading: a review of research evidence and real-world experience of a radical idea. *Energy and Emission*

Control Technologies **2**: 23–32, www.dovepress.com/personal-carbon-trading-a-review-of-research-evidence-and-real-world-e-peer-reviewed-article-EECT.

Park, J. (2016). Governing climate change policy: from scientific obscurity to foreign policy prominence. In P. G. Harris, ed., *Climate Change and American Foreign Policy*. New York: Palgrave Macmillan, pp. 73–87, https://link.springer.com/chapter/10.1057/9781137120809_4.

Parker, C. F., and Karlsson, C. (2015). Climate leadership. In K. Backstrand and E. Lovbrand, eds., *Research Handbook on Climate Governance*. Cheltenham: Edward Elgar, pp. 191–201, www.elgaronline.com/view/edcoll/9781783470594/9781783470594.00027.xml.

Patterson, M., and Stripple, J. (2007). Singing climate change into existence: on the territorialization of climate policymaking. In M. W. Pettenger, ed., *The Social Construction of Climate Change: Power, Knowledge, Norms, Discourses*. London: Routledge, pp. 149–72, www.routledge.com/The-Social-Construction-of-Climate-Change-Power-Knowledge-Norms-Discourses/Pettenger/p/book/9780754648024.

Pattyn, F., Ritz, C., Hanna, E., *et al.* (2018). The Greenland and Antarctic ice sheets under 1.5° warming. *Nature Climate Change* **8**(12): 1053–61, www.nature.com/articles/s41558-018-0305-8.

Pearce, F. (2019). Geoengineer the planet? More scientists now say it must be an option. *YaleEnvironment360*, May 29, https://e360.yale.edu/features/geoengineer-the-planet-more-scientists-now-say-it-must-be-an-option.

Peltier, E. (2020). Europe wants a "right to repair" smartphones and gadgets. *New York Times*, March 12, www.nytimes.com/2020/03/12/world/europe/eu-right-to-repair-smartphones.html.

Peters, G. (2020). How changes brought on by coronavirus could help tackle climate change. *The Conversation*, March 17, https://theconversation.com/how-changes-brought-on-by-coronavirus-could-help-tackle-climate-change-133509.

Pew Research Center (2020). As economic concerns recede, environmental protection rises on public's policy agenda, www.people-press.org/2020/02/13/as-economic-concerns-recede-environmental-protection-rises-on-the-publics-policy-agenda/#age-and-gender-differences-in-policy-priorities.

Phillips, T. (2018). Trump of the tropics: the "dangerous" candidate leading Brazil's presidential race. *The Guardian*, April 19, www.theguardian.com/world/2018/apr/19/jair-bolsonaro-brazil-presidential-candidate-trump-parallels.

Pickl, M. J. (2019). The renewable energy strategies of oil majors: from oil to energy? *Energy Strategy Reviews* **26**: 1–8, www.sciencedirect.com/science/article/pii/S2211467X19300574.

Plumer, B. (2020). Emissions decline will set records this year: but it's not good news. *New York Times*, April 30, www.nytimes.com/2020/04/30/climate/global-emissions-decline.html.

Podesta, J. (2019). The climate crisis, migration and refugees. Brookings Blum Roundtable on Global Poverty, July 25, www.brookings.edu/research/the-climate-crisis-migration-and-refugees/.

Pohl, B., and Schaller, S. (2019). Security Council debates how climate disasters threaten international peace and security. *Climate Diplomacy*, January 30, www

.climate-diplomacy.org/news/security-council-climate-disasters-threaten-inter national-peace-and-stability.

Pooran, D. (2018). GDP is destroying the planet: here's an alternative. World Economic Forum, May 31, www.weforum.org/agenda/2018/05/gdp-is-destroying-the-planet-heres-an-alternative/.

Popovich, N. (2020). Climate change rises as a public priority: but it's more partisan than ever. *New York Times*, February 20, www.nytimes.com/interactive/2020/02/20/climate/climate-change-polls.html.

Power, S. B., and Delage, F. P. D. (2019). Setting and smashing extreme temperature records over the coming century. *Nature Climate Change* **9** (July): 529–34, www .nature.com/articles/s41558-019-0498-5.

Pryor, L. (2020). Has Australia reached a climate tipping point? *New York Times*, international edition, February 24, www.nytimes.com/2020/02/24/opinion/austra lia-fires-climate.html.

Purdon, M. (2017). Neoclassical realism and international climate change politics: more and political constraints in international climate finance. *Journal of International Relations and Development* **20**: 263–300, https://doi.org/10.1057/jird.2013.5.

Radkau, J. (2008). *Nature and Power: A Global History of the Environment*. New York: Cambridge University Press, www.cambridge.org/hk/academic/subjects/his tory/environmental-history/nature-and-power-global-history-environment? format=HB&isbn=9780521851299.

Raftery, A. E., Zimmer, A., Frierson, D. M. W., Startz, R., and Liu, P. (2017). Less than 2°C warming by 2100 unlikely. *Nature Climate Change* **7**: 637–41, www.nature .com/articles/nclimate3352.

Ram, M., Bogdanov, D., Aghahosseini, A., *et al.* (2019). Global energy system based on 100% renewable energy. Study by Lappeenranta University of Technology and Energy Watch Group, http://energywatchgroup.org/wp-content/uploads/EWG_ LUT_100RE_All_Sectors_Global_Report_2019.pdf.

Rayworth, K. (2017). *Donut Economics: Seven Ways to Think Like a 21st-Century Economist*. White River Junction, VT: Chelsea Green, www.chelseagreen.com/ product/doughnut-economics-paperback/.

Readfearn, G. (2020). Antarctica logs hottest temperature on record with a reading of 18.3C. *The Guardian*, February 7, www.theguardian.com/world/2020/feb/07/ant arctica-logs-hottest-temperature-on-record-with-a-reading-of-183c.

Reed, S. (2019). Saudi Aramco is world's most profitable company, beating Apple by far. *New York Times*, April 1, www.nytimes.com/2019/04/01/business/saudi-ara mco-profit.html.

Richler, J. (2019). Effect of female representation. *Nature Climate Change* **9**: 801, https://doi.org/10.1038/s41558–019-0626-2.

Ripple, W. J., Wolf, C., Newsome, T. M., *et al.* (2020). World scientists' warning of a climate emergency. *BioScience* **70**(1): 8–12, https://doi.org/10.1093/biosci/biz088.

Ritchie, H. (2019a). Where in the world do people emit the most CO_2? *Our World Data*, https://ourworldindata.org/per-capita-co2.

Ritchie, H. (2019b). Which countries eat the most meat? *BBC News*, February 4, www .bbc.com/news/health-47057341.

Ritchie, H., and Roser, M. (2019). CO_2 and greenhouse gas emissions. *Our World Data*, https://ourworldindata.org/co2-and-other-greenhouse-gas-emissions.

Roberts, D. (2017). The key to tackling climate change: electrify everything. *Vox*, October 27, www.vox.com/2016/9/19/12938086/electrify-everything.

Robinson, M., and Shine, T. (2018). Achieving a climate justice pathway to 1.5°C. *Nature Climate Change* 8: 564–9, www.nature.com/articles/s41558-018-0189-7/.

Robinson, S. A., and Dornan, M. (2017). International financing for climate change adaptation in small island developing states. *Regional Environmental Change* 17 (4): 1103–15, https://crawford.anu.edu.au/files/uploads/crawford01_cap_anu_ edu_au/2017-11/robinson_and_dornan_international_financing_for_climate_ change_adaptation_in_small_island_developing_states.pdf.

Ropke, I. (2010). Ecological economics: consumption drivers and impacts. In C. Lever-Tracy, ed., *Routledge Handbook of Climate Change and Society*. London: Routledge, pp. 121–30, www.routledge.com/Routledge-Handbook-of-Climate-Change-and-Society-1st-Edition/Lever-Tracy/p/book/9780415544764.

Rosen, E., Valino, A., and Nowakowski, K. (2017). As billions more fly, here's how aviation could evolve. *National Geographic*, June 20, www.nationalgeographic.com/ environment/urban-expeditions/transportation/air-travel-fuel-emissions-environment/.

Russian Federation (2015). Russian Submission INDC, www4.unfccc.int/sites/submis sions/INDC/Published%20Documents/Russia/1/Russian%20Submission% 20INDC_eng_rev1.doc.

Russian Public Opinion Research Center (2017). Klimaticheskie kolebanija: teplo li, holodno li? [Climatic fluctuations: is it warm, is it cold?], https://wciom.ru/index .php?id=236&uid=116325.

Sandalow, D. (2019). Guide to Chinese climate policy 2019. Columbia Center for Energy Policy, https://energypolicy.columbia.edu/sites/default/files/file-uploads/ Guide%20to%20Chinese%20Climate%20Policy_2019.pdf.

Saryal, R. (2018). Climate change policy of India: modifying the environment. *South Asia Research* 38(1): 1–19, https://journals.sagepub.com/doi/pdf/10.1177/ 0262728017745385.

Satterthwaite, D. (2009). The implications of population growth and urbanization for climate change. *Environment and Urbanization* 21(2): 545–67, https://journals .sagepub.com/doi/pdf/10.1177/0956247809344361.

Saudi Arabia (2015). The intended nationally determined contribution of the Kingdom of Saudi Arabia under the UNFCCC, www4.unfccc.int/sites/ndcstaging/ PublishedDocuments/Saudi%20Arabia%20First/KSA-INDCs%20English.pdf.

Saudi Arabia (2020). Vision 2030, www.vision2030.gov.sa/en.

Sauer, N. (2019) Russia formally joins Paris climate agreement. *Climate Home New*, September 23, www.climatechangenews.com/2019/09/23/russia-formally-joins-paris-climate-agreement/.

Scarborough, P., Appleby, P. N., Mizdrak, A., *et al.* (2014). Dietary greenhouse gas emissions of meat-eaters, fish-eaters, vegetarians and vegans in the UK. *Climatic Change* 125: 179–92, https://link.springer.com/article/10.1007/s10584-014-1169-1.

Schapiro, M. (2010). "Perverse" carbon payments send flood of money to China. *YaleEnvironment360*, December 13, https://e360.yale.edu/features/perverse_co2_ payments_send_flood_of_money_to_china.

Schiller, P. L., and Kenworthy, J. (2017). *An Introduction to Sustainable Transport*. London: Routledge www.routledge.com/An-Introduction-to-Sustainable-Transportation-Policy-Planning-and-Implementation/Schiller-Kenworthy/p/book/9781138185487.

Schlosberg, D. (2012). Climate justice and capabilities: a framework for adaptation policy. *Ethics and International Affairs* **26**(4): 445–61, https://doi.org/10.1017/S0892679412000615.

Schor, J. (1999). The new politics of consumption: why Americans want so much more than they need. *Boston Review* (Summer), https://bostonreview.net/archives/BR24.3/schor.html.

Schreurs, M. A. (2011). Climate change politics in an authoritarian state: the ambivalent case of China. In J. S. Dryzek and R. B. Norgaard, eds., *Oxford Handbook of Climate Change and Society*. Oxford: Oxford University Press, pp. 449–63, www.oxfordhandbooks.com/view/10.1093/oxfordhb/9780199566600.001.0001/oxfordhb-9780199566600-e-30.

Schreurs, M. A., and Axelrod, R. S. (2020). Promoting environmental protection in the European Union. In R. S. Axelrod and S. D. Vandeveer, eds., *The Global Environment: Institutions, Law and Policy, 5th edition*. London: Sage, pp. 191–219, https://us.sagepub.com/en-us/nam/the-global-environment/book252391.

Schulz, F. (2020). Germany misses EU climate plan deadline. *Climate Home News*, January 8, www.climatechangenews.com/2020/01/08/germany-misses-eu-climate-plan-deadline/.

Schwartz, J. (2019). Major climate change rules the Trump administration is reversing. *New York Times*, August 29, www.nytimes.com/2019/08/29/climate/climate-rule-trump-reversing.html.

Schwartz J., and Popovich, N. (2019). It's official: 2018 was the fourth-warmest year on record. *New York Times*, February 6, www.nytimes.com/interactive/2019/02/06/climate/fourth-hottest-year.html.

Segal, J. M. (1999). *Graceful Simplicity: The Philosophy and Politics of the Alternative American Dream*. Berkeley: University of California Press, www.ucpress.edu/book/9780520236004/graceful-simplicity.

SEI (2019). The production gap, 2019 report, http://productiongap.org/wp-content/uploads/2019/11/Production-Gap-Report-2019.pdf.

Selby, J. (2018). The Trump presidency, climate change and the prospect of a disorderly energy transition. *Review of International Studies* **45**(3): 471–90, https://doi.org/10.1017/S0260210518000165.

Selby, J., Dahi, O. S., Frohlich, C., and Hulme, M. (2017). Climate change and the Syrian civil war revisited. *Political Geography* **60**: 232–44, www.sciencedirect.com/science/article/pii/S0962629816301822.

Sengupta, S., and Eddy, M. (2020). How hard is it to quit coal? For Germany, 18 years and $44 billion. *New York Times*, January 16, www.nytimes.com/2020/01/16/climate/germany-coal-climate-change.html.

Shapiro, J. (2018). As China goes, so goes the planet: the environmental implications of the rise of China. In G. Kutting and K. Herman, eds., *Global Environmental Politics: Concepts, Theories and Case Studies*. London: Routledge, pp. 143–54, www.routledge.com/Global-Environmental-Politics-Concepts-Theories-and-Case-Studies-2nd/Kutting-Herman/p/book/9781138895355.

Sharon, O. (2019). Nonterritorial exclusive economic zones: future rights of small-island states. In P. G. Harris, ed., *Climate Change and Ocean Governance: Politics and Policy for Threatened Seas*. Cambridge: Cambridge University Press, pp. 290–306, https://doi.org/10.1017/9781108502238.018.

Shearer, C., Brown, M., and Buckley, T. (2019). China at a crossroads: continued support for coal power erodes country's clean energy leadership. Institute for Energy Economics and Financial Analysis report, https://ieefa.org/wp-content/uploads/2019/01/China-at-a-Crossroads_January-2019.pdf.

Shepherd, A., Fricker, H. A., and Farrell, S. L. (2018). Trends and connections across the Antarctic cryosphere. *Nature* **558**: 223–32, www.nature.com/articles/s41586-018-0171-6#citeas.

Shepherd, A., Ivins, E., Rignot, E. *et al.* (2018) Mass balance of the Antarctic Ice Sheet from 1992 to 2017. *Nature* **558**: 219–22, www.nature.com/articles/s41586-018-0179-y.

Shepherd, A., Ivins, E., Rignot, E. *et al.* (2019). Mass balance of the Greenland Ice Sheet from 1992 to 2018. *Nature* (online), www.nature.com/articles/s41586-019-1855-2.

Sheth, J. N., Sethia, N. K., and Srinivas, S. (2011). Mindful consumption: A customer-centric approach to sustainability. *Journal of the Academy of Marketing Science* **39**: 21–39, www.researchgate.net/publication/226100566_Mindful_Consumption_A_Customer-Centric_Approach_to_Sustainability.

Shirk, S. L. (2007). *China: Fragile Superpower*. Oxford: Oxford University Press, https://global.oup.com/academic/product/china-9780195373196.

Shove, E. (2010). Social theory and climate change. *Theory, Culture and Society* **27** (2–3): 277–88, https://journals.sagepub.com/doi/10.1177/0263276410361498.

Shue, H. (2014). *Climate Justice: Vulnerability and Protection*. Oxford: Oxford University Press, https://global.oup.com/academic/product/climate-justice-9780198713708.

Simms, A., and Smith, J. (2008). Introduction. In A. Simms and J. Smith, eds., *Do Good Lives Have to Cost the Earth?* London: Constable and Robinson, pp. 1–23, www.worldcat.org/title/do-good-lives-have-to-cost-the-earth/oclc/909983922.

Singer, M. (2018). *Climate Change and Social Inequality: The Health and Social Costs of Global Warming*. London, Routledge, www.routledge.com/Climate-Change-and-Social-Inequality-The-Health-and-Social-Costs-of-Global/Singer/p/book/9781138102910.

Skjaerseth, J. B. (2017). The European Commission's shifting climate leadership. *Global Environmental Politics* **17**(2): 84–104, www.mitpressjournals.org/doi/abs/10.1162/GLEP_a_00402.

Sobczyk, N. (2019). How climate change got labeled a "crisis." *E&E News*, July 10, www.eenews.net/stories/1060718493.

Soper, K. (2020). *Post-Growth Living: For an Alternative Hedonism*. London: Verso, https://www.versobooks.com/books/3693-post-growth-living.

Speth, J. G. (2008). *Red Sky at Morning: America and the Crisis of the Global Environment*. New Haven, CT: Yale University Press, https://yalebooks.yale.edu/book/9780300107760/red-sky-morning.

Spratt, D., and Dunlop, I. (2018). What lies beneath: the understatement of existential climate risk. Breakthrough report, https://52a87f3e-7945-4bb1-abbf-9aa66cd4e93e.filesusr.com/ugd/148cb0_a0d7c18a1bf64e698a9c8c8f18a42889.pdf.

Springmann, M., Clark, M., Mason-D'Croz, D., *et al.* (2018). Option for keeping the food system within environmental limits. *Nature* **562**: 519–25, www.nature.com/articles/s41586-018-0594-0.

Stahel, W. R. (2019). *The Circular Economy: A User's Guide*. Abingdon: Routledge, www.routledge.com/The-Circular-Economy-A-Users-Guide/Stahel/p/book/9780367200176.

Stanley Foundation (2017). Setting an international policy agenda for just transitions. Policy dialogue brief, https://stanleycenter.org/publications/pdb/SPCCCPDB318.pdf.

Steffen, W., Rockstrom, J., Richardson, K., et al. (2018). Trajectories of the earth system in the anthropocene. *PNAS* **115**(33): 8252–9, https://doi.org/10.1073/pnas.1810141115.

Steininger, K., Lininger, C., Droege, S., et al. (2014). Justice and cost effectiveness of consumption-based versus production-based approaches in the case of unilateral climate policies. *Global Environmental Change* **24**: 75–87, www.sciencedirect.com/science/article/abs/pii/S0959378013001891.

Stephenson, J., Newman, K., and Mayhew, S. (2010). Population dynamics and climate change: what are the links? *Journal of Public Health* **32**(2): 150–6, https://academic.oup.com/jpubhealth/article/32/2/150/1610588.

Stevenson, H. (2016). Alternative theories: constructivism, Marxism and critical approaches. In P. G. Harris, ed., *Routledge Handbook of Global Environmental Politics*. London: Routledge, pp. 42–55, www.routledge.com/Routledge-Handbook-of-Global-Environmental-Politics/Harris/p/book/9781138953611.

Stewart, E., Pugh, G., and Jordan, M. (2019). Buildings are an ideal but overlooked climate solution. World Resources Institute blog, November 4, www.wri.org/blog/2019/11/buildings-are-ideal-overlooked-climate-solution.

Stewart, K. (2020). The religious right's hostility to science is crippling our coronavirus response. *New York Times*, March 27, www.nytimes.com/2020/03/27/opinion/coronavirus-trump-evangelicals.html.

Stoller, L. (1956). Thoreau's doctrine of simplicity. *New England Quarterly* **29**(4): 443–61, www.jstor.org/stable/362138.

Swim, J. K., Clayton, S., and Howard, G. S. (2011). Human behavior and contributions to climate change: psychological and contextual drivers. *American Psychologist* **66**(4): 251–64, www.apa.org/pubs/journals/releases/amp-66-4-251.pdf.

Tabuchi, H. (2020a). A Trump insider embeds climate denial in scientific research. *New York Times*, March 2, www.nytimes.com/2020/03/02/climate/goks-uncertainty-language-interior.html.

Tabuchi, H. (2020b). Japan races to build new coal-burning power plants, despite climate risks. *New York Times*, February 3, www.nytimes.com/2020/02/03/climate/japan-coal-fukushima.html.

Tarabay, J. (2020). Why these Australia fires are like nothing we've seen before. *New York Times*, January 21, www.nytimes.com/2020/01/21/world/australia/fires-size-climate.html.

Taylor, M. (2020). Fossil fuel pollution behind 4m premature deaths a year – study. *The Guardian* , February 12, www.theguardian.com/environment/2020/feb/12/fossil-fuel-pollution-behind-4m-premature-deaths-a-year-study.

Timperley, J. (2019). Denmark adopts climate law to cut emissions 70% by 2030. *Climate Home News*, December 6, www.climatechangenews.com/2019/12/06/denmark-adopts-climate-law-cut-emissions-70-2030/.

Titley, D. (2017). How did we end up with a 2C climate limit? *Climate Home News*, August 23, www.climatechangenews.com/2017/08/23/end-2c-climate-limit/.

Tollefson, J. (2016). How much longer can Antarctica's hostile ocean delay global warming? *Nature* **539**(7629): 346–8, www.nature.com/articles/539346a.

Trisos, C. H., Merow, C., and Pigot, A. L. (2020). The projected timing of abrupt ecological disruption from climate change. *Nature*, April 8, www.nature.com/articles/s41586-020-2189-9.

Trump, D. J. (2018). Remarks by President Trump to the 73rd session of the United Nations General Assembly, 25 September, www.whitehouse.gov/briefings-statements/remarks-president-trump-73rd-session-united-nations-general-assembly-new-york-ny/.

UN (1992). *United Nations Framework Convention on Climate Change*. Bonn: UNFCCC Secretariat, http://unfccc.int/resource/docs/convkp/conveng.pdf.

UN (1996). Report of the Conference of the Parties on its second session, held at Geneva from 8 to 19 July 1996 (FCCC/CP/1996/15/Add.129), https://unfccc.int/resource/docs/cop2/15a01.pdf.

UN (1999). Report of the Conference of the Parties on Its Fifth Session, Held in Bonn from 25 October to 5 November 1999, https://unfccc.int/cop5/resource/docs/cop5/cop5decis.pdf.

UN (2002). Report of the Conference of the Parties on Its Seventh Session, Held in Marrakesh from 29 October to 10 November 2001 (FCCC/CP/2001/13/Add.1), https://unfccc.int/resource/docs/cop7/13a01.pdf.

UN (2009). Copenhagen Accord (FCCC/CP/2009/L.7), http://unfccc.int/resource/docs/2009/cop15/eng/l07.pdf.

UN (2012). Report of the Conference of the Parties on Its Seventeenth Session, Held in Durban from 28 November to 11 December 2011 (FCCC/CP/2011/9/Add.1), https://unfccc.int/resource/docs/2011/cop17/eng/09a01.pdf.

UN (2014). Further Advancing the Durban Platform (FCCC/CP/2014/L.14), https://unfccc.int/resource/docs/2014/cop20/eng/l14.pdf.

UN (2015a). *Paris Agreement*. Bonn: UNFCCC Secretariat, https://unfccc.int/files/essential_background/convention/application/pdf/english_paris_agreement.pdf.

UN (2015b). Transforming Our World: The 2030 Agenda for Sustainable Development (A/RES/70/1), https://sustainabledevelopment.un.org/content/documents/21252030%20Agenda%20for%20Sustainable%20Development%20web.pdf.

UN (2017). Human rights and climate change (A/HRC/35/L.32), www.ohchr.org/EN/NewsEvents/Pages/DisplayNews.aspx?NewsID=21802&LangID=E.

UN (2019). Report of the Secretary-General on the 2019 Climate Action Summit and the Way Forward in 2020, www.un.org/en/climatechange/assets/pdf/cas_report_11_dec.pdf.

UN (n.d.[a]). Small Island Developing States, https://sustainabledevelopment.un.org/topics/sids/list.

UN (n.d.[b]). Sustainable Development Goals: about the Sustainable Development Goals, www.un.org/sustainabledevelopment/sustainable-development-goals/.

UN (n.d.[c]). United Nations Trust Fund for Human Security: climate change, www.un.org/humansecurity/climate-change/.

UNDESA (2018). *World Urbanization Prospects: The 2018 Revision*. New York: United Nations, https://population.un.org/wup/Publications/Files/WUP2018-Report.pdf.

UNDESA (2019a). World Population Prospects 2019: Graphs/Profiles, https://population.un.org/wpp/Graphs/DemographicProfiles/Line/900.

UNDESA (2019b). *World Population Prospects 2019: Highlights*. New York: United Nations, https://population.un.org/wpp/Publications/Files/WPP2019_Highlights.pdf.

UNDP (2011). *Human Development Report 2011: Sustainability and Equity—A Better Future for All*. New York: Palgrave Macmillan, http://hdr.undp.org/en/content/human-development-report-2011.

UNDP (2015). UNDP and climate change: zero carbon, sustainable development, www.undp.org/content/undp/en/home/librarypage/climate-and-disaster-resilience-/undp-and-climate-change.html.

UNDP (2017a). Rising tides, rising capacity: supporting a sustainable future for small island developing states, www.undp.org/content/undp/en/home/librarypage/poverty-reduction/rising-tides-rising-capacity-supporting-a-sustainable-future-for.html.

UNDP (2017b). Small island nations at the frontline of climate action, www.undp.org/content/undp/en/home/presscenter/pressreleases/2017/09/18/small-island-nations-at-the-frontline-of-climate-action-.html.

UNDP (2019). *Human Development Report 2019*. New York: UNDP, http://hdr.undp.org/sites/default/files/hdr2019.pdf.

UNEP (2014). *The Emissions Gap Report 2014: A UNEP Synthesis Report*. Nairobi: UNEP, www.unenvironment.org/resources/emissions-gap-report-2014.

UNEP (2016). *The Emissions Gap Report 2016: A UNEP Synthesis Report*. Nairobi, UNEP, www.unenvironment.org/resources/emissions-gap-report-2016.

UNEP (2018). *Inclusive Wealth Report 2018*. Nairobi: UNEP, https://wedocs.unep.org/bitstream/handle/20.500.11822/27597/IWR2018.pdf.

UNEP (2019). *Emissions Gap Report 2019*. Nairobi: UNEP, www.unenvironment.org/resources/emissions-gap-report-2019.

UNFCCC (1998). *Kyoto Protocol to the United Nations Framework Convention on Climate Change*. Bonn: UNFCCC Secretariat, https://unfccc.int/sites/default/files/kpeng.pdf.

UNFCCC (2002). Eighth Session of the Conference of the Parties and the Seventeenth Sessions of the Subsidiary Bodies, https://unfccc.int/cop8/.

UNFCCC (2020). Parties & observers, https://unfccc.int/parties-observers.

UNFCCC (n.d.). Party groupings, https://unfccc.int/process-and-meetings/parties-non-party-stakeholders/parties/party-groupings.

Unger, N., Bond, T. C., Wang, J. S., *et al.* (2010). Attribution of climate forcing to economic sectors. *Proceedings of the National Academy of Sciences* **107**(8): 3382–7, https://pubs.giss.nasa.gov/docs/2010/2010_Unger_un01100t.pdf.

UNHCR (2017). Climate change and disaster displacement: an overview of UNHCR's role, www.unhcr.org/protection/environment/5975e6cf7/climate-change-disaster-displacement-overview-unhcrs-role.html.

Union of Concerned Scientists (2020). Each country's share of CO2 emissions, www.ucsusa.org/resources/each-countrys-share-co2-emissions.

US (2015). US Cover Note, INDC and Accompanying Information, https://www4.unfccc.int/sites/submissions/INDC/Published%20Documents/United%20States%20of%20America/1/U.S.%20Cover%20Note%20INDC%20and%20Accompanying%20Information.pdf.

US Climate Alliance (2020). *States United for Climate Action*, www.usclimatealliance.org/.

US Congress (2019). H.R.763: Energy Innovation and Carbon Dividend Act of 2019, 116th Congress, www.congress.gov/bill/116th-congress/house-bill/763.

USGCRP (2018). *Fourth National Climate Assessment: Volume II – Impacts, Risks and Adaptation in the United States*. Washington, DC: US Government Printing Office, https://nca2018.globalchange.gov/downloads/.

US Senate (1997). S.Res.98: A resolution expressing the sense of the Senate regarding the conditions for the United States becoming a signatory to any international agreement on greenhouse gas emissions under the United Nations Framework Convention on Climate Change, 105th Congress, www.congress.gov/bill/105th-congress/senate-resolution/98.

Van Bavel, J. (2013). The world population explosion: causes, backgrounds and projects for the future. *Facts, Views & Vision in ObGyn* **5**(4): 281–91, www.ncbi.nlm.nih.gov/pmc/articles/PMC3987379/.

van den Bergh, J. C. J. M., and Botzen, W. J. W. (2016). Global impact of a climate treaty if the Human Development Index replaces GDP as a welfare proxy. *Climate Policy* **18**(1): 76–85, www.tandfonline.com/doi/pdf/10.1080/14693062.2016.1227954.

Vanderheiden, S. (2015). Justice and climate finance: differentiating responsibility in the Green Climate Fund. *The International Spectator* **50**(1): 31–45, www.iai.it/sites/default/files/vanderheiden.pdf.

Veblen, T. (2009). *The Theory of the Leisure Class*, M. Banta, ed. Oxford: Oxford University Press, https://global.oup.com/academic/product/the-theory-of-the-leisure-class-9780199552580.

Victor, D. G. (2020). Deep decarbonization: a realistic way forward on climate change. *Yale Environment 360*, January 28, https://e360.yale.edu/features/deep-decarbonization-a-realistic-way-forward-on-climate-change.

Vidal, J., Stratton, A., and Goldenberg, S. (2009). Low targets, goals dropped: Copenhagen ends in failure. *The Guardian*, December 19, www.theguardian.com/environment/2009/dec/18/copenhagen-deal.

Viola, E., and Hochstetler, K. (2015). Brazil. In K. Backstrand and E. Lovbrand, eds., *Research Handbook on Climate Governance*. Cheltenham: Edward Elgar, pp. 237–48, www.elgaronline.com/view/edcoll/9781783470594/9781783470594.00031.xml.

Viscidi, L., and Graham, N. (2019). Brazil was a global leader on climate change: now it's a threat. *Foreign Policy*, January 4, https://foreignpolicy.com/2019/01/04/brazil-was-a-global-leader-on-climate-change-now-its-a-threat/.

Vivid Economics (2013). Energy efficiency and economic growth. The Climate Institute, www.vivideconomics.com/casestudy/energy-efficiency-and-economic-growth/.

Vogler, J. (2015). Realism. In K. Backstrand and E. Lovbrand, eds., *Research Handbook on Climate Governance*. Cheltenham: Edward Elgar, pp. 14–24, www.elgaronline.com/view/edcoll/9781783470594/9781783470594.00010.xml.

Vogler, J. (2016). Mainstream theories: realism, rationalism and revolutionism. In P. G. Harris, ed., *Routledge Handbook of Global Environmental Politics*. London: Routledge, pp. 30–41, www.routledge.com/Routledge-Handbook-of-Global-Environmental-Politics/Harris/p/book/9781138953611.

Vogler, J. (2018). International relations theory and the environment. In G. Kutting and K. Herman, eds., *Global Environmental Politics: Concepts, Theories and Case Studies*. London: Routledge, pp. 9–27, www.routledge.com/Global-Environmental-Politics-Concepts-Theories-and-Case-Studies-2nd/Kutting-Herman/p/book/9781138895355.

Wallace-Wells, D. (2020). *The Uninhabitable Earth: Life After Warming*. New York: Tim Duggan, www.penguinrandomhouse.com/books/586541/the-uninhabitable-earth-by-david-wallace-wells/.

Waltz, K. (2001). *Man, the State and War: A Theoretical Analysis*. New York: Columbia University Press, https://cup.columbia.edu/book/man-the-state-and-war/9780231125376.

Washington, H. (2019). *What Can I Do to Help Heal the Environmental Crisis?* London: Routledge, www.routledge.com/What-Can-I-Do-to-Help-Heal-the-Environmental-Crisis/Washington/p/book/9780367342531.

Washington, H., and Cook, J. (2011). *Climate Change Denial: Heads in the Sand*. Abingdon: Earthscan, www.routledge.com/Climate-Change-Denial-Heads-in-the-Sand-1st-Edition/Washington-Cook-Oreskes/p/book/9781849713368.

Washington, H., and Kopnina, H. (2018). The insanity of endless growth. *The Ecological Citizen* **2**(1): 57–63, www.ecologicalcitizen.net/pdfs/v02n1-10.pdf.

Watts, N., Amann, M., Arnell, N., *et al.* (2019). The 2019 report of The Lancet Countdown on health and climate change: ensuring that the health of a child born today is not defined by a changing climate. *The Lancet* **394** (10211): 1836–78, https://linkinghub.elsevier.com/retrieve/pii/S0140673619325966.

WBGU (German Advisory Council on Climate Change) (2018). Just & in-time climate policy: four initiatives for a fair transformation. Policy paper no. 9, www.wbgu.de/en/publications/publication/just-in-time-climate-policy-four-initiatives-for-a-fair-transformation.

We Are Still In (2017). "We Are Still In" declaration, www.wearestillin.com/we-are-still-declaration.

Wei, T., Yang, S., Moore, J. C., *et al.* (2012). Developed and developing world responsibilities for historical climate change and CO_2 mitigation. *PNAS* **109**(32): 12911–15, www.pnas.org/content/109/32/12911.

Wewerinke-Singh, M. (2019). Remedies for human rights violations caused by climate change. *Climate Law* **9**: 224–43, https://doi.org/10.1163/18786561-00903005.

White House (2014). U.S.-China Joint Announcement on Climate Change, https://obamawhitehouse.archives.gov/the-press-office/2014/11/11/us-china-joint-announcement-climate-change.

WHO (2018). Climate change and health, February 1, www.who.int/news-room/fact-sheets/detail/climate-change-and-health.

Wijffels, S., Roemmich, D., Monselesan, J. C., and Gilson, J. (2016). Ocean temperatures chronical the ongoing warming of Earth. *Nature Climate Change* **6** (January): 116–18, www.nature.com/articles/nclimate2924.

Willett, W., Rockstrom, J., Loken, B., *et al.* (2019). Food in the Anthropocene: the EAT-Lancet Commission on healthy diets from sustainable food systems. *The Lancet* **393**(10170): 447–92 www.thelancet.com/journals/lancet/article/PIIS0140-6736(18)31788-4/fulltext?utm_campaign=tleat19&utm_source=hub_page.

Willsher, K. (2018). Macron scraps fuel tax rise in face of gilet jaunes protests. *The Guardian*, December 5, www.theguardian.com/world/2018/dec/05/france-wealth-tax-changes-gilets-jaunes-protests-president-macron.

WMO (2019a). 2019 concludes a decade of exceptional global heat and high-impact weather, https://public.wmo.int/en/media/press-release/2019-concludes-decade-of-exceptional-global-heat-and-high-impact-weather.

WMO (2019b). Greenhouse gas concentrations in atmosphere reach yet another high. Press release, November 25, https://public.wmo.int/en/media/press-release/green house-gas-concentrations-atmosphere-reach-yet-another-high.

WMO (2019c). The state of greenhouse gases in the atmosphere based on global observations through 2018. *WMO Greenhouse Gas Bulletin* **15** (25 November): 1–8, http://ane4bf-datap1.s3-eu-west-1.amazonaws.com/wmocms/s3fs-public/cke ditor/files/GHG-Bulletin-15_en.pdf?mQP5SDxBr_pHsQNJsAPrF8E5XnqkfHo2.

WMO (2019d). WMO confirms that last 4 years were warmest on record. Press release, May 7, https://public.wmo.int/en/media/press-release/wmo-confirms-past-4-years-were-warmest-record.

WMO (2020). WMO statement on the state of the global climate in 2019. WMO-No. 1248, https://library.wmo.int/doc_num.php?explnum_id=10211.

Woodward, A. (2020). Both the new coronavirus and SARS outbreaks likely started in Chinese wet markets. *Business Insider*, February 27, www.businessinsider.com/wuhan-coronavirus-chinese-wet-market-photos-2020-1.

World Bank (2016). *Shock Waves: Managing the Impacts of Climate Change on Poverty*. Washington, DC: World Bank, https://openknowledge.worldbank.org/bitstream/handle/10986/22787/9781464806735.pdf.

World Bank (2019). Fossil fuel energy consumption (% of total), https://data.worldbank .org/indicator/EG.USE.COMM.FO.ZS.

WWF (2018). *Living Planet Report 2018: Aiming Higher*. Gland, Switzerland: WWF, www.wwf.org.uk/sites/default/files/2018-10/wwfintl_livingplanet_full.pdf.

Wynes, S., and Nicholas, K. A. (2017). The climate mitigation gap: education and government recommendations miss the most effective individual actions. *Environmental Research Letters* **12**: 2–9, https://iopscience.iop.org/article/10 .1088/1748-9326/aa7541/pdf.

Xinhua (2019). China focus: leading with action in fighting climate change. *Xinhuanet News*, December 3, www.xinhuanet.com/english/2019-12/03/c_138602916.htm.

Xinhua (2020). China has over 200 million private cars. *Xinhuanet News*, January 7, www.xinhuanet.com/english/2020-01/07/c_138685873.htm.

YaleEnvironment360 (2019). CO_2 concentrations hit highest levels in 3 million years. *E360 Digest*, May 14, https://e360.yale.edu/digest/co2-concentrations-hit-highest-levels-in-3-million-years.

Young, O. R. (2009). Governance for sustainable development in a world of rising interdependence. In M. A. Delmas and O. R. Young, eds., *Governance for the Environment: New Perspectives*. Cambridge: Cambridge University Press, pp. 12–40, www.cambridge.org/hk/academic/subjects/politics-international-rela tions/comparative-politics/governance-environment-new-perspectives?format= PB&isbn=9780521743006.

Young, R. L. (2018). *Confronting Climate Crises through Education*. New York: Lexington, www.worldcat.org/title/confronting-climate-crises-through-education-reading-our-way-forward/oclc/1086210532.

Zhang, Z. (2003). The forces behind China's climate change policy: interests, sovereignty and prestige. In P. G. Harris, ed., *Global Warming and East Asia*. London:

Routledge, pp. 66–85, www.routledge.com/Global-Warming-and-East-Asia-The-Domestic-and-International-Politics-of/Harris/p/book/9780415315449.

Zhang, Z., Beggs, P.J., Bambrick, H., *et al.* (2018). The *MJA-Lancet* countdown on health and climate change: Australian policy inaction threatens lives. *Medical Journal of Australia* **209**(11): 474, e1–e21, www.mja.com.au/system/files/issues/209_11/10.5694mja18.00789.pdf.

Zheng, S. (2017). China now has over 300 million vehicles . . . that's almost America's total population. *South China Morning Post*, April 19, www.scmp.com/news/china/economy/article/2088876/chinas-more-300-million-vehicles-drive-pollution-congestion.

Index

Printed in the USA
CPSIA information can be obtained
at www.ICGtesting.com
CBHW050031150724
11582CB00005B/200